Easy Company Marines
More Than Brothers

Korea 1951–1952

Vito "Ted" Pileggi, USMC (Sgt-Ret)

Coho Publishing

Vito Pileggi – Easy Company Marines

Fourth Edition 2012

Copyright © Vito Pileggi 2008–2012

All Rights reserved.
No part of this publication may be reproduced, stored in a retrieval system, or transmitted, in any form or by any means, mechanical, photocopying, recording, or otherwise, without the prior written permission of the copyright owner.

International Standard Book Numbers:
Trade paperback 978-0-9830292-1-2
e-book 978-0-9830292-2-9

Design and production:
Cohographics, Salem Oregon
www.cohographics.com

Published in the U.S.A. by
Coho Publishing, Salem Oregon
www.cohopublishing.com

Printed in the U.S.A.

Also by Vito Pileggi:

Beginnings 2009

I'm Gonna Tell Grandma 2008

Dedication

To The Heroic Young Men
of
Easy Company
Second Battalion
Seventh Marine Regiment
First Marine Division

They Served Their Country
And The Nation Of South Korea
With Honor

Table of Contents

Prologue vii
Chapter I 1
Chapter II 25
Chapter III 45
Chapter IV 65
Chapter V 95
Chapter VI 123
Chapter VII 145
Chapter VIII 163
Chapter IX 185
Chapter X 195
Chapter XI 211
Chapter XII 229
Chapter XIII 241
Chapter XIV 263
Chapter XV 279
Chapter XVI 287
Battle Honors 305
A Tribute to a Valiant Marine 309
Acknowledgments 312
Marines E-2-7 roster, August 1951, Korea 315
List of photos and maps 318

Lest We Forget

They were all here and then no more.
These warriors, these Marines of our Corps.
They paid the price for you and me
That this nation would remain forever free.

They answered the call not thinking twice,
And we must never forget their sacrifice.
All rest here now as friends gather round
Paying respects at this hallowed ground.

What can we say to show that we care
As we bow our heads and say a prayer?
The sound of "Taps" played loud and clear,
An honor to all who will remain here.

So let us remember each Memorial Day,
As our time to pause, give thanks and pray.
We must always treasure our liberty,
And remember those who have kept us free.

And now that we depart this place serene,
We have rendered honors to a U. S. Marine.

Boyce Clark, USMC retired, author

Prologue

Easy Company Marines—More Than Brothers is a story about young men who fought in the Korean War during the years of 1951 and 1952. I was one of those young men. Our personalities are revealed through the hardships we endured fighting a determined, cunning enemy in unbearable weather. Most of us survived but, unfortunately, some of us died. The story recounts attacks on unnamed hills, our defensive positions during the peace talks, and the numerous patrols and ambushes that we prosecuted as well as the ones we repulsed. There are suspenseful moments, dreadful moments, moments of calm, and even moments of humor. Trusting my memory and that of many others who were in Korea, I have recorded the events in this story as accurately as possible. Only small amounts of dialogue can be remembered with any precision but the conversations in this writing reflect what happened at the time. There is no reason for me to believe that the anecdotes related to me by others are not true.

The story begins with my enlistment in the Marine Corps and the rigors of boot camp and combat infantry training. It continues with life aboard a troop ship and my assignment to Easy Company, Second Battalion, Seventh Marine Regiment of the First Marine Division. It describes my reactions and feelings at seeing dead people for the first time in my life, and seeing people, both enemy and friends, being killed. Several paragraphs are dedicated to individual men and their experiences. The story is from the personal viewpoint of a young Marine who had no idea where he was or what was happening. It is about actual combat, moments of fear, feelings and dreams, the reality of death, despair and relief.

Chapter I

Another War

Perplexed and troubled, my dad was listening to the nightly radio news broadcasts of the unsettling events that were developing in Asia when he asked, *"Where in the hell is South Korea?"* He wasn't the smartest bean in the pot but he knew that something horrendous was brewing, something that could eventually affect our nation, our entire family and, in particular, his oldest sons. But with the exception of Dad, none of us, including me, paid much attention to the reports of the invasion of South Korea by North Korean armies. Why should we? We had never before heard of North or South Korea and as far as I was concerned they were just two little unimportant countries somewhere on the other side of the world, far away from America.

But the reports of war persisted, and in just days this little skirmish seemed to erupt with a fury. Then the United Nations announced it was sending troops to fight the Communist North Korean aggression and the bulk of the troops, no doubt, would be from the United States. The thought of our nation becoming involved in another shooting war so soon after the end of World War II was disconcerting and frightening to me.

War! It was a small but ominous word. And this little war in far-off Asia that seemed so trivial at first was about to affect all of our lives, mine in particular. With mounting dread, I began to pay closer attention to this new war in the Far East, a war quickly becoming very deadly and very nasty.

Our military was woefully unprepared to meet this new threat to world peace. The numerically superior and well-trained North Korean forces had little trouble mauling and pummeling the hastily assembled United Nations forces as it drove deeper into South Korea. Nonetheless, our ill equipped and poorly trained soldiers put up a valiant, determined fight when they were thrust into the battle. Listening to the nightly newscasts and reading the newspaper headlines, it became quite obvious to us that this was no longer a small, insignificant skirmish.

Over time, the United Nations forces grew stronger and eventually they were able to stem the North Korean tide and take the offensive, shoving the Communists armies back to the north. Their progress seemed to be going so well that many of us believed the war would soon be over. But, then the Chinese Army entered into the fracas siding with the North Koreans. Massive numbers of fresh enemy troops routed the United Nations' armies and sent them reeling back to the south, inflicting huge numbers of casualties.

Near the end of the year, little doubt remained in my mind that my life was soon going to change and change drastically. Eighteen years old and unemployed I feared that I'd be drafted into the Army. I wanted to continue my education but I lacked the money to do so and I couldn't find any work, nothing but a few part-time jobs, certainly none that offered good pay or any permanency. Now that our nation was involved in this new war, employers were hesitant to hire young men who could be drafted into the service. Who could blame them?

However, there was a solution, a safe solution, so I thought. I could join the United States Air Force. Being in the Air Force

Chapter I

would likely keep me safe and out of combat and at the same time, I'd be fulfilling my military obligation and I could save my pay, attending college after the war. Heck, I didn't want to shoot at anyone and I certainly didn't want anyone shooting at me.

With my two best childhood friends, Alan Hanegan and Eddie Wager, I went to the Air Force recruiting office in Portland to enlist. Alan and Eddie both qualified for enlistment but the recruiters turned me down flat because I was a couple of pounds over their weight limit. I couldn't believe that they'd accepted Alan and not me because Alan was as pudgy as a fudge bar with a body the shape of a boiled egg and I was an athlete, in pretty fair shape. But there it was. My best friends would be going without me unless I could lose the weight in one week. The thought of being drafted into the Army was all the impetus I needed to go on a starvation diet and my mom made certain I did just that; she starved the hell out of me. But by the end of the week, and nearly dead from lack of food, I had, somehow, gained another pound. Frustrated and peeved by the entire set of events, I gave up the dieting routine and pigged out for the next three days.

"To hell with the Air Force. I don't care for their uniforms that much anyway."

With Eddie and Alan set to go, I began looking for work again, but it was the same old, frustrating story—no one wanted to hire an eighteen-year-old kid just out of high school who was eligible for the draft. I kept talking about joining the Air Force just to keep Dad off my back but I never once bothered to return to the recruiting office. Dejected and irritated by circumstances that I had no control over, my mind was muddled with uncertainty as I tried to make a logical and responsible decision. Since I had no money to go to school and since I couldn't find a decent job, enlisting in the service seemed the only option left to me. The folks knew there was a chance that I might be drafted but I don't think they ever gave thought to my enlisting in any branch of the service other than the Air

Force and most certainly not the Marines. And, because of my queasy stomach, I could never cope with life at sea so the Navy and Coast Guard weren't good options either. The only service left to consider, then, was the Marines.

Every time I read a newspaper article concerning the Army's involvement in Korea, I became more determined to stay out of that branch of the Armed Forces. But on the other hand, headlines about the Marines' participation in the war piqued my imagination. The Marines were outnumbered, outgunned and overwhelmed but continually made the enemy pay dearly. I knew little about them, about their traditions, their brotherhood, but I did know that they were tougher than hell. Joining the Marine Corps—now, that was an intriguing thought. And their dress blue uniforms were pretty enticing as well. Well, if the Marines wanted me, I was theirs. I'd made my decision, figuring that if someone was going to shoot at me, I might as well be trained by the best to shoot back.

Over the next five months, I asked myself many silly, inane questions. But this first question had to be the most stupid of them all.

"I wonder! Just how tough could it be to be a Marine?"

On a cold, rainy day in January 1951, Dad took me into Portland, as he had done for weeks, and left me to walk the cold, damp streets looking for work. Without a word to either of my parents about what I'd decided to do, I went to the Marine Corps Recruiting Office determined to enlist.

The recruiters made no promises, only that the Marines would make a man out of me. Heck, I thought I was a man: I'd played football, I could run up eight flights of stairs and I could shoot a gun. But I'm certain they knew exactly what they had on their hands—another dumb school kid. They took me anyway and they had no problems with my weight either. The only thing they seemed concerned about was that I walked upright and that I breathed air.

Another man to enlist the same day that I did was Norman Mann, a quiet fellow from Grants Pass and a few years older

Chapter I

than I. We weren't assigned to the same unit, not until long after serving in Korea, but our paths crossed many times. We became close friends and continued our friendship long after our service. Even our service numbers were close. Mine was 1166097 and his was 1166098.

That night, on the way home with Pop, I announced that I'd found work. Grinning from ear to ear, he seemed pleased, very pleased, and couldn't wait for answers.

"So, ya finally got a job, huh. When do ya start? Who hired you? What kinda work are ya gonna do? How much ya gettin' paid?"

I knew he would have a flipping fit when he heard my answer and I was right.

"I joined the Marines, Pa."

His eyes remained fixed on the road but he was visibly shaken, his face seemed to drain of color, as my statement took effect. After a few seconds, he took a deep breath and spoke almost pleadingly in a desperate, frantic voice.

"My God, Ted! Why in the hell did you join the Marines? I don't want you to go to war. I just wanted you to find a job."

Each one of my family reacted differently to the news of my enlistment in the Marines. Naturally, my folks were disturbed and extremely worried about what I'd done but they never once tried to talk me out of my decision. They were very patriotic people and they had no problem with me serving my country – but not in the Marines. It scared the hell out of them. It wasn't because they disliked the Marine Corps; it was because they didn't want their little boy in harm's way. And the Marines were always in harm's way. They felt deep concern just as other parents did when their sons went off to war. My brothers and sisters, on the other hand, were in awe that their big brother was going to fight in a war. And my poor grandmother, she cried and hugged me as if she were never going to see me again.

"Oh, Teddy! What ever possessed you to do sitch a fool thing like joinin' the Marines? Yore Uncle Jim was in the Marines and it was really hard on him. Oh, I wish you hadn't done this. Yore jist a kid, still wet behind the ears."

I loved my grandmother—I loved her dearly but she was always telling me that I was wet behind the ears, a statement that just peeved the daylights out of me. Being a dumb, naïve kid and not knowing the facts of life, I never really knew what the hell she meant by that.

On February 7, 1951, I left home on a train en route to the Marine Corps Recruit Depot in San Diego, California to begin boot camp training. I remembered the stupid question I had asked myself just a few weeks before.

"Just how tough could it be to be a Marine?"

I got an answer almost immediately. Oh, brother, did I ever!

Marine Corps Recruit Depot

The Marine Corps Recruit Depot was as foreign to me, an eighteen-year-old immature farm kid from Sherwood, Oregon, as the Sahara Desert would be to a penguin. My foolish question was answered immediately. Marine boot camp was pure hell and then some. The drill instructors harassed, ridiculed, demeaned and degraded us at every opportunity and they ran us into the ground, drilled us into the ground, and ground us into the ground. Everything we did was at rigid attention with eyes focused straight ahead. We ate at attention, took showers at attention, and even slept at attention.

After a couple of days, enough new recruits had arrived to form a platoon. Three Marines, a sergeant, a corporal and a PFC were assigned as our drill instructors. They were tougher than flank steaks cut from a 14-year-old Montana steer and each one spoke with a raspy, snarling, gravelly voice not easily understood. Our Senior Drill Instructor, Sergeant Cook, was every inch a Marine, ramrod straight and as trim as a Greek

Chapter I

athlete. In the end I came to respect and admire him as a good man, as did most of the other *boots*. But in the beginning I considered him an unyielding tyrant devoid of any sympathies for his fellow man.

Herding us across the parade ground to a warehouse, each of us received an issue of clothing, shaving gear and bedding. My shoes fit well but everything else was too large. The sleeves on my dungaree jackets were so long they hid my fingers. Laden with gear, we went to our new barracks but, instead of marching as a platoon, we ran as a mob. Most of us were in decent physical condition but running with an armload of gear wasn't at all easy. We were packing so much stuff that we couldn't see the man in front of us. And being slow afoot, I didn't want to be last, because being last for anything was certain to draw the ire of the DI's. Someone at the head of the crowd tripped and all of us to a man fell over him. It was pure pandemonium, bodies, clothing, bedding, all mixed in a large writhing clump in the middle of the parade ground and the DI's screaming at us from the top of their lungs that we were nothing but useless imbeciles.

Each of us got a *free* haircut, too, our heads shaved completely bald. I presumed every strand of hair was cut for two reasons. The first was to make us look alike—like a bunch of dumb hicks—and the second, and probably the more important of the two, was to make certain we had no head lice. With no hair on my head, my dungaree cap fit sloppily down to my ears and nearly over my eyes. But I wasn't the only one to look absolutely ridiculous. We all did but at least we looked ridiculous together.

We came from all walks of life and from states that I'd only read about in my high school geography and history classes: New York, Michigan, Florida, Texas, Arkansas. It was quite an experience meeting them and also quite an experience trying to understand some of them when they spoke, particularly those from the Deep South. Seven were from the same community: Moscow, Texas. Unfortunately, being from a place named Moscow gave the drill instructors an excuse to needle the hell out of them. For the first time in my life, I was truly thankful to be from Sherwood, Oregon.

We were ordered to write letters to our families no less than once a week. We looked forward to responses from home, but getting anything in return other than a letter, a Bible, or family photographs was certain to cause the recruit some grief. The Corps wanted us to maintain contact with our folks but they were determined to cure us of being a momma's boy. Within a few weeks of forming the platoon, two of the recruits each received a package that became a big, big problem for them. One of the guys got six candy bars in his package and had to consume all six within a minute. After gagging down the rich chocolate morsels, he had to dance about the squad bay in his skivvies flapping his arms like an idiot, screaming over and over in a falsetto-voice,

"I'm a pogey-bait pussy! I'm a pogey-bait pussy!"

Pogey-bait was the term that Marines used for candy. You can draw your own conclusion to what the rest of it meant.

The other guy got a package containing a few family photographs, two Roi Tan cigars and, of all things, a pair of striped under shorts. Wearing his new undergarment on the outside of his dungaree trousers, he stood at attention and smoked both cigars with a bucket over his head, nearly croaking from the suffocating cigar smoke. That night, every single one of us wrote a letter, begging our families not to send any packages.

During mail call, we stood at attention at the foot of our bunks while a drill instructor called out the names of those who had received mail. One of the Moscow, Texans named Allen, who had buckteeth akin to a beaver, stood at attention across the aisle from me. Every time I looked at him, I wanted to laugh. One day, the drill instructor bellowed out Allen's name. After acknowledging the drill instructor, he took a step forward to claim his letter and tripped, falling flat on his face, at attention. All I could imagine in my mind was Allen's buckteeth shattering like a porcelain dish on the immaculate squad bay floor. One corner of my mouth twitched upward just a

Chapter I

tiny bit and, unfortunately for me, one of our sour-faced drill instructors spotted it. I've no idea how he noticed but he did and he was immediately in my face yelling and ranting and screaming to wipe that stupid grin from my mug. After a few moments of verbal abuse, he ordered me to report to Sergeant Cook in the duty room for punishment. But because his voice was so hoarse and scratchy, I was quite certain he said to report to the *dirty room*.

The duty room also happened to be Sergeant Cook's quarters and before we could enter, we had to rap on the door and wait for permission. Some of the other recruits hadn't rapped loud enough and, as punishment, they had to run laps around the squad bay. So, I banged on Sergeant Cook's door with what I thought was some force. Surprised, the response from within was,

"I can't hear you."

If he couldn't hear me, then why did he make the comment? So, I reared back and I beat the ever-lovin' hell out of his door, hitting it just as hard as I could. The resounding thumps rattled the entire building. He angrily shouted,

"Get in here, meat head, before you break my damned door down."

Entering the room at a brisk pace, I stopped at attention in front of Sergeant Cook's desk, and reported in a loud, clear voice,

"Sir! The other drill instructor ordered me to report to the dirty room, Sir."

Sergeant Cook was already irritated as hell but when he heard me refer to his quarters as the *"dirty room,"* he went off like all the Roman candles in China. I spent the next thirty minutes with him screaming degrading insults one inch from my ear and doing push-ups with his foot on my butt. For the next two days, every spare moment I had was spent in Sergeant Cook's *"duty room,"* scrubbing the walls and floors to ensure that I remembered it was not a dirty room.

It was wise to keep a low profile and not draw attention to oneself. Out of sight, out of mind. But that wasn't always possible, and I managed to get myself into trouble on a few more occasions.

Every morning, about five o'clock, we were shaken out of our sleep by one of our barking, snarling drill instructors. It was the same routine every single morning.

> "Get the hell outa bed, you sweet little thangs. You girls got thirty minutes to get cleaned up before chow. Move it, you buncha idiots. Move it! Move it!"

Before falling outside on the parade ground in platoon formation and marching off to the chow hall for breakfast, we showered, shaved and made our beds. I always finished the routine as quickly as possible and usually sat down on the cold tiled floor in a corner, sometimes catching a few more winks of sleep, hoping not to get caught. But one morning, sitting on the floor, I fell into a deep sleep and no one bothered to wake me. Apparently, the drill instructor didn't notice that one of his sixty-plus recruits was missing and marched the platoon off to chow. When I awoke, I found myself alone and nearly went into a panic. I bolted out of the building and, avoiding anyone who remotely looked like a drill instructor, ran across the parade ground to the mess hall. A couple of the boots had already finished breakfast and had exited the mess hall, standing at parade rest on the drill field, waiting for the other men. I fell into place with them, preferring to skip breakfast rather than risk something far worse than the wrath of God.

We recruits had no idea why they were picking on us and forcing us to do things that seemed humanly impossible and possibly inhumane. It crossed my mind that this recruit training was far worse than war. What we didn't understand was that our Drill Instructors were gradually replacing the individualistic, self-centered and selfish person within us with a team spirit, the *esprit de corps* that's made the Marine Corps so famous. We were being taught that we were not just individuals; we were a team, and as a team we could endure anything.

Chapter I

Training indeed was the key and it formed the very basis for our survival in combat. Above all other things, boot camp taught us discipline, obedience and perseverance. We were taught to stand straight, our chins up and shoulders back, and to have pride in ourselves. It mattered not if we were short, tall, rich, poor, black, white, Jewish or Protestant. It mattered only that each one of us was part of a team that others could depend on.

After weeks of intensive training, drilling in formation, and doing calisthenics, the Marine Corps finally issued us M1 rifles…but no ammunition. I was eager to get my hands on one of the rifles but, after I got it, I wasn't so sure I wanted to keep it. First, we were given 60 seconds to memorize the serial number and, second, it was heavy as the dickens, weighing nearly ten pounds. Other than taking them into the showers and to bed, we carried them constantly and even did calisthenics with them. Extending our arms outstretched and holding a rifle for several minutes—well, that isn't exactly an easy thing to do. And no one in his right mind referred to his rifle as a gun, either, not unless he was willing to endure a half hour of humiliating punishment.

Several weeks into our boot camp training, we went to Camp Mathews for rifle training. Camp Mathews was another Marine Corps base not far from the Marine Corps Recruit Depot. Although discipline was still mighty strict, I felt a little more at ease. We spent most of the first week learning how to hold our rifles in the various shooting positions and dry firing at targets. To my surprise, many of the boots had never shot a weapon before. Well, I figured I had it made because I'd hunted and fired rifles and shotguns dozens of times while on the farm but that was another miscalculation on my part. To my chagrin, I barely qualified.

In the evenings while at Camp Matthews, we received specialized water training in a large swimming pool. Some of the boots didn't know how to swim and a few were terrified of the water, a sorry predicament because in only a few days they had to overcome their fears and learn. We practiced making floats out of our packs and swimming across the pool with all of our gear, including rifles. We also practiced the correct way to jump off a ship and some important life-saving techniques.

The first day we were to swim, we stood naked in the dressing room listening to instructions from one of our drill instructors. He stopped talking momentarily, staring at one of the boots standing some twenty feet from him. Then he blurted out,

"My Gawd, boy! You're loaded with crabs. You got a swarm of crabs on you."

His voice boomed and rose in a blaring crescendo with a warning.

"Anybody else in here got a problem? If you do, you better speak up now. Ah don't wanna find out later. Do you hear me?"

Every single one of us screamed a response in unison from the top of our lungs, rattling the glass in the windows,

"Sir! Yes, Sir!"

This naïve farm boy had no idea what the heck the drill instructor was talking about. Crabs? I'd never heard the term *crabs* used in this way. But I soon found out what they were because within the hour we all had been examined for these minute pests and deloused, whether we were infected with them or not.

We simulated leaping from a sinking ship by jumping into the pool from a fifteen-foot high platform. Another smaller platform had been constructed atop a tower perhaps twenty feet higher. To me, it looked more like a thousand. We knew that sooner or later, one of us was going to foul up and that poor soul would have to jump from the tower. And I knew if I were the one they picked to jump, someone would have to carry my limp body up there. Nearing the end of our final day of water training, the drill instructors surprised us, screaming,

"The last feather-merchant off the small springboard has to go off the tower platform."

Chapter I

Frantically, we clawed, scrambled, shoved and bulled our way onto the small springboard but most of us fell off before reaching the end of it. No one wanted to jump from the tower except for one person—an unpopular bully of a fellow named Hendon. He made certain that he was picked and he got his wish. I stood in awe, as we all did, watching Hendon climb, one rung after another up the ladder, to the top of that monstrous structure. He walked to the edge of the platform, extended his arms in front of him and made a beautiful, majestic swan dive into the pool. The completely dumbstruck drill instructors nearly swallowed their Adam's Apples.

Showing up the drill instructors fully exposed Hendon's stupidity and he didn't get away with it, not for one minute. A thirty-foot pole with a large box mounted on top was to be Hendon's perch for the next three hours. Wearing only his under shorts, he went up into the waist-high box and, with his thumbs tucked under his armpits, flapped his arms, and shouted over and over,

"I'm a shit-bird! I'm a shit-bird! I'm a shit-bird!"

Several weeks of doing calisthenics with rifles in our hands strengthened our bodies and prepared us for bayonet drill. We practiced thrust and parry, parry and thrust, until our arms ached with unbelievable pain. Several other recruit platoons joined ours on the parade field one morning to practice one final drill. I found myself facing a blond-haired brute, a fellow I recognized. His name was Lanny Johnson; he'd attended my high school, one grade behind me. The last time I saw him, he was a momma's boy, all baby fat and soft. But not now! His arms rippled with muscle and he had become as strong as a railroad gandy dancer's coffee. As we sparred with each other, we exchanged whispered messages but he never once smiled. Only after the drill was over did I cease worrying that he might remember that I was one of the kids who'd pulled his pants down while on the school stage and then opened the curtain revealing his bare bottom to the entire student body.

By the end of boot camp, our uniforms fit us very nicely because we had lost our baby fat and had become muscular, lean and fit. Our heads, no longer shaved bald, had hair but it was neatly trimmed. We had evolved from a bunch of scroungy, dumb oddballs into a platoon of sharp looking, fine young men. Other than having weather-beaten, leathery faces like our drill instructors, we all looked very much the same: ramrod straight, fit and determined.

Standing on the hot parade field during boot camp graduation, watching the heat waves rise from the red-tiled roof of my barracks, I felt relief that my training was over. But I also had some other feelings. I felt different and I looked different and I felt an immense pride in myself. I knew that an historic period in my life had just ended. I was physically stronger and mentally more determined and confident and I felt that I was ready to meet the challenges of the world head on. I felt that I had truly become a man and, most of all, a Marine.

Alan Hannigan, Vito Pileggi, and Eddie Wager

Chapter I

Ten-Day Leave

We new Privates-First-Class went home for ten days after boot camp graduation. For most of us this would be the last time we would get to see our families before going into combat. And for some, this would be the very last time they would ever go home at all. My ten-day leave passed by too quickly. My family and my friends noticed a difference in me—how respectful I had become of everyone, especially of older people and their comments made me feel good.

During this time I met Margaret Blaser, a cute little blonde who reminded me of the actress June Allison. No other girl affected me quite like her. She was simply breathtaking, as fresh and sweet as a bubbling mountain spring. There were several children in her family but I only knew her brother Benny. Everybody in Sherwood knew him. He was a good kid but he was hell on wheels...motorcycle wheels, that is. Maggie, on the other hand, was a quiet, lovely, young lady. Regretfully, I only got to see her a couple of times during my ten-day leave, but as far as I was concerned, she was for keeps.

Eddie and Alan had also come home from their boot camp but we only had a few days together. We tried to make the most of them and even though they were now in the service, they were still shy around the girls. One night, we drove through downtown Sherwood just once and then back home, just like we did when we were bashful 16-year-olds. I was happy to see them but I was glad that I had joined the Marines instead of the Air Force.

Combat Training

After my ten-day leave, I reported to the Advanced Infantry Training Center at Camp Pendleton, California. Unlike my cool, green Oregon, Camp Pendleton was a dry sagebrush covered desert, hot as the hubs of Hades.

"Advanced Infantry Training! Just how tough can that be?"

There were many, many times during the next two months that I thought I was going to die. Carrying fifty pounds of gear on one's back for fifteen miles in soft sand in blistering heat would cause any sane person to believe, with absolute certainty, his demise was near. If I didn't die from the heat, then surely it would be from thirst and if not from thirst, then from complete exhaustion.

The training was rigorous and grueling. We crawled through infiltration courses on our backs under barbed wire barriers while explosive charges detonated around us and live machine gun fire ripped through the air a few feet above our heads. We repeatedly raced through obstacle courses trying to break long established course records, performed hours of close-order drill, climbed hills, dug holes and practiced infantry tactics. We learned how to kill another human with our hands, with a stick, with wire or whatever item we could fashion into a weapon. It was tough, punishing and ugly but it was necessary.

As time passed, I got mentally tougher and physically stronger. As advanced infantry training neared an end, everyone began getting scrappy and cocky, confident that we were combat ready. For a time, knowing that I couldn't hit the broadside of a barn with a rifle, I thought it would be exciting to be a machine gunner but when I saw what those poor fellows had to pack on their backs my romantic notion quickly faded away. Another thing I didn't consider was that automatic weapons draw a lot of attention from enemy gunners.

Not many days before departing the United States, the men in my training platoon were given a series of shots. Shirtless and in single file, we entered a tent and were faced by two rows of grinning corpsmen, each one with a needle held at the ready. Passing between the corpsmen, we received four shots in one arm and three in the other. The pain and stiffness felt during the first few hours were tolerable but, by evening, it was a different story. My arms ached horribly and doing any kind of exercise was grievous torture. But, over the next 18 hours, the pain level gradually decreased until it was no longer a problem.

Chapter I

Not all of us in my group were going overseas. Many stayed in the States. Not all of us who were going overseas were going into combat. Me? This weed-pulling farm kid from Oregon was assigned to the eleventh replacement draft, sent to Korea aboard a troop ship and straight to the front lines. Heck, I thought all Marines went into combat. But that wasn't true even though we all had combat training. We were often reminded that there were six men behind the front lines in support of one man directly involved in combat. I became one of those lucky fellows who had the support of six guys who were somewhere behind me.

"*How could I be so darned lucky???????*"

Crossing The Pacific

Just how tough can it be crossing the Pacific Ocean on a ship?

The Navy gave us a little blue booklet entitled *Life Aboard a Transport* as we boarded the ship. The booklet contained rules of conduct while on board and a glossary of typical naval terms. Three of those terms are noteworthy and should be mentioned—the *Smoking Lamp,* the *scuttlebutt,* and the *Head.*

If one heard over the ship's intercom, *The Smoking Lamp is lit,* it meant that we were permitted to smoke – that is, we could smoke in specified areas. When we heard, *The Smoking Lamp is out,* that meant cigarettes had to be extinguished and smoking was no longer allowed. Period!

Now—the *Head* is a place where you put your butt and I'm not referring to a cigarette butt. The *Head* is the toilet.

The *scuttlebutt* meant two things. If someone was referred to as having the scuttlebutt, it meant that this person supposedly had the facts or knowledge about something that had happened or was about to happen. A drinking fountain was also referred to as a scuttlebutt, perhaps because people meeting at the water fountain often passed information to each other.

A small pamphlet stapled inside the back cover of the booklet immediately caught my attention. Printed in big bold letters on the face of the pamphlet were the words *Abandon Ship*. Now, that was all I needed to be reassured that this thing was going to get us across the ocean. Hell, I knew how to abandon ship. Jump!

According to the pamphlet, if the ship were attacked, all troops had to go below decks to their compartments thus allowing the sailors unrestricted freedom to defend their vessel. I thought to hell with the ship. Who wants to go below deck if the thing is attacked, blown up and might sink. I had a question that I didn't think was answered satisfactorily by the little blue book. Were we supposed to go below to our compartments if torpedoes were used to attack the ship? The U. S. Navy would have another thought coming if they thought I was going back down into the belly of this tub once it had been torpedoed. No way in hell!

For the next two-plus weeks we were held captive aboard the ship, with no place to go and nothing to do but train, train, train. Our non-commissioned officers kept us busy cleaning weapons, attending classes, and doing calisthenics. I must have field stripped and cleaned my M1 rifle ten times every day. The thing was immaculate. All of us knew we had to be mentally prepared and physically fit for combat when we arrived in Korea but the daily training routine was all so repetitive and boring.

The Tobacco Fairy

Even though the ship rolled around in the ocean like a basketball in a bathtub, and this was the very first time in my life that I had ever been on a ship, the first five days at sea were not difficult for me. Because I had a queasy stomach as a kid and often got car sick, it worried me that I'd get sick on the ship. But, I did fine. I did fine, that is, until the Tobacco Fairy struck me down. Most of my Marine buddies smoked cigarettes. Me? I despised cigarettes and had no problem turning

Chapter I

down a smoke when one was offered. However, on the sixth day some idiot offered me a chew from a plug of *Day's Work* tobacco. Although I'd never before tried chewing tobacco, for some stupid reason I thought I could handle it and bit off a healthy chunk.

After five or six chews, my stomach rebelled with a vengeance and I found myself at the rail of the ship throwing up everything I ever ate or owned. The combination of the tobacco and the ship's movement did me in. I covered the side and part of the deck of that grand old bucket, the U. S. S. Cavalier, with vomit. I spent the balance of the trip hanging onto and bending over the ship's railing, seldom daring to go below to my sleeping compartment or to eat meals. From that day on, no matter what ship I was aboard, I was never able to keep my food down—if I was able to eat at all. What normally triggered my stomach to give up its contents, other than the ship's movement, were an ugly mixture of odors: cigarette smoke, diesel fumes, the stink of vomit, and salt air.

There was always some wind because of the ship's speed, no matter how slow it seemed to be traveling. Therefore, it was a good idea to be upwind of anyone who was losing his lunch to avoid getting sprayed by a chunky mist.

A Texan who had also become seasick perched next to me on the rail. While visiting we occasionally took time out to throw up. He told me that he as well as several others had gotten sick the very first day out at sea. He was holding onto the rail, feeling horrible and looking as green as the ocean, when a chaplain stopped to console him.

"Got a weak stomach, son?"

Like all Texans, he had a quick comeback answer.

"No sir. My stomach's not weak at all. Heck, Ah'm throwin' it out there jest as fur as the rest of 'em."

I've heard that quip a couple of times since then and I'm not certain that he was the originator of it but I'll bet whoever said it first had to be a Texan.

The U.S.S. Cavalier

The sailors aboard her would probably have disagreed with me but in my estimation the U. S. S. Cavalier was a creaky old tub. Every piece of metal, painted gray, felt grimy, as if it had been coated with a thin layer of grease mixed with sand. The ship wallowed and surged as it chugged ponderously in the green, foamy swells of the Pacific Ocean. It had but one scuttlebutt (water fountain) that worked, and the water from it was warm and tasted stale. I had a feeling the water was pumped from the ocean and desalinated because it tasted so horrible. The mess deck also served as a movie theater and a place for training lectures and church services. When necessary, the tables and benches were folded and stowed out of the way. And because the benches folded easily, it caused us a few messy problems. They collapsed, sometimes without warning, even during church services. Several times, as a Marine was seating himself balancing a tray of food, his bench caved in. The guy's natural reaction was to throw the tray upwards. Thus, everyone in the immediate vicinity got showered with an extra serving of chow.

Although most of the men, three or four thousand in all, were Marines, there were also some Air Force personnel on board and all of us slept in the hold of the ship, crammed in like fish in a can. Each man's rack (bed) was really nothing more than a piece of canvas stretched inside a rectangular metal tubular framework. It measured about seven feet long and thirty inches wide, barely large enough to hold an average-sized person. The canvas was tautly suspended, laced with rope within the metal rectangle. Five or six of these racks were suspended, one above the other, about thirty inches apart and each sleeping compartment held hundreds of them. More often than not, someone trying to sleep four or five racks up got sick and vomited on the men sleeping below. I found it was always best to sleep in the very top rack, even though it was a climb getting to it and the temperature was a bit warmer. Not only was it safer, there also seemed to be a little more headroom and space to stick things among the pipes and electrical wiring.

The decks of the sleeping compartments were often covered with vomit, particularly so when the seas had become rough and the swells higher than normal. It was treacherous walking and it became a problem figuring out what to do with our shoes when sleeping, fearing someone might throw up on them. It wasn't unusual to see someone barfing into the same bucket he'd just been using to clean up the place. Unbearable at times, just the smell of vomit mixed with the odor of diesel in the stale compartmental air made me sick.

"How tough could it be crossing the ocean on a ship?"

What a fool question that was.

Horseplay

Pranks were common aboard ship so it was wise to be wary especially of the *old salts,* seasoned sailors and Marines, who knew every trick in the book. One was sending someone unfamiliar with sea duty to fetch a bucket of grommets. But my favorite of all pranks was a dandy one I witnessed several times.

The head (toilet) featured a long, slightly sloped, trough of fast-moving water with perhaps as many as a dozen seats. Salt water was pumped into one end of the trough and it gravity-fed out a drain at the other end, presumably emptying into the sea. The person pulling the prank always occupied the seat nearest the source of water. Being as inconspicuous as possible, the prankster gathered up toilet paper forming a large loose bundle, set fire to it and placed it into the stream of water. The flaming bundle, carried by the rapidly flowing stream, passed under each unsuspecting victim, searing their rumps and other precious parts of their bodies, causing them to sequentially leap straight up.

Kobe, Japan Harbor

In late July 1951, after more than two miserable weeks at sea, we at last arrived in Kobe, Japan for a short stopover. It was a relief to be docked and standing on something that wasn't rolling back and forth and heaving up and down but even at that I still walked spread-legged and tottered like a drunk. The Marines were allowed to leave the ship for a few hours to see the sights and to relax. The Air Force personnel also debarked but they never returned to the ship, staying in Japan.

Still feeling poorly and weak, I had no desire to plow through a mountain of sea-bags looking for my belongings just to go ashore and walk around Kobe. No doubt most of the Marines wanted to find women, knowing that it might be their last chance to see one for a long time. Fooling around with women in a foreign country often led to trouble, the kind of trouble I didn't need. I was quite content to stay aboard ship with no one to bug me. Besides, there were more than enough interesting things to see from my favorite perch at the ship's railing.

The harbor was a beehive of activity. Dozens of cargo cranes lined the docks busily loading and unloading ships. Their long, slow-moving booms reminded me of giant, mechanical praying mantises. Small fishing boats with tall, thin smoke stacks spouting black smoke rings chugged by in all directions. The stench in the air was considerably stronger than that of a typical fishing harbor.

Japanese children, with big grins on their faces, swam in the murky water around the ship waiting for the ship's crew and the Marines to throw small coins to them. Whenever they dove for a coin, the water churned as if a school of hungry piranha were fighting for a scrap of meat. The kids seemed to stay under water for remarkably long periods of time and, amazingly, when they resurfaced, they seldom came up empty handed.

On a nearby dock, I observed an old man and an old woman, who appeared to be visiting with each other. There was nothing strange about that except that they were squatting at the dock's edge, relieving themselves into the waters of the bay. And here these children were swimming around in that soup.

For a country boy like me, it was a captivating scene and quite relaxing. Going into combat was the farthest thing from my mind—for the moment.

Chapter II

The Korean Peninsula—Beauty and Tragedy

The boat ride to the harbor of Pusan in South Korea was short and uneventful. The seas were calmer and my stomach behaved itself, much to my relief. As we set foot on South Korean soil, I turned and bade farewell to the railing of the ship where I'd spent over two weeks of my life. Surveying the distant terrain, the sky, the buildings, the waterfront, I remembered Dad's query a year ago when this tiny Asian country first became involved in this war. *"Where in the hell is South Korea?"* Well, from first hand experience, his oldest son could now answer his question. And it wouldn't be very long before his oldest son could answer many more questions about the damned place ... from first hand experience.

We boarded trucks and rode to an airstrip at Masan. There, we climbed aboard C-47s, commonly known to civilians as DC-3s, old but sturdy two-engine tail draggers. My curiosity was piqued when I observed several round patches, similar to tin can lids, attached here and there to the wings and fuselage of the plane. The windows in the cargo and passenger bay were round like portholes. And in the center of each window was a hole, plugged by a rubber cork.

Getting as comfortable as possible, we waited. Presently, a truck carrying more Marines sped out onto the runway and, with a squeal of tires, stopped next to us. Quickly, the Marines and driver exited and climbed aboard the plane. The driver, who looked more like a civilian than anyone in the military, paused momentarily to discuss something with an officer and then climbed into the cockpit.

"For Pete's sake! That guy's gonna fly this plane."

It was a mite disconcerting when it sunk into my thick skull that a truck driver was our pilot, hoping he could fly better than he drove. Having flown only once in my life, I felt pretty darned uneasy wondering about the fellow's abilities. As the old plane lumbered down the runway on the way to becoming airborne, I took a deep breath and hung on. After being in the air a few minutes, I began to relax, feeling a little more confident in our truck-driver-turned-pilot. Actually, he flew quite well but never gained much altitude, flying between mountain ridges over small valleys, seldom any higher than the low surrounding hills. One of the men commented that the reason the pilot flew so low was to avoid sniper fire. When he said that, I knew then what the patches were covering. Bullet holes! We had arrived where people would be shooting at us. My stomach tightened in a knot, realizing that in minutes I'd be in the middle of a killing war.

Easy-Two-Seven, My Company

Our plane landed at a small airstrip near Yanggu, South Korea. The training, instructions and warnings we were given never mentally prepared us for what we were about to see: the complete obliteration of civilization. The town of Yanggu had been thoroughly destroyed by warfare. Only a few chimneys and walls were standing; everything else had been turned to rubble. This was my first vision of the results of war and even though I had half expected it, it was still a grim picture and a reminder that this was no game we were playing.

Crawling aboard trucks, we rode to a staging area where we received our company assignments. Mine was Easy Company, Second Battalion of the Seventh Marine Regiment in the First Marine Division. This was a combat line company and commonly referred to as Easy-Two-Seven. I soon came to feel that Easy-Two-Seven was the best outfit in all of the armed forces. *"Easy does it"* was our motto and it was heard often.

Caruso's The Name

Although I knew none of the other replacements personally, I recognized a few who had gone through advanced infantry training at Tent Camp Two in Camp Pendleton. One fellow I spotted, I vividly remembered telling myself at the time that the guy was nothing but trouble, a foul-up, and a goof ball. During problem exercises, I noticed the instructors were on him constantly, admonishing him for doing everything wrong. His name was Louis Caruso and, believe it or not, Louie became my best and closest friend while in Korea—and still is.

Louie Caruso

By luck of the draw, Caruso and I were paired together the very first night. He was from Brooklyn, New York and talked with that fabled Brooklyn accent. Louie had dark, curly hair, was every bit Italian, and a small bundle of energy. And when smoking cigarettes, he cocked his head to one side so the cigarette smoke wouldn't get into his eyes.

All of us developed nicknames. Mine was *Veep*. Caruso had several: Lou-Lou, Louie, Little Lou, and so on but some he earned should never be printed.

Eventually, I changed my mind about him being a foul-up. I actually came to believe, at times, that Louie was a genius. One thing was for certain: he was a survivor. He was always thinking of ways to make our lives more comfortable, more tolerable, even if implementing his schemes meant some risk to him. I credit him considerably for helping me survive the terrible ordeals of Korea, and in my eyes, Louie was a hero—although I would never admit it to him.

Louie's antics, pranks and schemes kept the rest of us entertained, if not a bit wary that one of us would be his next target. Concentrating on what he was up to kept us from worrying about the war and what we might be facing in the days to come. And some of the pranks that he pulled were things that only a great mind could conceive.

That first night together, Louie and I had to make a tent out of our shelter-halves. Two shelter-halves snapped together formed a small tent that presumably kept two people sheltered from the weather. However, the shelter-half tents were not all that large. Either your head or your feet stuck out of one end or the other if you stretched out full length. Sometimes the tent seemed to be more trouble than it was worth but for the time being, it was better than nothing.

With Louie constantly bossing me and telling me how to do everything in his Brooklyn accent, we got the tent up just about the time it began to rain. Then we discovered that we had to trench around the outside to keep the rainwater from running through the tent. This city slicker from Brooklyn, who was raised on concrete and probably never saw dirt until he joined the Marines, tried to tell me, a farm boy, how to dig a ditch.

That night we learned a lot about how NOT to put up a tent. Never put the tent pegs in the trench where the water runs. The ground gets soggy, the pegs pull out, and down it comes. Also, never touch the roof of the tent. The tent fabric seemed to collect moisture and wherever it was touched, it dripped water. We were wet for two days—maybe longer.

"I'm accustomed to rain because it rains a lot in Oregon."

Louie, puffing on a cigarette with his head cocked to one side, asked,

"Youse from Ory-gone? Ain't Ory-gone near Mishy-gone?"

Well, I could see right away that it was going to be a difficult task educating this guy. It seemed that, from that first night on, I had to tell him every day that the correct way to pronounce Oregon was to say *Ory-gun*, not *Ory-gone*. And we weren't referred to as lumberjacks either. We were loggers. They might have lumberjacks in Nova Scotia or in Buffalo but the folks who worked in the woods in the Pacific Northwest were called loggers. I kept trying and trying, but it never sank into his thick skull, no matter how much I preached.

It was a real adventure being in a leaky tent in a rainstorm, in a war in Korea, with a genuine nutcase like Louie. I wondered at the time what in the heck I'd done to deserve all of this.

Company Strength

Each line company was composed of a headquarters section, a machine gun platoon and three rifle platoons. The headquarters section included command officers and staff noncommissioned officers, a few office clerks, a sixty-millimeter mortar section, a 3.5 rocket launcher section, runners, corpsmen and radiomen.

The machine gun platoon, led by a lieutenant, was composed of three sections, two machine gun squads in each section. Most men in a machine gun platoon, over forty of them, were armed with thirty caliber carbines. Depending on the situation, from one to three machine gun squads were assigned to each of the rifle platoons. Not being in machine guns, I knew little about the guns other than they could lay down devastating fire.

A rifle platoon, over forty men when at full strength, was commanded by a lieutenant and assisted by a staff sergeant, a runner, a Korean interpreter and a corpsman. It was divided into three thirteen-man squads, each squad consisting of three four-man fire teams and a sergeant squad leader. The members of the fire team, the basic combat unit in the Marine Corps at the time, were a corporal designated as the fire team leader, a rifleman, a Browning automatic rifleman (BAR man) and an assistant to the BAR man. Except for the BAR man, everyone in a squad carried a Garand M1 rifle. The BAR man carried the Browning automatic rifle (BAR), a thirty-caliber weapon that used the same ammunition as the M1. The Assistant BAR man carried M1 ammunition clips for his rifle and extra ammunition magazines for the BAR.

Men of the Second Platoon

The day after our arrival, we replacements were assigned to units within the company. Louie Caruso, I, and several others went into the second platoon. The platoon was woefully short of men, some serving enough time in combat to be rotated home and others had become casualties, wounded or killed. There was no mistaking us as replacements; we were still clean and sharp while the veterans were scruffy, unkempt and appeared much older. We must have looked like snot-nosed kids to those guys. Most sported moustaches and hadn't had a decent haircut in some time not to mention the unmatched, soiled and worn condition of their dungaree uniforms. The company had just come off three months of intense, wicked, continuous fighting and their ranks had grown thin. During combat, the company rosters changed frequently as the leaders of the platoons shuffled men around trying to maintain complete and cohesive fighting units.

Our platoon leader was a redheaded second lieutenant by the name of John Lilley, sometimes referred to as Captain Jack. He was a native of Massachusetts with a very definite Bostonian accent. I loved to hear him say words like car and park, sounding more like *cah* and *pahk*. When I first met him, he was bearded, had a big bushy moustache, wore baggy clothing, and looked like he'd just crawled out of a boxcar. But regardless of his appearance, he was a true gentleman, one hell of a fine leader, and he had the utmost respect of every man under his command. He had been with the company five or six months before my arrival and had already been wounded twice. We eventually became very good friends, a relationship that would last for the rest of our lives.

Larry Pressley, Lt. John Lilley, and SSgt Quinones

The platoon sergeant was Manuel Hirata. He was small of stature but was a-tough-as-nails rooster of a man who wasn't beyond leading a charge directly into the face of machine gun fire. He, too, had the highest respect of his men always setting the best example of a good solid hard-charging Marine.

The Third Squad

Louie and I were assigned to the third squad, Louie in the first fire team and I in the second, both of us becoming Browning automatic riflemen. Our squad leader was Sergeant Larry Pressley, an Iwo Jima survivor. He instructed Louie and me to watch our fire team leaders and listen closely to their instructions and advice. He always had a few words of wisdom and, being a gregarious sort, recounted some very interesting stories about island fighting during World War II.

> "The Marines fight here in Korea the same way as we fought in the islands — brutal, head-on, frontal assaults. Nothin's changed much except for having better airpower. The rifles are the same, the chow's the same, artillery and mortars are the same. It's just another war but the same hell and nothin' but a stinkin' mess. The best advice I can give you is to stay off the skyline. And watch the shadows. If they move, well…I think ya got the picture."

A few World War II veterans, like Pressley, were sprinkled throughout the company, their leadership invaluable to the rest of us *kids* who had little or no combat experience.

My fire team leader was Jerry J. Miller, a tall, lanky, blond-haired kid from Minnesota. Everyone, including the officers, called him J. J. He was combat-smart and had the voice of a drill instructor. This guy I would have followed into hell. And there were several times that I thought I had. He'd already been in Korea five or six months and I figured if I stuck close to him, I might make it through this thing. But, sticking too close to him got me into a heap of trouble more than a few times.

Chapter II

Phil Meek was the team's rifleman. He was from Oklahoma and was part Sac and Fox Indian. He had fiery eyes. His small stature earned him the nickname *"Too Short to Squat"* but none dared call him that to his face.

Thomas Edward Bullock, a true southerner from Mississippi, had been the BAR man until my arrival. It was traditional that the newest man carried the BAR and the old BAR man become his assistant. Bullock couldn't wait. Grinning, he handed the Browning to me.

"Its all yorn now, pardner."

I cringed when he clamped his grubby mitts onto my clean and immaculate M1 rifle, claiming ownership.

Jerry Miller

Bullock was not a large person either but he was taller than Meek by a hair's breadth. Wearing clothing one or two sizes too large caused him to look somewhat like a vagabond. Because he was from the Deep South, some of the guys jokingly said he couldn't walk comfortably unless he had rocks in his shoes. Bullock was an easy-going type with a good sense of humor, laid back and cool-headed, but he wasn't someone to fool with when he was a bit upset, able to hold his own in a scrap. He was the one who gave me the nickname Veep. I got a big kick out of the way he talked, speaking with that thick Southern accent.

"Spell Mississippi for me, Ed."

"Hell, Veep! If ah could spell Mississipeh, ah woulda gone tuh high school."

Loren Tracy was Louie's fire team leader. He was a quiet, modest fellow from Kansas who had been wounded in previous action. Loren was fair skinned, had blond hair and was thin as a string. Being so skinny, I wondered how in the world enemy soldiers saw him well enough to take a shot at him.

New Jersey native Jack Bitting was the rifleman in Louie's team. A good-looking fellow with above average athletic abilities, he had a reputation for being a fine football player, good enough to play for a major college. He could throw a hand grenade farther than anyone else in the platoon and perhaps in the company, proving his athleticism.

Clyde Bridge, Louie's assistant BAR man, was from Texas. He was another Indian, an Apache. Because of his ancestry, one would expect him to be a fierce hombre but he wasn't. Instead, he joked constantly, his face lit up with a perpetual grin. Seldom combed, an unruly shock of coal-black hair hung over one eye.

Jack Wilkins Mills, the third fire team leader and a native of Alabama, was a dark-haired, stocky fellow with a neatly trimmed moustache. He carried side arms in addition to his rifle, earning him the nickname *Two-*

Loren Tracy

Gun Mills. He also carried every conceivable type of grenade issued to the U. S. Military and believed that a fragmentation grenade was much more effective if one could get an airburst. I spent some anxious moments with him when he demonstrated this feat during enemy probes of our defenses.

Once the spoon was released, the fragmentation grenade exploded in five to six seconds. The first time Mills pulled this stunt with me squatting beside him, he delayed throwing it for at least three seconds, a risky maneuver that nearly caused me to wet my drawers.

Every morning without fail he'd say,

Jack Mills

"The South shall rise agin."

The third fire team rifleman, Ebb Daughtery, was a round-faced blond-haired guy from Detroit. Immediately, I began referring to him as *Ebenezer* but he went by the name of Jack. He told me, and probably everyone else, that he'd changed his name and joined the Marine Corps because the mobs were after him. Over the next few months, I began to believe his story because of the things he told us about his involvement with the gangs in Detroit.

Richard Nelson or "Nellie" as everyone called him was the assistant BAR man. He'd been wounded in the leg during the Inchon Landing. A quiet fellow, he was a little distant, nervous and sometimes he acted confused.

J. J. Miller and Daughtery

Charles Creel, the BAR man, was a reddish haired fellow from North Carolina and another one who looked like a vagabond, wearing clothing too large. He was a rascal with a leprechaun twinkle in his eyes.

Some other notable characters in the platoon were Raymond Schaus, Don Young, William Jon Miller, most often called W. J., Roy Phillips, Lewis John Channey and John O'Malley.

Ray Schaus was from St. Louis, Missouri, a reservist who had been married for a little over one year when he was called to active duty. Three days after Ray's ship set sail for Korea, his wife, Glenda, gave birth to their first child. Affectionately, he had given his wife the nickname "Butch" and had stenciled it in bold lettering on the back of his jacket. Not realizing that it was his wife's name, the others called him Butch, a name that stuck and seemed appropriate.

Two who were native to the West Coast were Don Young and William Jon Miller. Don was a tough looking, snarling, redheaded grouch from Grass Valley, California and W. J. Miller, a tall, skinny, good-looking, dark-haired, con artist from Oregon City, Oregon.

Chapter II

"Aha! Two guys from the West Coast and one of them from Oregon! I can understand them when they speak. They don't talk like these other foreigners from Joisey, Mississippi and Detroit."

The veterans had been in Korea for some time and I half expected to find them older than me. But that wasn't true. I was greatly surprised when I discovered J. J. Miller, Bullock and Meek, all three members of my fire team, were only 18 and I was nineteen. Excluding the officers and staff non-commissioned officers, most of the men in the company were still in their teens and some had not yet completed high school. Having endured several months in battle, the strain of combat took its toll on them making them look older than their actual age—much older. These Marines were really nothing but kids who had been, not many months before, playing sports, studying literature and mathematics in high school, and had

Don Young manning a heavy .30 caliber machine gun

jobs delivering newspapers. Now, even though they were still teenagers, they were making horrendous life and death decisions and every one of them was very capable of fighting in this war.

The platoon corpsman, Navy Hospitalman Vance Kee, was called Doc Kees. In fact, the name "Doc" was the nickname given to all of our corpsmen. Some of the men told me that Doc Kees had been recommended for the Medal of Honor because he'd exposed himself several times to extreme danger to save wounded Marines during the past spring offensive.

Marines are fanatically protective of their corpsmen whether in combat or in a fistfight. They are probably the most important persons in a Marine's life during warfare. All that I met in Korea were courageous and seemed oblivious to the dangers of combat when they were called on to do their jobs. No matter the risk, they were always there to help us and every one of them who served in a war deserves to be recognized as a true hero.

Korean interpreters were assigned to most platoons and were men who had to serve their country for the duration of the war never getting a break from combat. Our interpreter's name was Charlie, a very likeable and educated man who spoke excellent English. For the most part, all of the interpreters spoke decent English and were very dependable people.

Doc Kees

Chapter II

Where's The Beer?

Even though we were in a reserve area behind the lines, we were still in a combat zone and in some danger of being attacked. But, strangely, some of the men had bottles of beer in their possession. Being curious, I thought it was logical to ask,

"Where in the world did you get this stuff?"

The answer was sensible. Command occasionally furnished a few bottles of beer to the troops to help bolster their morale, especially after a difficult period of battle.

The battalion had successfully taken several objectives during a series of running battles with the enemy, during the spring offensive, but had suffered numerous casualties. Constantly on the move and sometimes under heavy fire, the men had become exhausted, desperately needing a break. Upper command, realizing the danger, temporarily halted the advance allowing the battalion to regroup and get some rest. That evening, every man was issued several bottles of beer. Being dog-tired, not many of them drank their entire ration at once,

Caruso, O'Malley, and Pileggi

preferring to save some for the next few nights. However, their combat situation changed during the night and they had to move out to support another assault. Most of the men who still had beer just dumped it, not wanting to carry the extra weight. But that wasn't so with J. J. Miller. Instead, he drank as much of his ration as he could during the few moments needed to pack his gear. Unable to drink all of it, he dumped everything else he deemed not as important as the beer, such as socks, skivvies and water, preferring to carry the beer instead.

Learning About the Browning Automatic Rifle

If I was to be a competent and effective BAR man, I knew that I'd better learn as much about my weapon as I could. The veterans of my squad were astonished when they saw me reading my Guidebook for Marines. It wasn't so much because I was studying it; it was because I still possessed one. Most of them had discarded their guidebooks long ago, preferring not to carry the extra weight, packing something they thought useless in combat.

For hours on end, I read and re-read every passage in the book concerning the BAR until I could recite most of it from memory. I stripped the weapon, examined each piece thoroughly and reassembled it many, many times. It was amazing. My perseverance paid off, accumulating so much information that my guidebook was no longer necessary as a reference. So you can guess what I did with it. My reputation soon spread throughout the battalion that I was an excellent BAR technician and several times I was called upon to repair someone's weapon. I felt so comfortable with it that I didn't want to give it up, not even when a new man joined the fire team, voluntarily carrying it for well over eight months, somewhat of a record in the platoon.

Most men disliked carrying the BAR because of its weight, the reason why new replacements automatically inherited it. Equipped with a bi-pod, the weapon weighed twice that of the M1 rifle, nearly twenty pounds. Attached to the end of the

Chapter II

barrel by a flash-hider, the bi-pod was a mechanism that stabilized the weapon while being fired from the prone position. But in Korea, bi-pods were of little use and, oft times, a detriment in the hilly terrain. When moving as in an assault—and the Marines were always assaulting something—the bi-pods were a problem catching on brush, limbs and wire. One could fold the bi-pod legs, but there was little sense carrying them if they weren't needed. Being unnecessary and heavy, the men gladly dumped them.

An automatic firing selector permitted the shooter to select either of two rates of fire, 350 or 550 rounds per minute from twenty-round box magazines. I loaded four tracers in each magazine, spaced every five rounds beginning with the first, to help me pinpoint my target. Even though the weapon fired

Richardson, Phillips, Miller, and Daughtery standing in back; Pileggi (holding a BAR), Creel, and Bridge (holding an M1 rifle) in front

L to R: Name forgotten, Bullock, Meek, Pileggi, Name forgotten, Plick, Mills, and in front Creel and Nelson

automatically when the trigger was squeezed, I could accurately squeeze off single shots too.

Learning About Survival

The veterans, having endured weeks and weeks of horrific battles, were tired and beat and needed rest and the company needed to bolster its depleted ranks before getting back into the war. Most of the older veterans, who had seen a lot of action, shunned us new replacements during our first days in the company. One couldn't really blame them because we had taken the place of their friends, some who had been killed in earlier action. And, being fresh dumb kids, we asked some very insensitive and touchy questions such as,

"What's it like to shoot someone?" or *"How many gooks have you killed?"*

Chapter II

I listened intently to the vets when they conversed among themselves, trying to learn all that I could. Alertness was one of the keys to staying alive. Whenever we moved away from the camp, everyone was on the alert for anything abnormal. Our commanders constantly sent small patrols around the immediate vicinity of our camp, looking for infiltrators who were bent on doing harm and causing disruption. Every tree, hill and pathway was scrutinized over and over, even though we might have been there several times in recent days.

J. J. told me many times during my first weeks in the company that, while standing watch, I needed to be alert, especially at night, and not become too complacent.

> *"If you can make it through the first couple of months without screwin' up, Veep, you might make it all the way. So, keep your dumb ass awake, watch the shadows in the trees for movement and don't go to sleep when you've got the watch or you'll get a lot of us killed."*

He had reason to be blunt. Not long before my arrival, two members of our squad, who had fallen asleep, were shot to death. The company was on a fifty percent watch and one of the two men should have been on watch but both were sleeping. A North Korean crept up on their hole and riddled their bodies with an automatic weapon, a burp gun. A machine gunner in an adjacent hole downed the North Korean but too late to save the lives of the two men. Prior to the incident, one of them had been assigned to *bunk up* with J. J. but the fellow wouldn't stay awake during his watch. Jerry wanted no part of him and complained so much that his squad leader finally moved the fellow, assigning him to someone else. Jerry was lucky because it could have been he that was killed that night.

One man in the company had obtained a Russian burp gun and was keeping it as a souvenir. It was an ugly, bulky looking weapon that spit out lead at an incredible rate—close to a thousand rounds a minute. When it was fired, usually in short bursts, it sounded a little like a burp—*brrrrrrttttt, brrrrrtttt, brrrrtttt*. The mechanism was so loose that it rattled when the gun was shaken and it took half an army to reload the drum magazine. But the burp gun was reliable, seldom jamming or malfunctioning. It wasn't very accurate but enemy troops didn't have to be expert riflemen when shooting one, especially when they were in close.

Pileggi and Meek in back; Plick, Bitting, and Tracy in front

Chapter III

Into The Hills

Louie and I had been with Easy Company for about two weeks when the company was ordered to move toward the front lines. Sometimes we walked on muddy roads and sometimes we plodded over hills and up canyons where there were no roads or trails. I learned quickly about land mines, especially a mean little one in a wooden box called a shoe-mine that was meant to disable and possibly kill anyone who was unfortunate enough to step on it. Believe me, no one in his right mind voluntarily ventured off marked roads, trails or paths if he wanted to remain in one piece.

The landscape of the east coast of Korea where the First Marine Division was assigned is quite similar to that of the Oregon Coast Range: rugged, mountainous and yet picturesque. The trees looked like the firs and pines of the Pacific Northwest but they were smaller, some downright scrawny. Many ridges were steep and precipitous and not easily traversed. One could virtually stand with a foot on each side of a ridge, almost like straddling a sawhorse and walking on it was like doing a balancing act, reminding me of when I was a youngster walking the rails of a railroad track. Every hill we climbed only led to another one as high, if not higher. Had it not been for the war, Korea would have been a beautiful, peaceful, scenic country to visit.

The Company moved onto a densely forested, low-lying hillock and paused, taking a lengthy break. We were informed that we were standing atop a captured Communist command post, a huge cavernous control room, surrounded by several smaller rooms all connected by a maze of tunnels. Constructed far below ground and concealed by thick, natural vegetation, it couldn't be seen from the air. So, since we had the time, some of us took the opportunity to do a little exploring and were quite amazed at what we found. Half expecting anything made by the North Korean Army to be primitive, this command post was functional and very well made. Log beams supported the roofs and walls of the excavation and particular care was used to conceal the exits and air vents.

By late afternoon, the Company had moved to another hill, a much higher one, and set up a defensive perimeter, digging in for the night. I had no idea where we were, what we were doing or what we were about to do but, on occasion,

Moving forward and moving upward

Chapter III

I could hear the rattling sounds of machine gun and rifle fire in the distance. I don't think we were on the front line, face to face with the enemy, but we were darned close. This was my first night in an actual combat situation and the grim reality that this was the real thing and not a training exercise was setting in. It was gut-check time and time to get a little nervous. A real live enemy, an enemy that would kill me at the drop of a hat, was not very far away. The smug cockiness I felt not more than two months ago at Camp Pendleton had now been replaced by anxiety, uncertainty and a cold trembling fear.

We settled down, pulling ponchos over our fighting holes to keep out the dampness, and went on a fifty percent watch. It wasn't normal for two BAR men to bunk together but Louie and I did. When he was on watch, I wasn't able to get much sleep, worrying, sometimes fearing, that he might fall asleep but he, on the other hand, seemed to have no trouble sleeping when he was in the sack and I was on watch. He either had a lot of faith in me or he was a real cool customer.

Late into the night while on watch, I heard a slight rustling in the brush, down the hill in front of my hole. The hair stood up on the back of my neck. My only thought was to stay calm, if at all possible, and not move. Barely breathing, my chest felt heavy as if someone had placed a six-ton truck on it. Remaining as still as a rock, only my eyes moving, I scanned the darkness for the slightest movement and listened but heard nothing but the rapid pounding of my own heart. I hoped that if someone were there, he wouldn't hear the drum beat in my chest or the slow, labored, sucking of air into my lungs. Then I heard the rustling again as a cool breeze swept across my face. I relaxed. It was just the wind stirring the leaves. At least, I hoped it was only the wind.

I remained motionless for some time as my mind drifted back and forth between daydreaming of home and the reality of being here in Korea. I was dreadfully homesick and I missed my family. I wanted to be back home with them—to be in the arms of my mom and dad, to laugh and talk with my grandmother and my brothers and sisters. Daydreaming about my family made me feel warm and needed but it also made it difficult to stay alert and sharp. Daydreams gave me some respite from my current situation and the ugly war that I had yet to truly experience.

Puddles and The Pit

Sitting in this hole reminded me of the time when Dad wanted my brother Tom and me to dig a pit in the woods to bury garbage. Under normal circumstances, it would have taken an act of congress to get us to work but we jumped right on it, planning to use the hole as a fortress before anyone dumped trash in it. Working diligently, in a few days, we'd finished. It looked huge, large enough to bury a house but it was exactly what Dad wanted. Not only was it going to make a great fort, it seemed the perfect place to spend a few nights too. Using fir boughs, we covered it to keep the dampness out and laid sweet-smelling ferns in the bottom to keep us out of the dirt.

After supper, we headed for the woods and our hole in the ground, accompanied by our younger brother Dick and our dog Puddles. We packed a few burlap sacks and a couple of old blankets with us to keep warm and armed ourselves with a pocketful of rocks and a stick to ward off prowlers. Crawling into our new subterranean bedroom, we settled in for the night. But, unable to sleep immediately we recited stories, spooky ones, scaring ourselves silly. Finally, late in the evening with Puddles on watch, the three of us drifted off.

We'd been sleeping for some time when Puddles began scurrying in and out of the hole and barking her fool head off. Instantly wide-awake and a little frightened, we grabbed our rocks ready to repel invaders, wondering what the heck was going on. Without warning, one of our cows fell into the pit with us. Thrashing around, it completely destroyed the roof, our bed, and the remainder of our night's rest. Just as quickly as it had fallen in, it plowed its way out with Puddles nipping at its legs. We were lucky that our little dog had alerted us; one of us could have been stepped on but we escaped unharmed, only shaken.

The wind again stirred the leaves about me and brought me out of my daydream and back to my senses. As I peered into the dark, I wished with all my heart that Puddles were here with me, to keep me company and to help me keep watch.

A ruckus erupted down the line a short distance. Hearing another person's voice, especially someone speaking English, even though it was foul language, helped ease the tensions. I found out later that it was W. J. Miller trying to wake Don Young, his bunkmate, for his turn to take the watch. Don, a very, very sound sleeper, wasn't easy to rouse. W. J. found the only sure way he could wake the big redhead was to punch the hell out of him until his eyes were open and then back off before he could retaliate. The procedure was enacted twice every night while they remained in the Company.

Later during the night and again on watch and again daydreaming about home, I was suddenly brought back to reality by a faint musical sound carried by the wind. Louie hadn't mentioned any strange sounds or noises when I relieved him. And because it seemed so distant I wondered if he'd heard it at all. As the wind grew stronger, the sound intensified, becoming clearer. It was the music of a single bagpipe. Who in the world, I wondered, is playing bagpipes in these hills and why? It sounded so pitiful, so lonely. It was an eerie experience.

United Nations Forces

Eventually, I learned that men of the Commonwealth Division were the ones who were playing the bagpipes. They often played them when they were manning the front lines because the sound disturbed the North Koreans and Chinese, putting them on edge. After hearing them myself in the dark of night, I could see why. The Commonwealth Division was comprised of soldiers from England, Ireland, Wales, Scotland, Canada, New Zealand and Australia, and they had a reputation for being tough tenacious fighters. Later during my time in Korea I got to meet some of these folks.

The United Nations Armed Forces were also composed of units from several other countries, including Turkey. The Turkish soldiers had a reputation for allowing the enemy to come in close for hand-to-hand combat. They were knife fighters and believed that this gave them a huge advantage over their enemies. Even though I'd been trained in hand-to-hand combat and felt pretty confident that I could hold my own, I had no desire to experience that kind of fighting. None whatsoever.

Air Power

The following day, we found ourselves on the move again, climbing another hill and digging in for a short stay. Of course the hill was higher than the previous one. Moving up, we passed the wreckage of an American Bell helicopter that had crashed in a densely wooded area where a firefight had taken place earlier in the campaign. Since the cockpit bubble was intact, I assumed the pilot had escaped serious injury. This type of helicopter was used to evacuate wounded troops from the front lines. Able to transport two men simultaneously, each one strapped into a pod attached at the skids, once airborne, the chopper took only minutes to get them to a rear-area medical facility. Before the helicopter was introduced to evacuating wounded from the battlefield, the men had to be carried on stretchers sometimes taking hours to get them to a medical facility. Use of the helicopters flown by skilled, dedicated pilots saved many badly injured troops that would otherwise have died.

From where we had hunkered down, we overlooked a smaller hill a few miles to our front and north of us. Our Communist brothers occupied it. Friendly artillery had pounded it into powder and, while we watched, F-80 Shooting Star jets appeared overhead, continuing to destroy whatever was left.

Chapter III

For a half hour, we watched spellbound as the planes attacked, relentlessly, one after another. Smoke, dust and rubble filled the air. Some of the objects tossed up by exploding bombs and rockets were huge, appearing to be boulders and small bunker logs. And yet before it all fell back to earth, another plane zoomed in to drop more explosives. And after unleashing their load, some of the pilots, pulling out of their dive, did barrel rolls. Their skill and daring was absolutely amazing and no one could deny that they had plenty of guts and bravery. But I couldn't understand how in the world they could fly through all that stuff without hitting something.

We Infantry Marines were partial to the F4U Corsairs, a propeller driven aircraft. Usually flown by Marine pilots, they were the aircraft that supported many Marine Corps operations. The Corsairs often strafed and rocketed enemy bunkers in front of our positions and when they, or for that matter any type of friendly aircraft, were in the vicinity, we felt very confident that the enemy would stay hidden deep in their holes and leave us alone. Our pilots owned the sky and they raised some kind of hell with any enemy force they saw on the ground. The Corsairs were slow in comparison to jet aircraft but they did their work in a very precise and methodical manner.

We'd heard many stories about the historic acts performed by Air Force, Marine and Navy pilots while supporting us in battle but one story sticks out as being a classic. A North Korean MiG jet attacked a Corsair while the Corsair was strafing enemy positions in front of Marine forces. The MiG came in behind the Corsair at a speed twice that of its prey and as the MiG closed in and was about to fire, the Corsair pilot pulled on his flaps, or whatever was needed to slow the plane rapidly, dropping like a rock. As the MiG flew over, the Corsair pilot gunned his engine, pulled his aircraft's nose up and, with all guns blazing, destroyed the MiG. I would bet money that there isn't a Corsair jock in the world that hasn't claimed credit for being the pilot. Whether it happened or not, I really don't know.

52   Let Channey Do it

Whenever they were available, aircraft were called on to bomb and strafe North Korean emplacements. So the pilots wouldn't mistake us for the enemy, we identified ourselves by placing colored cloth panels, commonly referred to as air panels, in front of our positions. Our platoon had panels. But I never saw them…didn't even know who was packing the things and hoped we'd never have a reason to use them.

During the earlier spring offensive, though, they were used often. The man who'd packed them seemingly forever left the platoon, rotating out of combat to a rear area. When the platoon sergeant began looking for another man to carry them, one of the squad leaders made a recommendation.

"Let Channey do it."

Lewis John Channey, a quiet, light-haired fellow with a down-south Louisiana accent having been with the platoon for a short time, was given the air panels to pack. Packaged in an elongated roll, they were bulky but not very heavy and so he had no gripe or concern about carrying them. They were just another piece of gear to pack and soon he more or less forgot about them.

The battalion had been attacking and capturing enemy held territory at an incredible rate. But, one day when the attack bogged down, allied planes were called in to soften the enemy's defenses. But, no one thought about displaying the panels. Not until, one of the planes, making a run, accidentally strafed the platoon's position. For a few terrifying moments, no one could remember who had the panels until it occurred to Channey that it was he who was packing them. He was ordered to quickly display them in front of the platoon's positions. Now, John had no problem carrying the things but he certainly didn't take any pleasure in crawling out in front of friend and foe, especially when bullets were flying in both directions and planes were dropping bombs. But, Channey did it.

After securing the objective, the platoon set up defensive positions and the men began checking their surroundings for

Chapter III

problems. Channey ventured some distance up a small creek where he spotted what he thought was a dead North Korean soldier. As he neared the body, the North Korean, still alive and kicking, rolled over and pitched a hand grenade at him. Channey instinctively dove backwards. When the grenade exploded, the soles of his shoes absorbed the concussion from the blast, luckily not causing injury to his feet. He came up to his knees and fired seven rounds into the North Korean, killing him. A split second later, another grenade exploded but under the North Korean, causing his body to momentarily convulse off the ground. The enemy soldier, about to throw a second grenade, had fallen on it when Channey killed him.

As he was running back to rejoin the platoon, he stumbled and fell, severely twisting his knee. While rubbing his throbbing leg, he discovered that he'd also been struck in the arm by a piece of grenade shrapnel. Rejoining the squad, his buddies urged him to report the injuries to a corpsman. But Channey believed his injuries weren't serious enough and, like most of the men, didn't want to bother the corpsmen with a few little scratches when other men, who were injured far worse, needed their attention. Performing his own surgery, Channey dug the shrapnel out of his arm with his pocketknife and in time it healed but the knee injury continued to bother him, an ugly lump forming beside the kneecap. At times, it swelled as large as a tennis ball causing him to limp but never once did he report the problem to medical personnel, bothering him to the day he rotated home.

The platoon was without a sniper and the platoon sergeant asked for volunteers. No one stepped forward, so one of the squad leaders made a suggestion.

"*Let Channey do it.*"

And he did.

Channey was not a talkative person and spoke as few words as possible. As he was going out in front of the lines on his first sniping assignment, one of the squad leaders asked him where he was going to set up. Channey looked out at the hilly landscape and said in his normal, slow, southern drawl,

"Well, Ah'm gonna go up there on the side uh that there hill or ah'm gonna go down there on the side uh that there hill. Yuh can take yer pick."

Water, Cold and Mud

A few days later in a drenching downpour, we moved again, slowly walking uphill on both sides of a muddy road in two endless columns. We were all dog-tired and soaking wet. Two Army jeeps, each occupied by four soldiers, passed us going south. Some of the Marines had enough strength to bark like a dog and others jeered as the jeeps passed.

One of the soldiers in the jeep responded,

"U.S.M.C.! Yeah! Uncle Sam's Mountain Climbers."

As the jeeps rounded a bend and passed out of sight, I heard someone remark, with some disdain, that the men in the Army never walked and when they retreated, they either rode or they gave up. No matter the circumstances, we just had to torment any and all military outfits not our own and even though we were tired, we were still feisty as hell.

The word came back to take a break off to the side of the road and we all collapsed. With everyone else, I plopped down in a ditch that paralleled the road, so tired that I didn't care that I was sitting in running water. Some of the men instantly fell asleep even though they too were lying in water. I thought about being a kid at home during the summer and how I used to run barefoot in the plowed fields watching puffs of dust burp up between my toes. I loved walking barefoot in the soft, warm, plowed earth. But this place certainly wasn't warm and pleasant. Now I had mud squishing inside my shoes and I was wet and cold and miserable. I sure as hell didn't like this place, not one tiny bit.

An order came from somewhere up the line, passed along from man to man,

"On your feet! Saddle up and move it out!"

Chapter III

We were on the move again. About an hour later, the rain stopped and I seemed to get my second wind. As we climbed up a steeper part of the road, I saw a dead North Korean, his body lying in the ditch. This was the first dead person I'd ever seen in my life and he didn't look real, his body all bloated and yellowed. And then I realized that this was the same ditch that I had lain in a short time before and the water that had flowed around me had already passed around this dead body. At that moment, I would have given plenty for a nice warm bath and a change of clothing to rid myself of the sudden creepy, crawly feeling that engulfed me.

Being a boot replacement of only weeks, I had no idea what was going on or where we were going. In fact, during the entire time I was in Korea, I really had no idea what the heck was going on and seldom did I know where I was. I was reasonably certain that we faced the North Koreans on the Eastern Front and the Chinese Army on the Western Front and all of them were rabid-dog mad at us. I guess that was enough for me to know.

Finally, we arrived, dog-tired, at a staging area of sorts. Mess tents had been set up to feed us hot food and, glory be—of all things, the hot food included steak. By the time I got in line to get some food, it was dusk and I was really starved. Of course, no lights were permitted and that gave me a great idea. I was pretty good at swiping an extra piece of Mom's fried chicken when I was a kid, so why not an extra steak?

Fetching a tray, I waited my turn in the chow line and began to reminisce about the time my brother Tom and I planned to have a chicken cookout with some of the neighbor kids. Mom and Dad had gone to Sherwood to shop and left Grandmother to watch after us. She soon fell asleep while listening to one of her favorite radio programs so Tom took the opportunity to kill a chicken. Having no stomach for killing anything, my job was to clean it and do the cooking. We ran for the woods where four of the neighbor kids were waiting and had already built a small fire. I dry picked the feathers from the chicken as well as I could and cleaned it and in fifteen minutes we were cooking.

Watching me cook, the others formed a circle around the fire and conversed with each other about kid stuff. Looking up from my work, I realized that another kid, a big one, had joined us, standing there with a plate and a fork in his hand. It was my dad. No one heard him creep up on us and none noticed as he squeezed in among them. Stunned and speechless, my mouth must have dropped open as wide as a barn door. The other kids, when they realized that my pop was standing beside them, froze in place and stood motionless like numbed stumps.

Pop's face broke into a big grin as he gave us an ultimatum.

"If you kids give me the biggest piece, I won't tell."

What a relief it was that he had nothing more to say and that he was willing to keep our secret providing we shared with him. Happily, we obliged. But since Dad was head of the household, we should have asked ourselves a question. Who was he going to tell?

It was nearly dark when it was my turn to get a steak. In the dim light, I thrust my tray over the vat filled with meat and waited for the mess man to put a steak on it. As he was doing so, using my other hand concealed beneath the tray, I speared a second steak with my fork.

That night, I ate very well, stuffing myself like a Thanksgiving turkey. Thinking about our secret cookout and what a wonderful pal my dad had always been, I fell into a contented sleep like a small child and the sight of the dead North Korean lying in the ditch soon passed from my mind.

Poncho Parade

On the move again the next day, we left the road and began climbing up a hill, following a narrow trail. Then they came: South Korean Marines carrying their dead on two-man litters down the hill. My mind numbed at the unbelievably horrible sight. It was hard to conceive that all of these men had died in the last few hours. There must have been two hundred bodies, maybe more, each one covered by a poncho. The trail was slick with a mucky mixture of water, blood and dirt. I could see the back of the head of each dead man hanging over the end of the litter, his black hair dragging in the mud, and sometimes an arm or leg or piece of intestine dangled from the stretcher.

It was sobering to think that this could happen to us.

"It could happen to me."

We came upon one poor soul, a Korean Marine, with his stomach split wide open and his intestines spilled out on the ground. Lying just off the trail, he was conscious and talking to other Koreans. We couldn't help but look, wondering what his fate would be. A short time later I learned from our corpsman that he'd died. He, too, was covered with a poncho and his body joined the Poncho Parade.

Trained by members of the U. S. Marine Corps, the Korean Marines were tough fellows, seldom failing to take their objective and often fighting to the death. They paid a huge price for taking some hill—probably the same hill we were going to occupy. I tried to shrug off the sight of all this carnage, to drive it out of my mind by thinking of pleasant things but it wasn't possible. It's not something that one soon forgets.

Reaching the top of some unnamed but bloodied hill, we were assigned defensive positions. The hill had been occupied by elements of the North Korean Army before the Korean Marines took it from them. The North Koreans had dug a lot of fighting holes but we couldn't use them. They were on the wrong slope of the hill, most were far too small for us, some of them had been used as toilets and there was always the possibility that one or two could have been boo-by-trapped. We remained on the hill only a few days but before we left the place, I got a thorough indoctrination about warfare and a grim look at the brutal scenes of sudden death.

The Sniper

Two days after our arrival on the hill, our squad was assigned to patrol in front of the lines into an area not occupied by either side. It was called No-Man's-Land. This was my first patrol and, brother, I felt as jittery and nervous as if I were a target in a shooting gallery. I had no idea where we were going or why we were going or how I'd react if we came under fire. I had been trained for this but training exercises are not in any way the same as the real thing. I kept telling myself,

> *"Stay alert! Watch the tree line and the shadows for movement and listen for any noises out of the ordinary! Don't be thinking about home. Keep your mind on what you are doing here. Above all, stay close to J. J."*

We saddled up and, leaving our positions, we gingerly descended a densely wooded hillside to the floor of a valley, venturing onto an open, large, serene meadow covered with deep, lush grass. It was a beautiful place, like a picture in a magazine, making it difficult to believe that a war was being fought here. But this indeed was deadly territory.

J. J. took the point and I followed right behind him, as close as if I were his shadow. He didn't like it, me being so close. It made him nervous and he told me more than once in a stern, hushed voice to keep away from him. Actually, he said it more like,

> *"Stay off my ass, dammit. Maintain at least a five-yard interval like the rest of the squad. And keep the barrel of that damned BAR of yours pointed somewhere else."*

Bunching up close to each other made a much better target for enemy riflemen. I knew that but I didn't want to chance being separated from him if something happened.

We had gone part way across the meadow toward a wooded area on the far side before stopping. Everyone squatted down while the patrol leader received information by radio from men on the lines behind us. J. J. and I, talking quietly, scanned the area to our front for movement when suddenly there was a loud KABOOM that nearly deafened me. I turned and saw not one soul. Every man in the squad was flat on the ground, hidden by the tall grass. I didn't need an invitation to join them and dove to the ground as near as I could to J. J. An enemy sniper had taken a shot at us and because the rifle shot sounded so loud, the bullet was probably intended for J. J. or me. This was the first, but certainly not the last time, that I would actually be shot at. I was shivering like I had the flu, but I wasn't cold—just frightened—frightened beyond belief.

We remained hidden in the grass for a few moments before J. J. and I realized that we were alone. The rest of the squad had quietly bugged out and was heading back to the hill and our positions. J. J. yelled as he jumped up,

"C'mon Veep! Let's get the hell outa here."

Again, I didn't need an invitation, and I was probably running so close behind him that he might have thought I was in his shoes. I wasn't panicky—but I'll bet I was getting pretty darned close.

The safety and cover of trees at the base of the hill were only a few hundred yards away but those yards seemed like miles. We finally caught up to the rest of the squad just as they'd begun the ascent back up the hill to our positions. We were told to snap it up because North Korean soldiers were running down the hillside across the meadow from us.

I turned to see a group of men, perhaps fifteen, in a tight cluster, running in the open toward us about a half-mile away. Suddenly, in a resounding blast, they blew up. Their bodies flew into the air, as if someone had tossed little toy soldiers out of a box. One of our light artillery pieces, a seventy-five recoilless rifle, had fired a high explosive round from the hill above us and it hit squarely in the center of the group, killing nearly every one of them instantly. The survivors, if there were any, were immediately gunned down by machine gun fire. They were probably making an attempt to capture our patrol but had been seen by the defenders above us.

The sight of these people being destroyed looked so unreal, like a nightmare. Alive one moment and then in a flash they were gone, instantly snuffed out like candles. Nothing remained but mutilated bodies, pieces of torn flesh, and broken bones amid the dust, debris and smoke caused by the explosion. The same thing could have happened to us, but this time we were the fortunate ones. I wondered if these people—these ordinary men–I wondered if they had been as frightened as I was.

Our patrol had accomplished what it had set out to do—draw the enemy into the open. I never wanted to do that again, but this was just the first of many patrols that I would experience. Jerry was angry with the other members of the patrol because they'd pulled back to the lines without making certain that we had gotten the word, voicing his displeasure with a few choice but unprintable words.

We never caught sight of the sniper. I don't believe he fired at us a second time but I was running and panting so hard that I probably wouldn't have known if he had. I couldn't have cared less about what happened to him. I just wanted to get back to a safe place—my hole in the ground.

River Bottom

Not many days later, perhaps a week, we left the hill, withdrawing to a staging area situated on the rocky banks of a river somewhere behind the lines. The move to the river came none too soon for Bullock.

Just a few hours before leaving, the poor guy fell into a waist-deep hole, an abandoned honey pit that had been left open by the North Koreans to catch some poor unsuspecting farm boy from Mississippi. His shoes broke through something crusty and, immediately, a horrendous stench engulfed him. Before he could pull himself out, standing ankle deep in a smelly, gooey, stinking mess, some of the soupy waste oozed down into his *boondocker* shoes. Extracting himself, he tried to wash it from his shoes and pant legs but there just wasn't enough water in his canteen to do a thorough job. With crud on his fingers too, none of the others would share their water with him either, not wanting him to touch their canteens. So he resorted to using sticks, c-ration toilet paper, dirt and grass to do the job. He was still trying to rid himself of the awful crap when the Company saddled up to leave.

With pleading eyes, he looked around at the rest of us and asked,

"Why did this have tuh happen tuh me?"

Meek, walking a wide circle around him, remarked none too sympathetically,

"Gawd, Bullock. You stink bad."

Not one soul had any compassion for him and not one soul ventured near.

Bullock countered,

"You should talk, Meek, you crud-ball. Ah been downwind of you many a time and you don't smell none too good yoreself. At least, ah got some kinda excuse."

When we reached the river, Bullock walked directly into the water up to his hips and scrubbed his socks, his pant legs, his shoes and his hands and feet in the cold water but it didn't help much. The stink still clung to the poor guy.

Louie, Bullock, Meek and I were assigned to a position downstream from the main group to act as a listening post of sorts. There were signs that a mess tent had been erected there at one time and the distinct odor of fuel that the cooks used in their stoves and sanitation cans was noticeable. Louie, collecting some twigs and dry sticks, made a small fire and immediately there was a ground-shaking *ka-whump* under us. Seeing blue flame flickering among the pebbles and boulders, we surmised that some of the fuel had spilled, accumulating in small pockets among the rocks. The gaseous fuel continued to burn under us for some time, and although the round river rocks were uncomfortable to sleep on, we at least were warm.

We stayed but the one night at the river. I'm grateful that I wasn't able to foresee what we were about to do, where we were going, or what we were going to face during the next few days. Early in the morning, long before daylight, we prepared to move out again. J. J. was really in a bitchy mood.

"We're always on the move to some other damned place. They ain't never satisfied. Either we're walkin' somewhere because someone on our side wants us to or we're runnin' like hell because someone on their side is shootin' at us."

Rumors were as plentiful as grains of sand on a California beach. Something unsettling was about to happen but I had no idea what it could be other than we were probably going to be in a battle.

Although the mess tents had already been struck, two vats of food, one filled with a mix of hot gravy and ground beef and the other filled with toast, had been prepared for our breakfast. This particular food was called SOS, meaning *shit on a shingle*, and the stuff literally stuck to your ribs. Not being their favorite fare, a few of the guys grumbled. But not me! I liked the stuff and I always ate my fill. None of us, however, knew at the time that this would be our last hot meal for several days.

Filling our mess kits, our squad sat together among the river rocks in the dark to eat before moving out. Wrestling with my BAR and trying to balance a mess kit in my lap made eating in peace quite impossible. So I placed the mess kit on the ground in front of me and turned my attention to securing my BAR. Unbelievably, someone passing in the dark stepped smack dab into my mess kit and, momentarily glued to his shoe by the SOS, walked off with it. I could hear it *clunk-clunk-clunk* on the rocks for a half dozen steps or so before it fell off. As far as I could tell the guy never stopped, apparently not being curious enough to see what the heck he'd stepped in. Not having time to clean my kit, I got another batch of SOS and ate my breakfast from a canteen cup.

Before we finished, someone told us to load up on ammo, that we were going to attack some hill.

"What hill? What the hell's goin' on? Where the hell are we goin' now?"

That was the first time I'd heard that we were going on the offensive. As we checked our gear, preparing ourselves, each man was issued c-rations and, if they wanted it, extra ammunition. For good measure, I took another bandolier of thirty-caliber ammunition and a few more hand grenades. It was obvious as hell to me that this was not going to be something easy because the veterans of the platoon had become as tense as bowstrings and no one wanted to talk. Nobody knew the name of our objective and none of the older troops cared to know. It was just another hill with no name and we were going after it—tooth and nail.

Hand grenade

Chapter IV

Move to attack

I'm certain that it was September 10, 1951 when we went on the offensive. Our leaders at division headquarters, whom we seldom or never saw, were sending men that they personally didn't know into a battle that they hoped we could win. We combat troops, on the other hand, hoped that they knew what the hell they were doing and that the plans they had prepared for this battle were sound. It was a time when all of us had to have complete trust in each other from the top commanders down to the lowest infantry private.

With full packs, the Company moved throughout the day and late into the night, getting closer to our jump-off point. It had become as black as the bottom of a well as we moved single file into No-Man's-Land between enemy and friendly positions. Trying to maintain constant visual contact in the dark with the man in front of me was pure hell and, adding to the stress, we had to work our way through a minefield following a path marked with tape that was damned near invisible.

Even though we moved with extreme stealth, the North Koreans knew exactly where we were and opened up on us with seventy-six millimeter artillery. We were caught in the open with no cover and all we could do was lie on the ground and pray to God we wouldn't get hit and that the barrage would soon end. It was a punishing, frightening, gut-busting ordeal as round after round screamed in on us. It's pure hell receiving incoming mail while hunkering down in a hole or a bunker where at least there's some cover, some protection. But enduring an artillery barrage while in the open is downright terrifying and not being able to see anything makes it all the worse.

Even though I knew dozens of Marines were around me, I felt absolutely alone—as if I were the only person on earth—as I lay there in the dark, trying to shrink into my helmet. Mentally drained, Nellie Nelson began to sob quietly, his body shaking uncontrollably. He'd lost control. Two members of the squad crawled to him to let him know that he wasn't alone and attempted to reassure him, to hang on. He begged them for a cigarette but it would have been insane to light one even under the shelter of a poncho.

Trembling, praying and cringing with fear, I expected to be blown to pieces at any moment. Each exploding round caused me to wince and made my ears ring. Adding to that misery was the concussion that left me breathless as if I'd been kicked in the solar plexus. The pummeling was horrendous.

I tried to choke back the sobbing fear of dying by thinking about home. A strange, mixture of thoughts popped into my mind, Maggie, building a house, and what Mom had cooked for dinner.

> *"I wonder what the folks are having for supper tonight? I wonder if the old man fixed the barn roof yet? I wonder what radio program they are listening to? I wonder what will be left of me if I get hit? I wonder......oh, God......I wonder if I'm gonna die?"*

Praying helped and I thought it a good idea to be loaded up with an abundance of Hail Mary prayers—just in case I got hit—and to pray to God to save my dumb butt. One round hit so close that it bounced me off the ground and showered me with dirt and rocks. I felt as insignificant and helpless as an earthworm.

J. J., concerned about the members of his fire team, called to each one of us to determine if we were okay. Even when he spoke softly, his voice boomed like a bullhorn giving me concern that the enemy might hear him and further pinpoint our position. I managed to choke out an answer that I was unharmed, but my voice, no doubt, was quivering with fear.

Then he asked me the dumbest of dumb questions,

"Veep! What the hell are ya doing?"

He had to be off his cork to ask a question like that. We were being shot at with a big cannon—what the hell did he think I was doing?

"I'm praying."

"Well, say one for me."

I knew he was nuts. I was busy looking out for my own soul and he wanted me to pray for him, too. Why couldn't he just say his own prayers?

"For Pete's sake, Jerry! I've already said enough for the whole damned battalion. Say your own prayers."

To my surprise, from the darkness I heard some of the men chuckle. There was still life around me. I hadn't meant my remark to be funny but hearing the response it evoked helped me to cope. Maybe that's what Jerry had intended.

Paul Cranmer, assigned to the first platoon, was told to keep an eye on a new kid who had just joined the Company hours before our movement into No-Man's-Land. Going into combat for the first time, the kid was scared to death just as we all were but Cranmer told him he'd be okay if he stuck close and obeyed his every instruction. Sticking close to Cranmer wasn't easy even during daylight because he walked so softly that the others had given him the nickname *Creeper*. But the kid managed and when the artillery barrage began, he dropped down right next to Cranmer, so frightened that he threw up on the Creeper, covering him with vomit from head to toe.

Jerry Miller

After what seemed like an eternity, the shelling stopped but we stayed put for a short time. I knew that someone had been hit because I could hear a muffled, hushed call for a corpsman. But, otherwise, the wounded men themselves made little sound, stifling their groans and prayers and curses through gritted teeth. With the exception of Nellie's breakdown, our squad was still intact.

Slowly, quietly, we gathered ourselves and resumed moving along a riverbed toward a small hillock situated in the middle of No-Man's-Land. It was no more than a knob, rising a few hundred feet above the valley floor, covered by a few scrawny trees and thick brush. The plan was to hunker down there for a few hours before attacking our main objective. But there was a big problem getting to the top of it. The North Koreans had thoroughly mined the reverse slope with shoe-mines. Our command people decided the safest way to the top was to move up the north (forward) slope. That caused another problem. Some jittery Marines already occupying the knoll knew we were coming, but had it in their minds that we were coming up the reverse slope. When we neared their positions, they realized someone was out front of them, believing it was the North Koreans creeping up to attack. Not asking questions, they cut loose on us with a heavy dose of machine gun fire. Immediately there was confusion.

"What the hell's goin' on?"

Taking cover, at least thirty of us lay in an absolutely straight line behind a small tree with a trunk no more than six inches thick, as tracers zipped past us like angry bees. Someone in front of me yelled at the gunners above using some old fashioned military language, the really filthy stuff. Between bursts of fire, the gunners heard the profanity and ceased firing. They knew we were Marines because no North Korean could ever have learned to talk that dirty. We were lucky. Other than shaking the hell out of us, none of us suffered any harm.

Once we reached so-called *friendly* positions, our NCOs told us to dig temporary defensive holes and try to catch a few hours sleep. Almost immediately, there was an explosion and casualties. Someone had detonated a shoe-mine, either stepping on it or hitting it with an entrenching tool. We realized too late that the entire hilltop, not just the reverse slope, had been saturated with mines but we couldn't see the damned things because it was so dark.

No one dared move far from his position during the night, not even to relieve himself. Unable to sleep, we waited uneasily for the coming dawn, knowing that we were going into the fires of hell.

The Attack on Hill 749

Just before daybreak, Easy Company moved out. Our objective was Hill 749, a hill and a number that I will never forget. Moving in single file, we descended to the valley floor, crossed a small river, and crept northward on an ancient path that paralleled a small stream. Our progress was slow, at a snail's pace, because booby-traps and anti-personnel mines had been planted everywhere, particularly in the trail. We did everything possible to find them: probing, searching, praying. We even stepped in the footprint of the fellow in front of us hoping not to trip one. But even that didn't always work. Mysteriously some mines exploded only after being trod on several times. It wasn't unusual for some poor unsuspecting sap bringing up the rear to be the victim of a mine that had been passed over by several others.

Shoe-mines and mortars were the two things I feared most, even more than artillery and snipers. A split second before impact, mortars make a swishing sound that sounds something like a duck's wings as it flies by. You definitely know it's coming, but there isn't much time to take cover. The shoe-

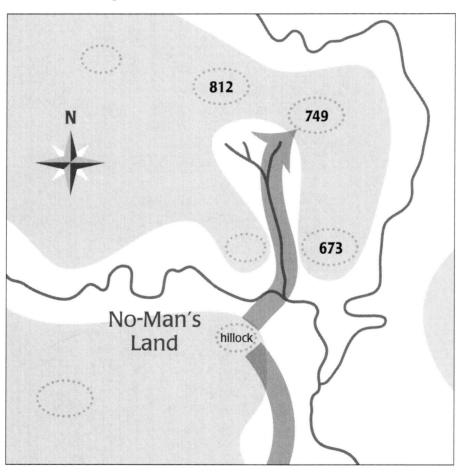

Assault route to Hill 749

Chapter IV

Moving to attack Hill 749, September 1951

mine was made mostly of wood in the shape of a small shoebox, thus the name *shoe-mine*. It couldn't be detected by mine detection equipment because there were no metal parts. They were most effective when they were buried just below the surface of the ground and covered with dirt and natural vegetation to hide them. If we saw a small depression in the dirt, one was certain to be there.

Trying to locate every mine was a hopeless task because there seemed to be no pattern or reasoning for the way they were planted. Whenever the point fire teams detected one, it was marked with whatever was at hand to warn the others that a mine was there. On this day, pieces of c-ration toilet paper held in place by a stone or a stick were used as markers. Dozens were marked this way but, unfortunately, many of the pieces of paper blew away in the wind and by day's end, toilet paper littered the valley and no one could tell which piece marked a mine and which piece was just litter.

The point man leading the Company had the nerve-wracking job checking the trail for mines, trusting the men behind him to keep a wary eye out for snipers. It was a grueling task, one that a person couldn't continue doing for any length of time. Since crossing the river, Otto Pavelcik had been the point man but growing weary, Butch Schaus, his squad leader elected to relieve him, selecting another man to take over the job. So as not to step off the narrow trail and to keep his balance, the man squeezed by Otto, wrapping an arm around him for balance. The fellow took a couple of steps beyond where they had stopped and stepped on a mine blowing his foot to shreds to the ankle and severely injuring the other leg. Knocked into the brush beside the trail by the concussion, Otto was shaken and, except for bits of dirt embedded in his face, was unharmed. Without hesitating, another man voluntarily took the lead and resumed probing. The Company continued moving forward leaving the wounded man in the care of a corpsman. Otto, shaken by the incident, knew that he might have missed spotting the mine too and could easily have been the victim

Fortunately, few men in our platoon became casualties of mines, but the platoons following us took a beating losing several men. None of us felt very confident that the trail was completely safe, no matter how closely it was checked. But it didn't matter. We had to move forward and move with determination, hoping and praying not to lose a foot or a leg or our life.

The hills above us echoed with the sounds of exploding artillery but for the moment nothing fell near us. We knew with absolute certainty, though, that sooner or later we were going to encounter North Korean regulars. I scrutinized every bush and stump, like everyone else, feeling almost certain that there was someone hiding there and if anything had moved, it would have been annihilated.

The First Contact

The lead fire team, cautiously probing the trail, encountered some difficulty and halted the column. John O'Malley, another member of the second squad, heard what he thought was a machine gun bolt slamming home and at the same time saw the barrel of a gun protruding from the

Chapter IV

port of a well-concealed bunker to his right. The bunker, occupied by North Koreans infantry, was hidden among the bushes on the side of the hill, mere yards from his squad. O'Malley screamed a warning,

"Machine gun!"

His squad hit the deck at the same instant, very much like a flight of birds changing direction simultaneously. All hell broke loose. A small embankment that paralleled the path and streambed offered meager cover as the gun opened up, raking the area with a steady sweeping burst of fire. O'Malley thought he'd been hit several times as rocks and dirt, kicked up by machine gun, peppered and stung the nape of his neck. There was just enough cover from the embankment to keep the point squad from certain annihilation but the men, prone on their stomachs, were still carrying their packs and the packs were protruding above the embankment. The North Koreans knew exactly where each man was lying and shredded the packs with machine gun fire before the men could slip out of them. Enemy soldiers heaved a couple of hand grenades but they bounced into the creek away from the squad, detonating harmlessly. Butch's squad tried to return fire but, being pinned down, they were not able to do much maneuvering and, to make matters a lot worse, mortar rounds began to fall. Time was running out for them.

Our squad, back down the trail, was still out of sight of the enemy machine gun bunker and in good position to flank it. Pressley led us up a small, wooded ravine to our right moving no more than fifty yards before we too encountered bunkers hidden in the trees to our left, all manned by enemy infantry. The fight was on. Jack Mills and Loren Tracy's fire teams lay prone directly in front of the bunkers and engaged them in a firefight while our fire team lay prone facing up the ravine, ready to engage any enemy troops coming down to support their comrades.

Exposed to enemy fire from the bunkers, I scooted up closer to a small tree trying to find a little more protection. Then an explosion came from up the ravine 50 yards from us. It was a mortar. Another enemy mortar team somewhere above joined the fray, firing sixty-millimeter mortar rounds. They "walked" them down the ravine toward us in fifteen to twenty-foot increments. A round hit sixty feet in front of us, the next forty feet. Then one hit exploding in a shallow depression not more than twenty feet in front of me. The small tree that I lay by took most of the blast but the concussion blew the helmet off my head and sent it spinning down the hill. These were small mortars but the blast and concussion were still violent enough to bounce a person's body off the ground. I knew the next round would be right up my chute. I steeled myself, covering my head with my arms, waiting for the impact, hoping I could survive it. But for some reason it never came.

A piece of shrapnel from the last mortar impact, however, hit Loren Tracy in the chest and although wounded, he persisted in continuing the attack on the bunkers. Jack Mills, with a live grenade in one hand and his revolver in the other, charged the nearest bunker, shooting into the opening to keep the enemy inside pinned down. He flipped the grenade into the bunker, neutralizing it. Caruso caught sight of a North Korean darting out of another bunker and, before he could shoot at Mills, Louie downed him with a burst from his BAR, hitting him three times.

Within a few minutes, the mortars and all firing stopped—at least for the moment. Except for the men shifting around and positioning themselves in the brush ready to repel a counter-attack and the officers and NCOs giving orders in hushed voices, it had become quiet, unnaturally and eerily quiet. The entire sequence of events seemed a blur. All the enemy soldiers had been killed or captured, but unfortunately we also took a few casualties in the fight.

As we were attacking the bunkers, a Marine with another squad, moving to support Butch's squad, took the full impact of a mortar round right in front of where John O'Malley lay. Luckily, John escaped being struck by shrapnel. The nauseating odor of warm blood and burned powder hung heavy in the air. This one skirmish was just the beginning of a long, hellish, bloody fight.

Shooting erupted behind us, echoing through the valley causing our command people much concern. Then we received a startling radio communication that the Company had penetrated too deep into enemy territory and we were in danger of being cut off. Backtracking some distance, we finally began our ascent up the hill toward our objective, toward the summit of Hill 749. At first, the platoons moved in single file with fire teams on the flanks, and then broke into smaller units, gradually forming a skirmish-line. I recalled the ominous comment that Pressley had made only a few weeks before about how rough it was to make a frontal assault.

I didn't think I could ever become more frightened than I had been the night before when we were getting shelled in No-Man's-Land but I was getting pretty darned close. I watched Jerry and Bullock and Meek like a hawk and every move they made, every flinch they made, I made also, reacting more out of instinct than from thinking.

As we continued to climb higher and higher, snipers began taking potshots at us, mortars fell with more frequency, and firefights continued to break out in the hills around us as other units engaged the enemy. At times, enemy mortar men found us with devastating accuracy and sometimes their barrages fell harmlessly far behind us. Artillery from both sides devastated the countryside. As we neared our objective, the fighting and shelling intensified until it was non-ending.

Some mortars struck close enough to cover me with dirt, when they exploded. Fortunately, that was all that happened. After each close call, squad leaders called out to their men to determine if they were okay. After one mortar exploded extremely close, causing me to grimace from the concussion, I heard Bullock call to Bridge,

"Air yuh okay Clyde?"

Clyde answered quite seriously and with a quiver to his Texas drawl,

"Hey Hoss! If I don't answer, y'all oughta know I'm not alright."

The bullets from an automatic weapon suddenly pinged off the ground and butchered the trees near me. I dove into a shell crater landing on J. J. and before he could give me hell for being too close to him, Meek and Bullock joined us in quick succession. Pinned down momentarily, a man from another squad dispatched the shooter with Browning automatic rifle fire and we were on the move again.

With heavy packs on our backs and under intense fire, we moved persistently, sometimes crawling, sometimes running, but always forward and upward. Finally, we got into position to make our final assault. Miraculously, our squad was still intact, with no casualties other than Tracy and Nelson. Other squads in the Company were not so fortunate though and some had to merge to make an effective fighting unit. Several good men were gone, most of them wounded but a few dead. Some were my friends.

Machine Gun Duel

Our objective was in front of us—a bluff covered with brush and small trees. There seemed to be no thin line of bunkers but a deep maze of fortifications, most of it concealed. The place was honeycombed like an anthill and when one bunker was destroyed another immediately behind it had to be assaulted. I had no idea if this was the top of Hill 749 or not, but whatever it was the enemy soldiers occupying it were shooting at us and we were going after it. The base of the bluff lay about seventy yards in front of us, across a flat, sparsely treed, grassy space, and all of it covered by enemy machine gun and rifle fire. It would take an additional three or four hundred yards of steep climbing to get to the top.

Our platoon, spread out on line, was ready for the final assault. Raked by continuous small arms fire, we managed to crawl, scramble and leapfrog squads to get into position along a small ridge that offered, at most, scant cover. I crawled up beside a small tree in view of the bluff to get a good look at what we were attacking. One of our machine gun squads had set up some thirty yards to my right and was engaged in a battle with an enemy machine gun on the bluff, their tracers pinpointing the enemy's emplacement. Once in a while I could see what I thought were puffs of smoke on the bluff as enemy gunners returned fire.

Even though mortars exploded around us and the two machine guns clattered away at each other, I hardly noticed any sound feeling as if I were in a vacuum. Twigs, leaves, limbs, and at times small trees fell, shattered and torn by withering fire from every type of weapon imaginable.

I watched the ammo carriers run forward to the machine gun with cans of ammo and then run back to take their positions behind the gun, preparing to take more ammo when needed. One of them, crouching as low as he possibly could, ran forward with a can of ammo in each hand. Before he reached the machine gun position, one can fell to the ground but the man kept running. He threw the remaining can to the assistant gunner and ran back, passing by my position. He was holding his left wrist, blood dripping from his palm. His fingers were gone. I couldn't believe it. A bullet had cleanly nipped off his fingers and that's why he'd dropped the can of ammo.

As he passed, he looked over at me, his face drained of all color, and said with a weary voice,

"I'm going home. Oh, God! I'm going home."

Just Peachy

The only food left from my issue of c-rations was a can of peaches and a shirt pocket stuffed full of powdered milk, coffee and sugar packets. Each issue of c-rations contained one can of fruit and it was usually fruit cocktail, bland and tasteless as Hawaiian poi. My favorite fruit was peaches because they were juicy, sweet and tasty but it was rare to get them. I figured this might be the last chance to eat my peaches and, besides, if I got killed I didn't want some other jerk getting them.

Small bits of bark and chips of wood falling into the can interrupted my sweet repast. Rolling onto my side, I looked up at the trunk of the small tree that I was lying beside and discovered that the enemy machine gun was chopping hell out of it only a few feet above my head. In a split second I turned into a big old *crawdaddy* and scooted backwards down the hill to a safer spot so I could finish eating my peaches in peace.

We finally got the word to go over the ridge and head for the base of the enemy-held bluff. One man after another leaped up and ran across the ridge from the very same point. If the enemy gunners had noticed that we were all taking the same path, they needed only to zero in and take each one of us as we left our cover.

When it was my turn to go, my stomach churned and I felt like throwing up my peaches. Nothing seemed real, as if I were having a horrible dream. Struggling to my feet, I began to run as fast as I could but my feet felt like they were bogged down in deep mud. Crossing the crest of the ridge some thirty yards behind Phil Meek, I could see dirt and rocks jumping off the ground where machine gun and rifle bullets were striking. Brush and limbs fell to the ground, chopped from trees, and it was all happening directly in front of me, right where I was going to run. Ricocheting bullets, sometimes as deadly as direct fire, buzzed past me like bumble bees.

Having a horrible, dreadful feeling that if I kept going I would surely die, I stopped dead in my tracks. At that very instant, someone or something rammed into me from behind and propelled me forward. Again, I found myself sprinting as fast as I could. Nothing was on my mind but getting across that open space as quickly as possible and finding some cover with the rest of the squad. Dodging through that rain of deadly fire was like dodging droplets of water in a three-foot by three-foot shower stall.

My lungs felt like they were about to burst when I flopped down beside Meek. I half-expected Bullock to be right behind

Chapter IV

me, believing it was he who had bumped into me. But he wasn't. No one was. Looking back, I saw that he was just leaving his place of concealment behind the ridge. I was confused wondering who or what it was that had knocked me forward. If an enemy bullet had hit my pack, the impact would have knocked me backwards and there would have been damage to my equipment. To this day, I've not figured it out but I've often wondered if it might have been something divine.

Our machine gunners deserved most of the credit for saving our hides. They put a blistering, withering fire on the enemy positions, forcing the North Koreans to keep their heads down and fire blindly. Remarkably, we made it, every single one of us in the squad made it without being hit. But, again, some of the men in the other squads were not as fortunate.

We gathered in our fire teams, lying prone on the ground behind bushes and small trees, concealed at the base of the hill. We were now beneath the enemy guns, making it impossible for them to put direct fire on us. They couldn't see us and we couldn't see them. But the new position we now occupied put tremendous pressure on them and, in addition, other units were attacking them using different routes.

After several minutes nervously waiting for the word to make a final assault on our objective, most firing from the enemy above us ceased. Other squads from the Company had overrun adjacent enemy positions, forcing the withdrawal of the enemy above, leaving only a few suicidal squads to harass us.

As we swarmed over the top of the hill, the remaining North Koreans put up a furious fight but they were quickly dispatched. The place was a maze of bunkers, tunnels and trenches. Killed by our artillery, small arms, and mortar bombardments, dozens of bodies of enemy soldiers lay among the debris. They were shot several times by wary Marines who took no chances that they could be playing 'possum ready to shoot us in the back as we passed.

Roy Phillips and his squad were attacking to our left. Roy's fire team leader, racing ahead, ran past an unseen hole where a North Korean soldier was hiding. The team leader caught sight of the fellow out of the corner of his eye just as he popped up and, believing that he was surrendering, screamed over the racket of gunfire,

"Take him, Roy."

Phillips, already swinging his BAR around, put a short burst of three or four rounds into the North Korean's chest and the soldier slumped back down into his hole. Phillips' squad, down to eight men, pressed on with the attack.

What seemed to take an eternity, the final assault was over in just a few minutes, the last of the enemy captured, killed or routed. Several had run off to the north over the crest of the hill and into a brush-filled valley beyond. Once we had taken our objective, it was time to defend it against a counter-attack. Officers and non-commissioned officers shouted orders directing the men to quickly set up defensive positions. Several of us watched for enemy stragglers as the others began digging in.

There had been some confusion from the time we began the attack early in the morning until we gained the top of this hill, however, it wasn't as if nothing went right. Men who had become separated from their units merely joined another unit and continued to fight. Partial fire teams merged with other partial fire teams and PFCs took charge of their squads when their NCOs went down. Some fire teams were out of contact with their squads and some squads were out of contact with their platoons. Hand and arm signals were used when the men could no longer hear voice commands because of the deafening roar from the intense firefights and mortar barrages. Confusion happens but Marines are trained to deal with it.

It was a horrible fight and like a blur in my memory. We had attacked like a pack of hungry wolves taking a deer carcass from an opposing pack. Our forces gradually but ever so persistently forced the enemy, bloodied and beaten, off these ridges and hills and now it was time for us to hold and hold on tight.

We had been under fire from mortars and machine guns all day but for the moment, to our relief, most of it had ceased. The odor of burnt powder hung heavily over the area and again there was the nauseating odor of fresh blood—blood from our

Chapter IV

men and from the enemy. The corpsmen, those who were still standing upright, were busy tending to wounded men, some in desperate, critical condition. They had scrambled right along with us through some withering, tree-shattering barrages, seemingly with little regard for their own lives, to help our buddies who had fallen from gunfire.

I had no idea where we were: on top of Hill 749 or on some hump beside it. Daylight was fading fast and we all expected a maniacal banzai attack at any moment. I had not yet experienced an all-out assault by the enemy, but I was told they would come en masse, blowing bugles, screaming and shouting threats at us in broken English. It was an unpleasant thought and I just hoped I had the guts to face it. The biggest concern for all of us now was having enough ammunition and hand grenades to repel them. Our officers, trying to establish a better and stronger defensive perimeter, shuffled us about more than once. I'll bet our fire team moved at least four times during the next hour and every time we moved, two things happened—we got shot at and we had to dig new fighting holes. In the meantime, our platoon sergeant took Meek out of our fire team, giving him a different assignment, and replaced him with Ebb Daughtery.

Phillip's fire team leader crawled to where Roy was digging a hole and asked why he'd shot the Korean. Phillips rolled onto one side facing his fire team leader, a bit puzzled by his question.

"Geez, you said to take him, didn't you?"

"No, I didn't mean for you to shoot him. I meant take him prisoner. He was trying to surrender."

Roy, in his defense, said,

"Geez! All I saw was this little gook coming out of a hole and you yellin' to get him. He sure as hell didn't look like he was trying to surrender to me."

Their squad leader, ducking and dodging to give the snipers a poor target, dropped down beside them, having witnessed what had happened.

"You know that little bastard that Roy shot? Well, he had a live grenade or somethin' and when we started pulling his body out of that hole to search him, it fell out of his waistband and exploded. If it hadn't fallen into the hole, we'd a got our stupid heads blown off. He was prob'ly gonna commit hara-kiri and figured to take some of us with him. It's a good thing Roy took him out. He prob'ly saved our hides."

Roy's fire team leader was nearly speechless but not quite.

"The dirty little bastard!"

Counterattack

Lieutenant Lilley crept over to where we had hunkered down. He had an assignment for our fire team. He told Jerry he wanted the four of us to move about two hundred yards beyond the Company's temporary line of resistance, dig a couple of two-man holes, and man them throughout the night. Our job was to intercept and *thwart* an enemy counterattack if it came from that direction. J. J. wanted a little more information, asking how large an attack was expected. The Lieutenant shrugged,

"Hell, J. J., I don't know—squad size, platoon size, maybe even a battalion. What the hell difference does it make? Get going! Get 'em out there right now."

J. J. murmured something incoherent under his breath that was no doubt ugly profanity as we went post haste into the darkness. I also heard him say,

"Intercept and Thwart? Thwart, my ass!"

Our assignment meant that we were going to be a buffer to slow an enemy attack against our main force and hopefully to momentarily confuse them. It also meant that we were expendable, something that J. J. probably realized immediately. Thank goodness I was green and stupid and didn't think of that myself, otherwise I'd likely have wet my drawers on the spot.

Chapter IV

The four of us made our way into No-Man's-Land through chest-high brush that was quite similar to the wild Salal shrubbery of the Pacific Northwest. It was thick and trying to move through it quietly without making noise was nearly impossible. We were a good two hundred yards in front of the Company, just over the crest of a steep slope, before we stopped to dig defensive positions. It was nearly pitch black by then but somehow the entire stinking North Korean Army knew exactly where our little four-man fire team was about to hunker down. That wasn't surprising; they always seemed to know exactly where we were.

Daughtery and I commenced digging a two-man hole as J. J. and Bullock moved thirty yards to our left and began digging theirs. Somehow, every time I dug in, I managed to get a difficult piece of earth. My end of the hole was all brush roots and rocks and hitting the stuff with my entrenching tool made all kinds of noise. If the enemy didn't know where we were before we began to dig, they most certainly knew it then.

Ebb Daughtery

We had dug down six to eight inches when a round of seventy-six millimeter artillery screamed in on us, impacting nearby. Diving into our shallow pit, we lay as flat as possible, hoping our butts weren't exposed. The North Koreans were bent on blasting us out of there and began systematically blowing the hell out of the hillside around us. The next round burrowed into the earth just a few yards below us and exploded, propelling both of us out of our hole. I found myself lying on my back in the brush just above our position, frightened and confused and dazed by the concussion.

Through a buzzing noise in my ears, I heard Daughtery call in a low raspy whisper,

"Veep! Where the hell are you? Are you okay?"

Trying to get my bearings and determine which end was up, I answered,

"Yeah, I'm okay but I can't find my BAR. It's gone."

My Browning automatic rifle had been thrown away from me by the blast. My head spinning, I was disoriented and frantic, crawling around in the pitch-black dark of night, searching for my weapon. Another round hit above us and to the right. Except for my helmet, I had no cover or protection. I couldn't just jump back in my hole and hide from the artillery because I needed my BAR. I had to find it. Fear gripped me like a vice, feeling as if the entire North Korean Army was only after me. Without the BAR, I'd have little chance surviving an enemy charge.

After what seemed like an eternity of frantic searching but was probably only seconds, I found it and scrambled back into what was left of our position. We resumed digging, like a pair of coolies, deepening our hole for better protection. I prayed to God that they would leave us alone, to stop shooting at us, but the shelling continued. We knew Miller and Bullock were unharmed and continuing to dig because we could hear the sounds of their entrenching tools and J. J. cursing everyone but the Pope.

The enemy gunners eventually gave up trying to destroy our little four-man fire team and turned their attention back to the top of the hill. Both sides dueled all night with mortars and artillery. Sporadic rifle and machine gun fire echoed throughout the hills and sometimes we heard an occasional rifle shot behind us, causing us some real intense concern. Flares launched from mortars constantly floated into the valley below us, illuminating the rugged hillside. We waited and waited, daring not to doze off even though we were near exhaustion, listening for the slightest sound of the enemy creeping up on us. When dawn came, we were still waiting for the counterattack but thank the good Lord it never materialized.

The terrain before us, now visible with daylight, was a mass of brushy defiles where snipers could easily move about and hide. The crater made by the artillery round that nearly killed us was plainly visible just yards below our hole. Now that it was daylight, I wondered why we couldn't leave, why we couldn't rejoin the Company.

"When are we going back to the platoon?"

"Your guess is as good as mine, Veep. They probably forgot about us."

Ebb's answer was not very reassuring. He seemed edgy as he scanned the ravines to our front looking for anything suspicious. He probably didn't like me pressing him for answers.

"Does J. J. have a radio with him?"

The expression on his face clearly revealed his irritation with my pestering questions but before he could answer, we heard noises, a rustling in the bushes, behind us. Daughtery swung his rifle around to face up the hill. We caught a glimpse of a figure, ducking and dodging, running through the brush down the hill toward us. It was my little buddy, Louie Caruso, coming with a message. Diving into our hole, he peeked down the hill and asked,

"Hey Pledge, how youse doin'? See anything out there?"

I was really glad to see my little goofball friend especially when he told us we were to rejoin our platoon. More men, behind Louie and hiding in the brush, were ready to cover our withdrawal. Nothing could be seen moving in front to concern us, so, during a lull in the mortar and artillery bombardments, we made a quick exit back to our lines.

Rejoining the Company, we found that our platoon had been repositioned—again. We quickly scraped out new fighting holes, crawled into them, hunkered down and waited, still expecting a counterattack. Not one man slept during the night but now that it was daylight, we were on a fifty percent watch. Some of the men were catching a few winks but they had to put up with the sounds of artillery and mortars flying overhead. We were starved, thirsty, exhausted and nearly every one of us had suffered an injury of some sort: cut, bruise, sprain, or scrape. And some of us were just plain sick.

Running in a zigzag fashion to another position, one of our men was shot by a sniper. The bullet sent his helmet flying and him sprawling into the dirt. But the fellow wasn't dead. He rolled over and, in a swirl of dust, scrambled after his helmet and crawled into a nearby shell crater already occupied by too many men. Examining the helmet, he found the bullet had made a deep crease in it and neatly slit the camouflaged helmet cover like a knife. A lucky near miss and a reminder to the rest of us that there were still plenty of live North Korean soldiers out there ready to take us on.

A squad from one of the other platoons was assigned the very dangerous task of eliminating the sniper—and they did. But none in the squad, including a Texan named Bob Couser, were at all thrilled about going out there into No-Man's-Land where snipers had the advantage. Not long after they left, a nasty mortar barrage hammered us again. When the patrol returned, Couser was devastated to learn that the platoon runner, a black kid by the name of Nelson, had been killed when a mortar round struck the kid's hole. They were friends and he'd dug in next to Couser. Had Couser not been on the sniper hunt, he too would probably have been killed. Not only did Nelson's death affect Couser, it affected many of the men who knew him to be a likeable young bashful kid. But none felt any worse about it than Captain Schmidt, our Company Commander.

Chapter IV

I glanced over at Louie, sitting in a hole not more than thirty yards from me. He was scrutinizing the terrain in front of our positions and was smoking a cigarette. Smoke was rising from his hole like it was coming out of a chimney. If a sniper sees that smoke, I thought, he's apt to pick off that Brooklyn nut. Instead of extinguishing it when I warned him that the smoke was visible, he merely blew it down into his hole. What a jerk. He was a hopeless idiot.

Since we had no solid food, I shared my packets of powdered milk, coffee and sugar with the fire team. With a few drops of water, I mixed a packet of coffee, sugar and powdered milk. It wasn't much but it tasted delicious. Louie looking over from his position asked,

"Hey, Pledge! What are ya eatin'?"

"Ham and eggs, Louie. Ya want some?"

"Ya know, Pledge, I've been thinkin'. Maybe we should sneak over there and steal some food from those Gooks. I'm so hungry I could eat some of their stinkin' fish and rice."

I think he was kidding but, with Louie, one could never be certain.

When darkness came, everyone went on watch just as we did the night before. And thank God there was no need for our little four-man fire team to return to the so-called listening post in front of the lines. The enemy came, though, just as we knew they would, probing our lines and stirring up trouble, attacking at several points. But every probe was repulsed. Whenever a flare popped open, I was certain that I'd see a horde of them coming at us.

Half of the men remained on watch the following morning while the others tried to get some much-needed sleep. We were really beat. Those who were awake kept a wary eye open for our little Commie friends and yet, at the same time, were able to improve and strengthen their positions. Communications wire, strung from platoon to platoon, gave us instant contact with our leaders and eliminated the need for runners, who were tempting targets for snipers. Every fighting hole had a good field of fire and our line of defense grew stronger and stronger. And with the passing of every hour, the possibility that the enemy could kick us off the hill grew weaker and weaker.

A tally of ammunition was taken and some units were found to be woefully short. Since there was no indication when we would be re-supplied, redistribution of the ammo was necessary. Strangely enough, I realized that I hadn't fired my Browning, not one time, and, as far as I knew, no one in my fire team had discharged his weapon. We just never had the opportunity. Reluctantly, I gave up the spare bandolier of thirty-caliber ammunition and the extra hand grenades that I had taken before we jumped off.

> "Isn't that ironic, Louie? I brought all that extra ammo, packed it up here just in case I needed it, and I never fired one damned round or threw one lousy hand grenade. You other guys did all the shooting and all I did was make a dumb-ass target of myself. What a bunch of crap! Now that I've given up all this damned stuff, all hell's gonna break loose and I'll wish I'd kept it. You just wait and see if I'm not right."

The North Koreans were just as busy as we were and their snipers continually harassed the hell out of us. As soon as a sniper fired, our sixty mortars fired a few rounds into the area where the sniper was thought to be hiding. Then, their artillery tried to hit our mortar sites. Then our artillery retaliated pasting their artillery. It would stop and be quiet for a short time and then some damned sniper would shoot at us again and the entire sequence of events would start all over.

Ebb had been crawling around trying to find some branches and small tree trunks to cover our hole when the enemy suddenly unleashed a heavy volley of artillery fire, blistering the hill with high explosive rounds. Asleep for about an hour, I was jolted awake by the earth-shaking explosions and Ebb diving into the hole to take cover. I'd been having a horrible, surreal nightmare, dreaming about shrieking, murderous banshees attacking me, trying to tear me apart. Being awake was not any better because this bombardment was a real gut-buster and a couple of close impacts shook the meager makeshift roof so hard that it collapsed on us. I cringed and clenched my teeth and tried to replace the dread and fear that gripped my soul by thinking of home.

It's strange what a person thinks when under fire, knowing he might be maimed or blown to hell in the next split-second. With me, it was usually food. I just wanted to have another chance to eat one of Pop's fabulous Sunday morning breakfasts.

> *"If I hadn't eaten so damned many of Pop's Sunday morning breakfasts, I would probably be in the Air Force with Eddie and Alan instead of here. I wonder if he cooked eggs with onions and garlic this morning? Boy, when I get home, I'm gonna insist he cook some of his slumgullion chow for me."*

Pull Off

We had endured several days of intense firefights, snipers, frenzied counterattacks, mines and mortars and, surrounded for a time, some units had to fight hand-to-hand. But we hung on and we accomplished our mission. And my misgivings and worry about giving up the extra ammunition was for naught. Five days after beginning the offensive, we were relieved by other units and left the hill. On the way out, we saw what had happened on Hill 673, a hill adjacent to Hill 749. It, too, had been decimated by artillery, bombs, mortars, and had been the scene of one hell of a battle. The place was littered with remnants of military gear. No vegetation was left – not one single blade of green grass on the ground or leaf on a tree. The greenness of the earth had been destroyed just as if it had been devoured by a huge threshing machine. Here and there were the telltale brown splotches in the dirt and the remnants of first aid packs where someone had fallen victim to the fighting. I couldn't believe the maze of enemy bunkers that the Marines had to fight through to get to the top of the hill. The place was a dirt and log fortress manned by human fanatics. Hill 749 was horrible but Hill 673 might have been worse, if that could have been possible. I was glad that our unit hadn't been assigned the task of taking it.

We left the lines carrying our wounded and dead on stretchers, over and down some brushy and incredibly steep terrain. The weight of the stretchers pulling on our arms was nearly unbearable. The wounded men grimaced with pain with every step we took but no matter how serious their wounds, I cannot remember any of those tough, heroic kids crying out or complaining. Some of them, even though they were terribly injured, encouraged us with jokes and quips to keep us going. Some of them prayed and some of them died.

We finally reached the floor of a valley where medical attention awaited the wounded and food and water provided to all of us. I think I ate an entire daily issue of c-rations at one time. C-rations weren't the tastiest food in the world, but at that particular time we stuffed ourselves as though we were eating a banquet. Something else occurred to me that seemed very strange. I couldn't remember going to the bathroom one single time during those five hectic days—no, not one single time.

Rumor had it that we had suffered nearly a hundred casualties, mostly wounded but some killed. A bare majority of the Company somehow avoided being hit. There were many joyous reunions when old friends and buddies found each other still alive. Our squad, except for Tracy and Nelson, came through okay and, thankfully, Tracy wasn't too badly hurt. The first two squads in our platoon, and other units in our company, however, were not as lucky and our machine gunners took a terrible beating.

Bobby Ogden from Portland, Oregon and Al DeLuise were the only two members of the third squad, third platoon, left standing. Most of them had become casualties the night we waited on the little hillock in No-Man's-Land before making the assault on Hill 749. One of Bobby's squad members, Bob Harding, stepped on a shoe mine, destroying his foot. Bobby was standing nearest to Harding and was bowled over by the blast but fortunately he was spared any injury. But the others weren't as fortunate including John Roseland. He was injured so severely, he nearly died. Ogden and DeLuise spent the remainder of the night carrying their friends to an aid station.

When the two survivors returned to rejoin their platoon many hours later, we had already begun ascending Hill 749. They came upon an eighty-one-mortar outfit that had set up their tubes by the creek at the base of the hill. Members of the mortar crew advised Ogden and his buddy to wait there with them until they received orders and directions to where their unit was located.

Bobby Ogden

Waiting with the mortarmen, they felt some security because the fighting had now progressed up the hill far beyond them. But they soon found out that their location wasn't so secure after all. The mortar outfit had fired several rounds into the hills and almost immediately drew return enemy mortar fire. The two infantry Marines, not having a hole to crawl into, were forced to dive into the creek for cover as mortars exploded all around them, rattling their teeth and showering them with river rock.

A young Minnesota lad named Bobby Johnson, who had been in my boot camp platoon, was also killed in the fighting. Bobby was a freckled-faced, redheaded kid with a squeaky voice, barely old enough to enlist. Our drill instructors, trying to get him to speak in a deeper, manlier voice, often pushed down on his chin with their swagger sticks. During a firefight, an enemy soldier lobbed a grenade into the shell crater that Bobby had just jumped into. It exploded, killing him instantly. Another fellow who had been fighting on Hill 673 was Norman Mann, the fellow who enlisted with me in Portland. Luckily, he came through it without getting hit.

We walked, stumbled and struggled down a road that was muddy yesterday but had turned dusty today. A couple of Army jeeps driving slowly down the road passed through our column. Upon seeing "USA" painted on the jeeps, everyone straightened up and fell into step, trying to look proud and tough. A couple of the kids began singing the Marine Corps Hymn and before the jeeps passed by us, we had all joined in. As they drove on, one of the soldiers, God bless him, stood up in his jeep and gave us a smart military salute, paying us high tribute. For the moment, we were all brothers in the same lousy war and none of us, Marines or Army, made any derogatory remarks about the other.

We found our way to a meadow nestled among the hills where we could erect our shelter-halves and try to recover from the brutal week we had just endured. Some of us were sick, all of us were filthy, stinking like manure and we desperately needed sleep, shaves, baths and clean clothing. Many of us had lost gear and personal mementos. As soon as we had encamped, our chaplains passed the word that the various faiths would hold church services to give thanks to our Creator for getting us through the previous five days. J. J. Miller told Daughtery that he was going to attend a Catholic mass. Daughtery, a person who professed no belief in a higher deity, asked if he could go along. J. J. was somewhat surprised.

Chapter IV

"Ain't you an atheist?"

Daughtery replied,

"I think so but I'm beginning to think there might be a little something to this God stuff after all and I don't wanna take any chances, just in case. What do you do when you go to church, J. J.? I've never been to one before."

Now, Jerry Miller was far from being the most devout person in the world and hadn't attended church very often, himself. So, he suggested,

"Just watch the guy in front of you and do what he does. That's what I'm gonna do."

Chapter V

A Short Rest

The area where we bivouacked was quiet and peaceful, like the war hadn't found this little piece of paradise. It rained a few times but not enough to bother us and, for the most part, the weather was warm and enjoyable. We treated our scratches, cuts, sprains and scrapes, bathed in a creek, cleaned our weapons and gear, slept like babies and relaxed. The fellows from the Deep South even managed to set up a small liquor-still in a tent. But when new replacements began to join us, we knew that in just a few days we'd be going right back into the lines.

In the meantime, we got paid. The money wasn't in American dollars however but in military script. Except to servicemen, it had no value. We used it to buy stamps, get haircuts, gamble, and occasionally buy some item of personal gear. I'd taken out an allotment sending most of my pay home to Mom and Dad, collecting only five dollars each payday. And not being a gambler, five bucks was far more money than I could spend.

Ed Bullock, Jack Mills, Butch Schaus and both Millers were huddled around a small fire, sipping coffee and munching on crackers and jam when I joined them one evening after mail call. Bullock had brewed a batch of coffee in his helmet. It was horrible stuff, so strong that it could pull a road-grader. Slurping down a few chunks of something, I wondered what the heck I was swallowing. He must have used at least a half dozen coffee packets for each cup he made.

They'd been talking about the close calls they'd had during the spring offensive. Of particular interest to me was an incident that occurred in early June when the outfit was being relieved after two-plus months of running battles with a retreating enemy. They'd halted to allow another regiment to pass though their positions to take up the attack when, about eight in the morning, enemy mortar-men opened up with 120 mm mortars, heavy stuff, inflicting an enormous number of

Script money

casualties on both units. One of the wounded was Earl Boyce Clark, a married veteran, from the great Northwest, the state of Washington. He'd been wounded once before but this time he'd been hit hard, his left arm shattered so badly that surgeons were unable to save it. Boyce was gone before my arrival but I'd heard about him a few times when the older vets talked about some of their friends. Losing a limb is tough for anyone to endure but his devoted wife and unwavering Christian faith gave him the strength to cope with it.

Earl Boyce Clark

Little did I know that one day we'd meet, that one day I would have the honor to know him personally.

My fellow Oregonian, Jon Miller, produced a packet of photos he'd just received. They were developed from a roll of film that he'd found on the body of a North Korean soldier who had been killed during a firefight only days before they'd been relieved. Viewing the pictures, as we sat around the campfire, was a weird experience. They were of the dead North Korean and a few of his Communist friends as they, too, were sitting around a campfire and eating a meal.

On the day that Jon found the film, the company had been engaged in a furious four-hour-long firefight attempting to overrun a heavily defended hill that other units had previously tried to take. Leading the assault, the platoon was successful in accomplishing their mission, rooting the enemy off the hill and capturing a few prisoners. But they'd suffered casualties too.

During the skirmish, Jon's second squad topped the crest of the hill and spotted a handful of enemy soldiers escaping down the reverse slope. Veering off to his left and around a small knoll, he saw two of the enemy fleeing some three hundred yards downhill from him. As he was about to fire at them, he heard a noise from behind. He whirled about to see a young North Korean soldier standing directly behind him with his hands at his sides. He apparently wanted to surrender because he made no effort to go for a weapon that was lying on the ground close by. With the barrel of his rifle, Jon motioned to the Korean to raise his hands. A big grin broke out on the young soldier's face as he nodded in the affirmative, lifting his hands high over his head, wanting no more of the war. As Jon took a step toward him to secure his capture, an enemy machine gun from across the valley opened fire, spraying the area with bullets, stitching the ground around his feet. He instinctively dove into the dirt, seeking cover. But with an unsecured enemy soldier on his hands, he realized how tenuous his position was. He looked toward his captive to determine if the fellow had gone for his rifle and saw that he hadn't. Instead, the young soldier had thrown himself to the ground also and was lying near Jon, his arms covering his head and his body shaking uncontrollably from fear.

Recounting the incident, Jon said that the North Korean could easily have killed him had he not wanted to give up, that it was his lucky day, and it just wasn't meant to be.

For some time I'd wondered about a bullet hole in Jack Mill's helmet, a hole just above the front brim. Surely, I thought, he couldn't have been wearing that thing when the bullet hit. But, I was wrong in that assumption.

On the same hill where Jon Miller found the roll of film, the third squad, employing a different tack than other units had previously used, followed a stream wading chest deep in water, trying to flank the enemy positions. When they figured

Chapter V

they'd penetrated deep enough, they left the stream and ascended a steep slope toward the top, creeping and crawling to a point very near their objective, certain that they hadn't been detected. But the enemy combatants knew they were there and opened up on them with a fusillade of small arms fire, blistering the trees, brush and ground around them.

Mills, running for better cover, tripped causing his helmet to rock forward and down over his eyes. At that very instant, a bullet, probably fired from a burp gun, struck the helmet just above the brim knocking Mills to the ground, falling as if he'd been shot dead. The projectile penetrated the metal helmet and the fibrous liner inside the helmet but stopped before it drew blood, wedging in the helmet sweatband. However, the impact was like a hammer and knocked Jack unconscious.

William Jon (W. J.) Miller, the Oregon con-artist

The others in the squad, not having time to check his body, believed that he'd been killed outright and continued to fight their way upward toward the enemy, leaving him where he fell. But the enemy defenders held on tenaciously forcing the small band of men to temporarily withdraw.

Platoon Sergeant Manuel Hirata made his way to Mills, who had regained some of his senses and was sitting upright. Still dazed, he said that he thought he'd been shot in the head, that when the bullet hit his helmet, it sounded as if his head were inside a bell. Hirata lifted Mills helmet and, finding no blood, told him he was okay and to get ready for another try at the hill. While examining the helmet, the bullet fell into Mill's lap, a souvenir of a close call that the lucky Alabaman pocketed. But feeling too wobbly to get to his feet, he decided he'd better stay put for a few more minutes.

Butch Schaus, Mill's fire team leader and the other two members of the team returned to where he was sitting and were stunned to see that he was still alive. When they asked if he'd been hit, he pointed to the hole in his helmet and said, with a trace of a grin, that he'd been shot right between the eyes.

Regrouping, another attempt was made to take the hill. Other squads, making a frontal assault, began drawing most of the fire as the third squad struck from the extreme right flank again. The squad's third fire team moved to a better location to provide covering fire as the other two teams began their ascent.

Nearing the summit, they were pinned down again by another wicked hailstorm of small arms fire. Forrest Payer, the BAR man in the third fire team, found an excellent spot from which he could fire upon the enemy positions, forcing them to keep their heads down. Crawling close enough now to throw grenades, Butch rose to his knees and, just as he lofted one,

Sgt. Manuel Hirata

a bullet creased his helmet knocking him down. But luckily, just like Mills, he was unharmed, only shaken.

As Payer continued to blast away with the BAR spewing bullets just a few feet over their heads, Schaus's fire team frantically continued flinging grenades, one after another, blasting hell out of the nearest enemy positions. One of the machine gun squads joined the fracas, moving into the position where Payer lay and, setting up their gun, began ripping the hilltop apart with short accurate burst of automatic fire, adding to the enemy's woes. The grenades and the blanket of small arms fire killed a number of enemy combatants and soon routed the others from their positions. Schaus decided it was time to make a banzai attack over the hill and to do it as quickly as possible before the enemy soldiers could gather themselves and counter the assault. Other units joined in the final assault hitting the enemy positions from the front.

O'Malley, Schaus, and Miller, December 1951

Butch went around a clump of brush to his left and Mills and the other two team members went right, tossing grenades into bunkers and driving the remaining enemy defenders off the hill. Pursuing a group of North Koreans down the reverse slope, they suddenly came under direct fire from a machine gun emplaced on another hill across a ravine from them, probably the same gun that had fired at Jon Miller. Putting on the brakes, they figured it wise to give up the chase and rejoin the rest of the platoon.

Jon Miller

Under sniper and machine gun fire, the platoon, quickly setting up a line of resistance, dug in and waited for a counter attack. The platoon did well, particularly the squad, routing the enemy, killing several and taking a few prisoners. But tragically they, too, suffered some casualties. Nonetheless the hill was finally and firmly under control of the Marines and never again did the North Koreans occupy it.

After the hill had been firmly secured, J. J. Miller squatted down beside Mills and asked,

"Didn't you get hit, Jack?"

Mills pointed to the hole in his helmet and whimpered,

"Yeah! I got it right between the eyes!"

"You gotta be shittin' me! You've gotta be dead if you got hit between the eyes."

W. J. Miller, also hearing that Mills had been killed, made his way to where J. J. and Mills were sitting and dropped down beside them looking a bit surprised that Mills was still breathing. Before Jon could ask a question of Mills, though, J. J. blurted out,

"He's still alive, Jon. The jerk's not even hurt."

Instead of acting happy, Jon acted disappointed, mumbling,

"Shit! I wanted his peaches."

Mills, Doc Kees and a few other men were recommended for citations for their bravery, daring, courage and dogged determination for routing a well-entrenched superior enemy force while under constant deadly fire.

Seamen Kirk and Rice

John O'Malley was running an errand when he spotted two guys coming up the path toward the platoon's encampment. He was startled to see how they were dressed: black Navy shoes and a mix of Marine Corps and U. S. Army gear. They asked John where they could find Easy Company, informing him they were looking for a friend named Don Young. By coincidence, Don Young was John O'Malley's squad leader.

John led them to Don's tent. A number of us, seeing these strange-looking fellows, were curious and gathered around them. Young, hearing the racket and people shouting his name, crawled sleepily from his tent, growling like a bitchy old bear. His mouth dropped open in disbelief when he realized an old childhood friend, someone he hadn't seen in a couple of years, was standing before him. With joyous whoops and huge grins on their faces, they gave each other bone-crushing bear hugs and teeth rattling slaps on the back. W. J. Miller was astonished. He'd never seen Don Young so happy. And he was smiling too. Usually, he was in a foul mood, bellyaching and grousing about everything under the sun.

Young introduced his good friend, Robert C. Rice. He too was from Grass Valley, California and they'd known each other all their lives. Rice, in turn, introduced his buddy, Donald Francis Kirk, a member of the Klamath Indian Tribes in Oregon. Oregon! I knew right then and there that I was going to like the guy. His family and friends called him "Bear." No wonder—he was one big fellow.

"Where the hell did you guys come from? Why the hell are you here?"

They proceeded to tell us an incredible story and the reason for their visit. The first thing we learned was that they were sailors assigned to the U.S.S. Estes, AGC 12 Amphibious Group-1, anchored in the bay at Inchon and that they'd jumped ship. When we heard that little bit of news, we huddled around them even closer.

Rice liked the Navy but he wanted to go to school to be a corpsman so he could see combat with the Marines. But the Navy turned his request down and, instead, sent him to engineering school. After finishing, he was assigned to the Estes. Duty aboard the ship was boring. Nothing exciting ever happened with the exception of an occasional visit by a North Korean plane that had earned the nicknames *Midnight Charlie* and *Piss-Call Charlie*. He always came in the dead of night, dropped a bomb or two, and then flew quickly back into

Seamen Robert Rice with his childhood friend, Marine Corporal Donald Young, September 1951

Chapter V

North Korea. Kirk added that the guy couldn't hit his ass with a stick.

So, Rice decided to jump ship, find his good friend Don Young, and join Young's Marine unit hoping he'd get a chance to go into battle. Devising a plan, he discussed it with several of his shipmates, hoping to entice a few to go along with him. Some were interested but when it came time to actually go, they decided not to be so adventurous. All backed out with the exception of Don Kirk. After performing an Indian ritual becoming blood brothers, they departed. It was September 15, 1951, when they began their trip eastward across the Korean Peninsula, to the area where they knew the Marines were fighting, confident they could find Young's outfit.

The two men hitched a ride in a truck with Army engineers driving east from Inchon. That night, as they bunked down with the engineers, they told them of their plans to join the Marines. Because military police regularly patrolled the roads, they needed a change of clothing to hide their identity. Eager to help, the engineers obliged them and, with the exception of their shoes, swapped their Navy attire for Army clothing. The following day they caught a ride in an eastbound ammunition truck and the third day they rode in a truck loaded with rockets. Finally, in a torrential downpour of chilling rain, they arrived at a location near the front lines and were given directions to Marine positions. The terrain that lay before them was steep and the ground wet and terribly slippery. Immediately they had trouble climbing in the soft muck and found it necessary to use ropes to pull themselves the first few hundred yards up the hill.

After hours of climbing, they came across Third Battalion's Item Company dug in on the reverse slope of a hill. The nearest thing they had to a weapon was a pocketknife and, needless to say, they felt pretty darned nervous being so close to the front lines without a rifle to defend themselves. Asking where they could get one, two of the Marines pointed up the hill and told them there had been a horrendous dogfight up there earlier in the day and that gear was strewn all over the landscape including weapons. But there was one problem. The area was in No-Man's-Land and it was likely they could draw fire from either side. Figuring they had little choice if they wanted to be armed, they very gingerly and very quietly, worked their way over the hill.

They found the area where the firefight had taken place and it was, indeed, littered with gear and debris, pockmarked with shell craters, and stinking of strange odors and burnt powder. They told us how very nervous and wary they were as they searched through the graveyard of gear, worrying that they might encounter North Korean troops. They found two usable M1 rifles, helmets and ammunition belts, plus some other gear they knew they would need.

As they were about to retrace their steps, the North Koreans suddenly opened up on them with small mortars. Rice quickly jumped into a shell crater that was partially filled with rainwater. Protection and cover were the only things on his mind at the moment and getting soaked didn't matter. When he peeked over the rim of the crater looking for Kirk, he saw him dodging from one hole to another. Rice yelled at him to get down. Kirk, hearing Rice's warning, made a beeline for him and jumped into the same hole. After the shelling stopped, Rice asked him,

> "Why in the hell were you dodging around out there from one hole to another?"

Kirk's simple reply was,

> "I was looking for a dry one."

We soon learned that Kirk seldom spoke, but when he did, it was usually something very simple or quite profound.

The pair of adventurous swabbies, probably wondering if they'd made the right decision about going into combat, remained in the crater long after the last mortar had fallen, trying to make a decision whether or not to chance leaving. Getting wetter and wetter and feeling more nervous by the minute, they finally decided it best to run for it and take the risk of being shot at again. They scurried back down the hill without

Chapter V

further incident and, rejoining Item Company, dug in for the night. The rain kept falling. Everyone was trenching and trying to keep the water out of their holes, but it was hopeless.

One of the Marines remarked,

"Welcome to the war, boys."

Only Rice and Kirk could ever say whether they were shivering from the wet and cold or from the harrowing experience of being under fire for the first time. After a few days, Item Company was relieved from the lines. So, the two sailors followed the Marines to the rear and soon found where Easy Company was camped.

Since they wanted to fight in the war with us, who were we to deny them that experience? Every one of us to a man decided to keep his mouth shut, hoping that none of our command people would find out. The decision was made and Kirk moved into W. J. Miller's tent and Rice with Young. And then we proceeded to have one hell of a party, thanks in part to the boys from the Deep South and their liquor-still. Little did our new friends know that, by joining up with us, they would soon be going right back to the front lines.

The day before leaving, seven of our shelter-half tents caught fire. It was rumored that the liquor-still had gone bad and had caused it. Lieutenant Lilley's tent was one that went up in smoke, burning most of his possessions. Mumbling to himself, he was standing among the burned remains surveying the damage when Alan Murphy, another Marine from Massachusetts, approached him to offer him some solace. Jack thanked him for being concerned, but it wasn't the loss of his personal mementos that Jack regretted most. It was the loss of his liquor ration

Murphy's speech and accent were identical to Jack Lilley's. Of course, everyone who knew him called him *Murph*. He was a Ninth Replacement Draft reservist and was assigned to Easy Company's mortar section. Murphy had a very close relationship with his mother and wrote letters to her nearly every day, no matter what the circumstances. More concerned about her health than about his, Murphy frequently reminded his mom to take her medication. And she did her best to make him happy, sending him packets of Kool Aid and tea bags in the envelopes, with her letters. Never missing an opportunity to scribble a few words, Murphy wrote the following while crouched down in a hole during a firefight.

Dear Mother,

There's not much to write about today. I'm lying in a hole right now behind a rock. We're in a push and we attacked some hill and now we are pinned down. The gooks have been shelling us with artillery and mortars and this machine gun raked the hill right in front of me. It was close but I'm still here. Now, some snipers are shooting at us and our guys are shooting back. At least it hasn't rained on us. In fact, if it wasn't for all the noise, it would be a pretty nice day.

Loren Tracy recovered from his chest wounds and returned to the company, but not to our platoon. He was assigned to 3.5 rockets, a somewhat safer unit not as likely to be involved in many direct firefights. He was awarded a Silver Star for his gallantry and leadership while under fire and another Purple Heart for his wound. As for Nellie Nelson, I never saw him again.

Alan Murphy and Ken Moody

Chapter V

Mortar Valley

We went on line, occupying existing bunkers constructed by previous units. The place was so pockmarked with mortar craters, it looked like the moon. And we certainly knew what they meant when the men we relieved commented as they pulled out,

"Keep yer hats on, boys."

Ebb Daughtery, now the platoon sniper, and redheaded Sergeant Osborne were my bunkmates. The bunker that we were assigned was situated in the bottom of a small valley on the east side of a large creek, flowing from north to south through our lines down the hill to our rear. The valley was densely forested with brush and trees and the trees were the largest I'd seen in Korea, reminding me of the fir trees at home. Communications with each other wasn't a huge problem because each bunker including the Company Command Post was equipped with a voice-activated sound power telephone, attached to a continuous communications wire.

A machine gun bunker manned by men from another company was positioned to our right and Louie Caruso and another Marine rifleman occupied a bunker across the creek to our left. From our positions, Louie and I could lay down a cross fire on the banks of

Red and Daughtery

the creek in front of us with our Browning automatic rifles and the machine gun could sweep the side of the hill in front of and beyond Louie's bunker, thus making the area a deadly place for our enemy to venture into. However, the creek bottom was another matter. It wasn't easily defended against individual enemy infiltrators.

We nicknamed the place *"Mortar Valley"* because every blessed day, without fail, we received mortar barrages. Most of them were horrendous, teeth-grinding, nerve-wracking poundings and the unpleasant smell of burned powder, always present in the air, was the only reminder needed for us to *keep our hats on*. The lid on our bunker was five feet thick, made of bagged dirt and logs. Sergeant Oz occasionally suggested that we add more to it but we never did. It seemed to be more than sufficient to take a direct impact from a small mortar. But then when those things began to drop on us, the roof never seemed to be thick enough and doubts and misgivings always surfaced.

The floor of our bunker was constantly wet and muddy. The previous owners had covered it with small limbs and empty sand bags but it did no good. Daughtery and I dug deeper and discovered that we had running water—a tiny trickling spring. We dug a small ditch out through the bunker opening to drain the water into the creek. Then, to keep the water running, we laid rocks in the ditch and covered it with logs and cardboard from our c-ration boxes. We did the same to the floor inside the bunker and finished it off with a layer of dry dirt and leaves. It worked beautifully. We slept comfortably but we could still hear the faint musical sound of trickling water under us, a sound that made me want to pee all the time.

The enemy's line of defense, quite a distance to our front, was not visible from our position in the valley but it could be seen from the positions farther up the hill to our left. Seventy-five to eighty yards beyond us, the terrain in No-Man's-Land was brushy and dense with foliage, an enemy sniper's paradise and a dangerous situation for us.

Chapter V

We found the enemy to be quite active in this sector, constantly probing and patrolling and snooping near our lines. We didn't have to go out looking for trouble. It came to us. Sometimes, without trying, we found ourselves embroiled in brief skirmishes. I felt uneasy nearly every moment in Korea but the uneasiness escalated considerably while in this area. We knew that any North Korean who wanted to do us harm could sneak in pretty darned close whenever he desired.

Five or six unarmed North Koreans actually surrendered to Ebb, Sergeant Oz and me while we were in Mortar Valley, a couple of them getting as close to us as fifty yards before we knew they were there. None carried anything that could have been construed as a weapon—no bullets, grenades, not even a pocketknife and every one of them had a look of apprehension and uncertainty on his wrinkled and weather-beaten face, probably wondering if he was going to get shot. But regardless of what they looked like or how they acted, none of them could be trusted. We had to be constantly on the alert for trickery.

Every North Korean I saw, alive or dead, wore a quilted uniform and Ked tennis shoes. I thought to myself at the time,

"What the hell, Ked tennis shoes? I think they're made in the United States and here these guys are wearing them."

Two older and very nervous North Koreans surrendered to us one afternoon. Unseen by any of us, they had gotten to within a hundred yards of our positions before one of them tripped a wire attached to a hand-illuminating grenade. The pop of the grenade alerted all of us and immediately rifle fire was directed at the two individuals, who had crouched down behind some brush and debris. I leveled my Browning automatic rifle and had one of them squarely in my sights, ready to kill him, when I heard someone yelling,

"Cease-fire! They're surrendering. Cease-fire! Cease-fire!"

For a split second I gave serious thought to killing him anyway. These North Koreans were not very high on my list of protected creatures, but nonetheless, I let up on the trigger because I knew it wouldn't be right. The guy never knew

North Korean surrendering

that he'd come within a whisker's width of dying. At the time, I doubt that I would have cared much had I killed him. But thinking back on the incident now, I'm glad that I held my fire.

One young North Korean, who appeared to be about fifteen or sixteen, cautiously approached the wire in front of W. J. Miller's bunker and surrendered. Realizing that the kid was frightened to death, Jon tried to reassure him that he was not going to be harmed by offering him some c-ration chocolate. Miller, being an opportunist, felt certain that the boy was harmless and decided to keep him as his personal *washy-washy boy*. Washy-washy boys, kids who did laundry for the servicemen, were common around the reserve camps but certainly not on the lines. Miller's scheme lasted about half a day before he was found out and ordered to turn the lad over to company command.

Johnny Pompeo, manning his thirty-caliber machine gun and standing watch inside his bunker, was just about to eat his noon meal of c-ration chow when he experienced a hair-raising surprise. As he was spooning the first bite of food into his mouth, he caught sight of a movement that he thought was a hand waving a piece of paper. Dropping his lunch, he swung the

Chapter V

barrel of his thirty-caliber machine gun into position. Then he saw it again. And it was a hand. It was a North Korean soldier, a mere 30 to 40 yards in front of Johnny's bunker, trying to get the machine-gunner's attention without getting shot. Johnny yelled out a warning and the soldier hesitatingly rose up from his prone position with a surrender leaflet in his hand, pleading,

"No shoot! No shoot! No shoot!"

When Johnny yelled to the soldier to put his hands in the air, three more North Koreans rose up from concealed positions, startling the soup out of him. The four enemy soldiers, wanting to surrender, had crawled much too close to our positions without being detected. Each man, their arms outstretched, nervously waved a surrender leaflet as they squatted in front of Johnny's bunker. His voice trembling, using the sound power phone, he called requesting assistance, screaming that he had four prisoners on his hands.

Marine riflemen manning adjacent bunkers moved cautiously into position to cover the enemy soldiers, watching for any kind of trickery. Two of the Marines moved forward, motioning to the North Koreans to come closer but with hands up. Another Marine slipped into the bunker with Johnny. Feel-

Safe Conduct Pass

ing much relieved, he nodded toward the enemy soldiers and smugly remarked,

"Looky what I got."

The other Marine, not very impressed by Johnny's so-called *capture,* asked,

"Did you search 'em, Pompeo?"

The smart-ass question irked Johnny.

"Search them? Hell no, I didn't search them. I'm in here. They're out there. How'm I gonna search them? I just caught them, fer cryin' out loud! You want me to do everything? Fer cryin' out loud!"

The other Marine continued to give Johnny a bad time,

"Ah, quit yer bitchin', John. You're just lucky as hell these guys didn't pitch a grenade in here and blast your dumb butt to hell."

Johnny, continuing to defend himself, said,

"Aw, fer cryin' out loud! Isn't anybody ever satisfied in this stoopid outfit?"

In the excitement, John's can of c-ration had been kicked over on the bunker floor and not until after the North Koreans had been secured and led away for interrogation did he realize that his chow had been trampled into the earth. He felt unappreciated, insulted and put upon and he was still hungry. Using the sound power telephone, he called out a plea asking if someone would share some food with him. But not one soul had any sympathy for him. Immediately, we heard a number of the guys answering him from up and down the line, making remarks like,

"You need to skip a meal now and then, John, and lose a little more weight."

"Ya want some of my hash?"

"Why don'tcha make like a cow and chew yer cud?"

> "If you're hungry, Pompy, I got somethin' fer you to chew on."

> "Fer cryin' out loud!"

The stern voice of the company Gunnery Sergeant boomed over the sound power telephone system from the command post ending Johnny's plea for food and stemming the insults being cast his way.

> "Knock off the chatter! If you jokers were more alert, this kinda crap wouldn't happen. You guys had better be more alert. If you keep letting these gooks get in close like these did you're gonna have bigger problems. Now, knock off the chatter and every one of you jokers keep your eyes open."

Within the week, more enemy soldiers came calling on us but not to surrender. It was another beautiful, quiet and peaceful moonlit night but it wasn't to remain that way very long. Just after midnight, one of the men in the first squad issued a warning on the sound power telephone.

> "You guys better wake up. I think I just saw some movement out there."

The first squad was positioned across the creek some distance up the hill. The area in front of them was barren and not dense with brush like the area in front of our hole down in the valley. After a few seconds, the man again spoke but this time his voice sounded hoarse and raspy, filled with nervous excitement.

> "Holy gee! Look at that, you guys! There's a bunch of gooks out there."

The fellow in an adjacent bunker asked,

> "I don't see nuthin'. Where the hell you lookin' anyway?"

> "Dammit! Right out there, in front of my bunker – maybe a hundred yards out. For cry sakes, they're all over the place. If the sixties get on 'em right now, they could really raise some hell."

Someone from sixty mortars joined the conversation and seconds later, I heard the familiar hollow *ploop* sound made by a mortar firing. A flare popped open up the hill but because of the trees, it did little to light the area in front of our bunker.

"Ya believe me now? Look at those little bastards divin' for cover."

Our mortars went to work. I woke Oz and Daughtery with some frantic prodding and hearing the sounds of explosions not far off, they wasted little time scrambling out of their sacks. Uneasy but trying to remain calm, I whispered to them that we were being probed somewhere up on the hill but nothing had happened, as yet, in front of us. We heard no rifle shots, only the booming of our sixty mortar impacts. Listening to the voices of excited men on the sound power, the three of us stared nervously into the dark and waited, hoping that the North Koreans wouldn't attack our bunker, that the probe wasn't a prelude to something bigger.

Calling on the sound power to the mortar section, someone asked,

"Hey, Murph! Are you awake?"

"Hell, yes, I'm awake. Who the hell do you think is shootin' this damned thing?"

"You guys are right on target. Keep it coming, buddy, hot and heavy."

During the remainder of the night, more than one mortar crew worked as they fired nearly eighty rounds, bombarding the area in front of the first squad's positions. Flares constantly streamed into the air. For some reason, the racket that the mortars made was consoling to me. I figured as long as those things were shooting, the goonies would be too busy ducking for cover to mess with us. And that's exactly what happened. The mortar-men did a great job preventing the Communist soldiers from getting any closer and eventually drove them off.

When daylight came, the lifeless bodies of a few North Korean soldiers could be seen some distance in front of the lines. Because they were lying in an area that was mined, a decision was made to let the North Koreans have their dead if they wanted to crawl out there and risk getting shot. But they didn't want the bodies any more than we did and they remained where they fell, eventually decomposing and filling the October air with a nauseating stench.

Two new replacements joined our platoon, Louis Racca and Lehman Brightman. Louie was a stout, comical, dark-haired fellow of Italian descent, born and raised in Massachusetts. Lehman was a true-blue, full-blooded Sioux Indian from Oklahoma, a big brute with huge, broad shoulders. With Don Kirk here, we had us another big Indian in the platoon. He'd played football for a couple of years at Oklahoma A & M before enlisting. Lehman and Louie teamed up with each other and hit it off right away, becoming good friends.

A few days after being assigned to our platoon, their squad was scheduled to go on a patrol in front of the lines. Of course, this being his first combat patrol, Lehman was quite nervous and wondered what it would be like to be in a firefight. As the squad was preparing to go through the wire, Lehman's squad leader told him to take the point and lead the patrol.

Puzzled, he asked,

"Why me? Why are you putting me on the point? I'm new here and I haven't had any experience at being a point man."

The reply from his stoic squad leader was,

"You're an Indian, aren't you? You got natural instincts, don't you? Take the point."

Lehman figured that the white man was still determined, one way or another, to get rid of all Indians and for the next fifteen minutes, he spoke nary a word that's printable. Lehman often professed that he spoke two languages fluently—English and profanity—and, to be honest, his English wasn't that good.

The creek was handy, providing water for drinking, water for washing our clothing and to bathe. One day, while working beyond the wire clearing brush and becoming acquainted with the lay of the land, we found a small side creek running into the main stream. About twenty feet up the small creek, and partially lying in the water, was a dead North Korean soldier. The body was in the advanced stages of decomposition, the stomach cavity full of maggots. Looking at a rotting corpse didn't upset my stomach near as much as the realization that I'd been drinking water from this stream. Some of the guys continued using the water but added iodine tablets for purification. Not me! Ebb, Oz and I and a few others elected to use the water from our own private spring, the one running through our bunker.

Every so often we were re-supplied by South Koreans, a human mule train of about thirty men that carried supplies, including c-rations and ammunition, on their backs for some distance from behind the lines. The loads these little people carried were huge. For some reason, we referred to these folks as Chiggy Bearers or Chiggy Bears, a name I never figured out. The Chiggy Bearers themselves were not armed, but were always escorted by a few armed South Korean or American soldiers. To bring supplies to us, they used a well-traveled trail coming up behind our bunker and then crossed the creek following the line of bunkers up the hill to the company command post

One day the Chiggy Bearers were passing through our position with supplies when mortar rounds began to fall on us. Most of them had already crossed the creek and were going up the hill toward the Company command post. Two of them scrambled into our bunker seeking shelter and the remaining few who had not yet reached us turned and ran back down the trail. We were in luck because the two fellows who sought safety in our bunker were carrying food, one a thermal-vat filled with hot chili and the other a box of apples. As soon as we saw the food we were determined to keep it with us. Relieving them of their loads, we told them as best we could, during a lull in the shelling, to vamoose down the hill. They understood and very gladly obliged, not wanting to be there

Chapter V

Chiggy bearers

any more than we did. We ate heartily for several days and no one at company headquarters ever had the slightest idea what had happened to their chow.

Most of our reconnaissance and combat patrols crossed the concertina wire in front of our bunker and followed the path upstream along the creek into No-Man's-Land. It was handy but it was also dangerous because the North Koreans often booby-trapped it after dark. We also booby-trapped it trying to catch them. It was always cat and mouse, with the careless becoming the loser.

A patrol from one of the other platoons went out before dawn, intending to probe the enemy's defenses. They crept up on the Communists soldiers, catching them unaware, and bayoneted several while they slept. When one of the survivors sounded an alarm, the patrol withdrew, avoiding a firefight, and made its way back into the lines without sustaining any casualties. Only after they'd secured did our enemy retaliate bombarding us for an hour with an extra dose of mortars.

The first platoon went on another, much larger, patrol two or three days later, passing through the wire in front of our bunker, using the same trail. They had penetrated into No-Man's-Land some distance up the valley before coming under rifle fire. This time the enemy was awake and waiting. Within moments, they supplemented their rifle fire with another heavy barrage of mortars. It was deadly, many rounds exploding among the men, injuring several as they hurriedly retraced their steps back to our lines. They came pouring over the concertina wire, diving into the nearest bunkers for cover. Two or three crowded into our bunker with the three of us as mortars rained down thick and heavy, some striking so close that we could feel our bunker shudder from impacting shrapnel.

We thought the entire patrol was back but, while watching through the gun port for an enemy banzai attack, we saw two Marines, one of them wounded and the other trying to help him, struggling to get through the concertina wire. It was a lousy, hairy situation but they needed help. Without thinking of what might happen, I bolted out of the bunker and ran to them. Together, the other Marine and I freed the wounded man from the wire and practically dragged him to the bunker as mortars continued to burst around us.

The injured man had been hit in the backside by a piece of shrapnel, a painful wound but not life-threatening. Eventually, a hospital corpsman, darting through the bombardment, crawled into our already crowded hole and quite efficiently treated his wound. The corpsman, probably no more than nineteen years old, was about to go out to find more wounded men to help when we realized that he, too, had been hit by shrapnel—not once but several times. Two of his wounds were nasty and must have given him considerable pain. We couldn't let him go like that so we barred the entrance preventing him from leaving, forcing him to stay with us until the shelling stopped. He objected but we were adamant and wouldn't give in.

Chapter V

A few hours later, some very grateful Marines carried the young corpsman to an aid station to the rear of our lines. We told our officers what the lad had done, how he had performed, and how willing he was to risk his life to continue helping others even though he too had been wounded. Because of his gallantry and bravery, he was recommended for and received a silver star, a well-deserved reward.

These corpsmen were something else. Most of them were just snot-nosed kids who were scared to death, but there was no quit in them. They just kept going, exposing themselves to brutal and perilous conditions, sometimes suffering terrible injuries as they responded to the calls of our wounded. Some of them died trying to keep us alive.

Dog tags

Chapter VI

Platoon Leader For 8 Hours

The word came to us that a new second lieutenant had joined the Company, replacing Jack Lilley as our platoon leader. Not one of us wanted to hear that kind of news. We wanted to keep Jack. We had the highest respect for him, valuing his leadership. He was assigned to a safer unit within the company and, even though he probably didn't request the move, he more than earned it.

That night, just hours after joining the company, our new platoon leader, whom I'd not yet met, volunteered to lead a squad-sized patrol in front of the lines. Rice, one of our transplanted sailors, and John O'Malley were two members that went with him. Unless encountering enemy resistance, their objective was to patrol up to one thousand yards in front of our lines before returning to friendly territory.

Fifteen minutes after departure, they discovered their hand-held radio was inoperative. The lieutenant ordered the patrol to stay put while he and his runner returned to the lines to fetch another one. Finding the correct re-entry point, he obtained another radio and immediately went back into

No-Man's-Land. They became disoriented in the dark, lost their way and bypassed the patrol. Discovering their mistake, they circled back. Hearing noises in front of them, the members of the patrol quite reasonably assumed that an enemy patrol was approaching, not expecting the lieutenant and the runner to be coming from that direction.

The BAR man positioned at the deepest point of the patrol's perimeter fired a short burst at the figures creeping toward them. Both men went down, the lieutenant killed instantly by the deadly fire and the runner hit hard in the upper arm and shoulder. When the mistake was discovered, one of the veteran Marines took charge and prepared to withdraw. But the portable stretcher they had taken with them was so flimsy that it collapsed under the weight of the dead lieutenant's large body. Rice volunteered to take the wounded runner back to the lines, fetch another stretcher and return with additional men.

Helping the wounded man over the rugged terrain, he somehow made it safely back without tripping any booby traps or stepping on mines. He made a hurried report to the men in the bunkers at the re-entry point, obtained another stretcher, and, with a few more Marines following him, he returned to where the patrol had hunkered down. After securely strapping the dead officer's body to the stretcher, Rice again took the lead and, carefully skirting some abandoned enemy bunkers, they eventually made it back into the lines without suffering further mishap.

Rice later related that he could vividly remember the password and countersign as being *cotton* and *tail*. Never taught the correct procedure for giving a password or for receiving the countersign and really not knowing what to do, he repeatedly yelled *"Cottontail! Cottontail! Cottontail!"* over and over as he approached our positions praying that he wouldn't be shot by some edgy, trigger-happy Marine.

The wounded man, a very religious person, constantly read the Bible and had been nicknamed *Bible Back* by some of the troops. Religion, according to Rice, was the fellow's strength and it helped him survive his terrible injuries. Sometime later, we received word that surgeons were unable to save Bible Back's shattered arm. It was a hell of a way to go home.

They brought the dead lieutenant's body to my bunker and I helped carry this man, to whom I'd never been introduced, down the trail with a poncho draped over his body.

Louie's Goose

It was an exceptionally dark night when Don Kirk, our other transplanted sailor, began to get nervous feeling that someone or something was out front of the wire barrier near his position. He was in a bunker across the creek, one or two bunkers up the ridge above Louie's position. Using the sound power telephone, he told us of his uneasiness but he also related that he hadn't actually heard anything. It was so black that we could see absolutely nothing and none of us had heard anything strange, either. The consensus was, though, that since Kirk was an Indian he could likely sense things that the rest of us couldn't. Someone decided that it was better to be safe than sorry and called for flares. We could hear the *ploop* sound of a mortar and the night suddenly lit up. Strange shadows moved across the brush and tree covered landscape as a flickering flare slowly drifted down to earth. A grenade exploded, a burst of automatic fire that sounded like a burp gun, and then another grenade echoed throughout the valley, proving the enemy was there. A couple of our sixty mortar rounds exploded in front of the concertina wire on the other side of the creek. Everyone hunkered down but continued to communicate with each other in hushed, tense voices on the sound power telephones. Everyone, that is, except Louie Caruso. He wouldn't answer our repeated calls to him. I hoped and prayed that the North Koreans hadn't gotten to him and, frantic with concern about the little imp, I strained, peering into the darkness toward his bunker. After the initial exchange of gunfire, not another shot was fired. For the next hour, an occasional flare popped open above us but its light revealed nothing. We settled down, waiting for daylight, hoping to hear something from Louie. Even though no movement was detected in the area of his bunker, Marines in the bunker above occasionally lobbed a hand grenade near his position, hoping to fend off and discourage any infiltrators that might have gotten through the wire.

Then, in the dim light of dawn, there stood Louie behind his bunker, stretching and yawning as if he was just rising from a good night's sleep on a feather mattress. At first, I was elated to see that he was safe but then, after thinking about all the worry that he had caused me, I wanted to kick his lousy butt.

"Just look at him. He doesn't even know what the hell's going on. I should shoot the dumb jerk myself."

Even though he denied it, I just knew he'd slept through the entire night, including that hell-raising racket made by the shooting, exploding grenades and mortars. Louie claimed that he was awake all the time but couldn't answer our calls because his sound power telephone had malfunctioned. He squirmed out of trouble again and eventually 'most everyone forgot about it— 'most everyone but me.

Just beyond Louie's bunker, near the concertina wire, lay a dead North Korean soldier killed by grenades and mortars. Kirk's alertness and instincts probably saved Louie's *bacon*. But for scaring the hell out of me, I wanted to cook his lousy *goose*.

Return To The Navy

With the passing of each day, more people became aware of the presence of Kirk and Rice. For nearly a month, Jim Stanley, one of our sergeants, scratched his head many times trying to figure out why the platoon needed two additional boxes of c-rations every day. But, he trusted the squad leaders were reporting an accurate count to him and shrugged it off. Gunnery Sergeant Virili knew something was amiss, also, and had asked Stanley if the platoon wasn't getting more rations than it deserved. However, other things were more worrisome and pressing at the time and they let the matter slide.

Chapter VI

Finally, Sergeant Stanley and one of the officers found out. After confirming their presence, Stanley reported to an astonished Company Commander and Gunnery Sergeant that the men of the platoon had been hiding two sailors in their bunkers and that these two stowaways had actually been pulling ambushes and patrols.

"You gotta be shittin' us, Jim."

"No I'm not, Gunny. Honest to God! The guys have been hidin' them in their bunkers. They come off some ship. Hell, they've got rifles, helmets, everything. They look just like Marines."

Now that the company's officers knew about them, the jig was up. Kirk and Rice were informed that they had to return to their ship and regardless of what they wanted they could no longer stay with us. Every one of us, especially our officers, would have been in serious trouble with the Department of the Navy had either one or both of our swabbies suffered an injury, or worse been killed. They seriously considered sneaking off and joining up with another outfit, but, after being reminded of the consequences, they grudgingly gave up the idea. They'd proven to be good troops and every last one of us was sorry to see them leave.

Several days after their departure from the platoon, a Navy Lieutenant came to the lines to determine if Kirk and Rice were telling the truth about fighting with the Marines. The man was stunned when he heard our stories. We laid it on a little thick and even Captain Maxson, our company commander, gave high praise to the two wayward sailors. He didn't mince any words, either, when he told the Navy Lieutenant how heroic he thought they were. After answering the officer's questions, we asked what the Navy intended to do with them. His reply was not something we wanted to hear. They were each facing a court-martial for being away from their duty station without permission. Every one of us tried to impress upon the lieutenant that both of them deserved medals for their bravery, hoping to throw a monkey wrench into the Navy's plan

AWOL Seamen Robert Rice and Donald Kirk, serving with Easy Company in September 1951, prior to returning to the Navy

for the court-martial. It took some intense persuasion to prevent Don Young, who was pretty hot under the collar, from telling the lieutenant what he thought of the Navy and its court-martial plans for his friends. Since Rice's departure, Young had reverted back to being his old self; the grumpy grouch that the rest of us had become accustomed to seeing.

Before he left, the lieutenant himself experienced one hell of a mortar barrage. After being pinned down for nearly an hour inside a bunker, he left the lines shaken and probably wondering why in the world two of his sailors wanted to live like we did—enduring sleepless nights, crummy tasting food, artillery, snipers, mines and mortars.

Kirk and Rice each received a court-martial. They were found guilty by a military court, fined some of their pay and sentenced to some time in the brig. We Marines were not very happy with the Navy's decision and believed our Navy mates deserved to be rewarded for their willingness to put their lives on the line for us. We thought the penalty blatantly unfair, considering what they tried to do for their country. These two sailors were heroes to us and even now they deserve to be recognized as such.

Not many days after Rice and Kirk left us, Butch Schaus informed his squad to clean their weapons, that he was going to inspect them. Inspection was seldom done on the lines but the platoon had a new lieutenant and Butch figured it best to make certain everyone's rifle was clean and in good condition. Since Schaus and Don Young were bunker mates, Young's rifle was the first weapon to be checked. Young, sullen and pissed off at the world since Rice returned to his ship, stared at Butch as Butch gave the rifle a close examination. Finally, thrusting the rifle back into Young's hands, Butch informed him that his rifle was filthy, so damned dirty that he was to clean it again and that meant immediately.

> *"I'll be back in a few minutes, Don, and it had better be clean or you'll be fetching water for the squad in those five-gallon cans. And if it isn't clean then, you'll have to get another five gallons of water."*

Young, his voice steady but barely audible, said,

> *"When we get out of the Marines, Schaus, I'm gonna kick the crap out of you."*

Butch knew that Young's bark was bigger than his bite. It was really Young's stare that was unsettling. The guy could stop a grizzly bear fight with it.

The Souvenir Hunter

Nearly everyone collected souvenirs of some type: Communist red star hat emblems, spoons made from brass ammunition casings by Korean civilians, opium pipes, surrender leaflets, weaponry of all sorts, and various coins and currency. We named the brass spoons *itiwa spoons*. According to a Korean friend, the correct pronunciation should have been *iriwa*, the Korean word for *come here*, but we couldn't understand the language. When speaking, the Korean people flip the "r" in *iriwa*, making it sound like a "t" to us. The spoon surface was large and, being sturdy, they didn't break. The long, thin handles were slender and resembled an ice pick. The very popular *itiwa* spoons were preferred over the flimsy c-ration utensils. Therefore, nearly every one of us Infantry Marines carried one stuck in the pencil pocket of our shirt.

Everett Partridge was a souvenir hunter extraordinaire. Among other things, he collected dud ammunition, including a small mortar and hand grenades. Not many of us who had any sense cared to be around his bunker knowing the danger his souvenirs posed. One of the strangest things he had, though, was a human finger bone, hung from a chain around his neck. His finger-bone souvenir gave me the willies. And I had no desire whatsoever to know how he came by it.

A few weeks after taking up positions in Mortar Valley, Everett suffered a grievous injury and had to be evacuated. He was dismantling one of the many booby traps that he'd placed in front of his bunker when he accidentally stepped on a forgotten Bouncing-Betty flare. The blast viciously drove one of his feet up into his face, shattering his leg. I didn't know Everett very well; he was assigned to another squad and we seldom had a chance to visit with each other. But nonetheless, when I heard what had happened, I went to his bunker to bid him

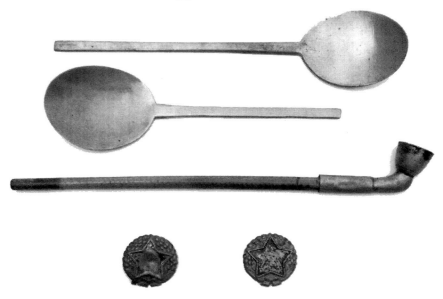

Souvenirs: "Itiwa" spoons, opium pipe, Communist red star hat emblems

Chapter VI

Korean Bank note

good luck and farewell. There was no doubt in my mind that his injury would cause him grief for the rest of his life. I can still remember him as he lay on a stretcher waiting to be evacuated. He was in considerable pain but yet he was grinning, perhaps because he knew he was going home. Since he couldn't take his souvenirs with him and the stretcher-bearers refused to carry them, he tried giving them away to his buddies. But not one person wanted anything to do with them.

Bouncing-Betty flares were not used with the intention of killing people. But, nonetheless, they did considerable harm to anyone unfortunate enough to step on one, as Everett found out. When triggered, a hefty explosive charge, with as much power as a grenade, sent a flare package skyrocketing several hundred feet into the sky. At its apex, a chute deployed and it slowly drifted back to earth, with a flare dangling beneath, illuminating the surrounding terrain like a searchlight. They were a Godsend on dark nights. But, unfortunately, those things also pinpointed our positions.

Unfortunately, Everett wasn't the only one to suffer an accident because of carelessness. I came close to blowing my fingers off one day in Mortar Valley because of a stupid mistake. Unscrewing the detonating assembly from a fragmentation grenade, I intended to play a trick on some Chiggy Bearers as they passed through our position. Like an idiot, I forgot that the detonating assembly also contained an explosive device, powerful enough to destroy one's hand. I pulled the pin, let the spoon fly, and watched the Chiggy Bearers scramble away in fright across the creek. Lucky for me, I tossed it aside just an instant before the thing detonated. The small blast peppered me with dirt but, other than scaring the hell out of me, and everyone else that was close, it caused no harm. Immediately, someone from above was on the sound power telephone wanting to know what was going on. I lied like a dog and told them that one of the Chiggy Bearers had accidentally tripped a flare, but that everything was under control. No one ever brought up the incident again and I kept my dumb mouth shut, hiding my stupidity.

Johnny Pompeo had tied a long pull-wire to a hand grenade, pulled the pin and inserted the grenade into a can that was anchored to a tree, making a booby trap in front of his position. As he returned to his bunker, he accidentally tripped over the wire, pulling the grenade from the can. He heard the spoon fly and, realizing what he'd done, yelled,

"Fire in the hole!"

But he couldn't duck because he'd lost his balance and was unable to throw himself to the ground. The grenade exploded and although Johnny was still in a partially upright position and within yards of it, none of the shrapnel hit him. Luckily, he suffered nothing more than a good heart-stopping fright and a lot of razzing from his friends.

Texans

Jimmy Richardson from Grand Prairie and Roy Phillips from Dallas took great pleasure in teasing the guys from the Northeast, and especially the ones from Massachusetts, New York and New Jersey, about their speech and accents. Richardson and Phillips spoke with a very strong Texas drawl. For some reason, Richardson seldom bragged about Texas and if he did say anything, he certainly didn't crow about it like Phillips.

Chapter VI

If one happened to venture anywhere near Phillips, he never failed to give you an earful about his native state.

Vernon Roll, a small shy kid, was reminiscing with Phillips about his home. Vernon asked Roy if he'd ever visited Deer Park, Washington where he lived. Roy, replying with his customary Texas wit, said,

> "Yep, ah shore have. Ah passed through that neck-a-the-woods one time when ah was out mendin' fences on muh Uncle's Ranch. Yuh gotta know, though, that as fur as ranches go in Texas, it wuz jest a itty bitty place."

My little Brooklyn friend Louie Caruso and Phillips got into an argument one day about who could speak the clearest and most understandable English. What a riot. We folks from out west could hardly understand either one of them and just sat back enjoying ourselves listening to those two *foreigners* speak their *y'alls* and *youses* to each other.

Nearly every time Phillips or I went on a patrol or an ambush, we made five-dollar bets with each other about which one of us would be the first to get shot. Of course, neither of us wanted to collect that kind of bet but we played this little game anyway just to reinforce our determination to get back unscathed. Someone figured out that neither one of us could have collected the bet, anyway, had the other one gotten killed. Well, we already knew that with no intention of collecting. That's why we made them.

Jimmy Richardson kept hounding the guys to find him a girl with which he could correspond. Now this guy, a stocky fellow with reddish, curly hair, was certainly no prince as far as looks were concerned. One of his nostrils was at least four times larger than the other and his feet would have rivaled Sasquatch in size.

I got a bright idea one day to play a joke on him and, borrowing a picture of a very nice-looking young lady from one of the troops, I showed it to Jimmy, bragging that she was my cousin. I gave him a name and address but the name and address was that of my grandmother, a woman in her seventies and living with my mom and dad. Jimmy told me a few days

Jimmy Richardson, October 1951

later that he'd written a letter to her, introducing himself, that he was in my outfit, and that he would like to visit her one day in the future.

But my trick never came off as I had intended. I received a letter from my mother several weeks later and she was mad as hell at me—like a disturbed hornet—because I'd given Grandmother's name and address to Jimmy. And you can't believe how angry she was with him for what he had written. She wanted to know if this fellow, Richardson, had been shell-shocked or was suffering from some kind of mental condition. His letter to my fictitious cousin was enclosed.

He wrote in part,

"When I get out of the Marines, I'll come up to Oregon and maybe I can get a little 'poon tang' off of you."

I couldn't believe the idiot wrote *that* to my grandmother. As if he were standing there before me, I bellowed,

"Jimmy, you stupid jackass! Why the hell did you write that to her? Oh, my God! What the hell have I done to my Granny? She's gonna just kill me when I get home"

Mom was upset, Grandma was confused and Jimmy was salivating. To end this quickly, I told him that my cousin was marrying a policeman. Thank goodness that put a screeching halt to his romantic missives to my dear old granny. And you can bet your last dollar that I never did anything like that again.

A Bright Man

Brightman and Racca had been with the company for about two weeks when they were dispatched to man an overnight listening post several hundred yards in front of the lines. Just after dark, they moved down the hill and crawled into their positions, shallow holes covered by brush. Even though Brightman's hole was too small for his bulk, something that really irritated the big guy, they quietly hunkered down. It rained on them all night. In the dawning hours of the following morning, Lehman, numbed by the cold night air, found himself ankle-deep in water. As he extracted himself from the mud-sucking hole, he began to bitch. First, he believed himself to be an idiot for enlisting in the service

Lehman Brightman, our own Indian Chief

when he could have remained in Oklahoma playing football. Then, as they began making their way back to the lines, he vented his frustrations about the cold, the mud, the war, and everything else in general.

> "I haven't even been here a month and I'm already sick of this damned place. You know why I joined the Marines, Louie? The damned coach! That dirty slope-headed bastard benched me just because I dropped a damned kickoff. So, I got mad and quit. That's the reason I joined the damned Marines—because that jerk coach benched me. Why in the hell did I ever leave college?"

Incoming artillery was frequent, but most rounds screamed over our positions, crashing into the valley behind us. One round, however, that might normally have cleared the ridge did not. Caught in the open, Racca dove to the ground when he heard it coming but Lehman merely crouched down expecting it to clear the hill. He was mouthing curses when the round hit the top of a tree, exploding. Knocked to the ground, his head ringing, Lehman felt a stinging sensation. He'd been hit in the neck, back and shoulder by shrapnel and his helmet, lying on the ground near him, had a huge hole in it. Somehow Racca had escaped injury. After a few more rounds whistled over them, they bugged out for the lines and their bunkers.

Lehman was taken to Easy Company's command post for treatment and preparation for evacuation to a rear-area hospital. He was hurt, but his wounds were not severe enough to keep him out of action very long and he would soon return to the Company. As he lay on a stretcher, he started complaining again about the rain and mud, but, surprisingly, not about his injuries. The company gunnery sergeant asked,

> "Didn't you hear the artillery coming in, Brightman?"

> "Yeah! I heard it, Gunny. But I thought it was gonna go over us like the rest of that damned crap. I guess I just wasn't paying that much attention to it."

The gunny, his compassion gone, barked,

Chapter VI

"Geez, Brightman! Them guys were shootin' at you with a cannon and you weren't payin' attention? Well, look at you now. You got your dumb ass shot off."

Wincing, Lehman snapped back,

"Well it sure as hell doesn't help much, you chewin' on what's left of it, Sarge." 28

Reserve and Patrols

We finally left Mortar Valley and pulled a little reserve time before going back on line. But being in reserve didn't mean we could sit around and relax. Searching for enemy infiltrators, we patrolled frequently. Usually, two out of three units (battalions and regiments) stayed on the front line for a couple of months while the third unit took about a month off in reserve to bolster their ranks with replacements, to recuperate, and—you know it—to patrol.

Korean hut

Bridge and Miller

We had only been in reserve a few days before we pulled a reconnaissance patrol to search the surrounding hills for guerrillas. Not one of us had any desire to go traipsing around in the boondocks just yet.

We'd been making our way along a ridge when the lieutenant, a new replacement, motioned that he wanted us to halt. We hoped that he just wanted to take a break but taking a break wasn't on his mind. A few hundred yards below us in a small valley lay an old, dilapidated and supposedly abandoned Korean hut. The lieutenant was concerned that guerrilla troops could be hiding there and wanted to make certain that the hut was unoccupied. He told J. J. to check it out while the rest of the patrol provided cover for him from the ridge.

Jerry didn't want to crawl down there but he dutifully began to descend the steep slope, realizing that it was going to take the better part of an hour to get there, check the place and then crawl back up the hill to rejoin the patrol. And then, there was always the chance that the place might be mined or rigged with booby-traps. He'd have to be extremely careful.

Beginning his descent, he muddled over the lieutenant's instructions remembering that he only wanted to make certain the hut was unoccupied. Just out of sight of the patrol, J. J.

Chapter VI

made a decision, a decision that wasn't going to set well with our new platoon leader.

Hearing rifle shots, we ducked, looking for cover, believing we'd come under fire. But, it was J. J. He'd fired his rifle, shooting a handful of tracers into the hut's dry, thatched roof, setting the place ablaze. Moments later, as the hut flamed in the valley below, he reappeared on the ridge reporting to a speechless lieutenant that the hut was definitely unoccupied.

Larry Pressley told a story about a daylight reconnaissance patrol he led into No-Man's-Land not many months before. For several hours, the patrol moved stealthily through high grass and brush, up onto a small ridge. Upon nearing the crest, he halted the patrol while he crawled forward. Reaching the crest, he peeked over the ridge, surveying the area beyond with field glasses. As he focused them, he spotted a figure not more than fifty feet lying directly in front of him. It was a North Korean soldier and he too was using field glasses and looking

Ray "Butch" Schaus and Don Young on the old two-holer

directly back at him. Realizing they were each looking at an enemy, they jumped up and ran in opposite directions. Reaching his squad, Pressley told them that they had better get the hell out of there before the North Korean called mortars in on them. I mused that perhaps the North Korean patrol leader said the same thing to his men, as they too were bugging out.

Another story about patrols involved Butch Schaus and Don Young. Butch was leading a squad sized recon patrol when a sniper shot at them. The squad immediately dove to the ground, seeking cover. Butch lay on his stomach next to a large stump, looking up a small ravine from where the shot had come trying to determine where the sniper was hiding. Don Young, sitting with his back against the stump and looking down the defile, was discussing with Butch in hushed voices what to do next. Butch believed that if the sniper fired again he could probably pinpoint his location. In jest, he suggested to Don that he rise up just enough to draw the sniper's fire. Don didn't stir or reply to Butch's suggestion but, instead, gave his squad leader a one-fingered salute.

Pulling another reconnaissance patrol searching for guerrillas, we made our way into an area of brush-covered, rolling hills that Clyde Bridge recognized. This place was an objective that Easy-Two-Seven had taken in a terrible firefight in the month of May. Although the vegetation was recovering rapidly from the devastation inflicted on it by mortars, napalm bombs and grenades, it was easy to see the rotting gear that still littered the landscape. Clyde also remembered, sadly, that this was the place where a friend, Bobby Mills, had been killed.

Bobby, who had gotten into a bad spot, had been hit hard by small-arms fire. He was able to crawl to where Bill Brannon, one of the older veterans, and some of the others had set up a base of fire. Doc Kees managed to get to Bobby, but his wounds were so severe that the corpsman was unable to keep life in him. Bobby, asking for his mother, soon died in their arms.

During the skirmish, Clyde Bridge and Lieutenant McNerney, the platoon leader, lying on the ground within three feet of each other, suffered a frightful experience. The enemy was *walking* eighty-two millimeter mortar rounds up the hill toward them in fifty-yard increments. Being exposed and unable to take any cover, they gritted their teeth and held on for dear life knowing that the next round was going to be damned close. They cringed, covering their heads with their arms, as they heard it coming down. It hit the ground right between them and buried itself up to the tail fins in the soft dirt but it failed to explode. The thing was a dud. Had it detonated, both Clyde and the lieutenant would have been history, killed instantly. And even though it was a dud, had it physically struck either one of them, that man would have died anyway.

Firing a few more rounds that exploded behind them, the enemy gave up, ending its barrage. Weakened by the horrible thought of what could have happened to them, Clyde and the lieutenant did nothing for a few seconds but stare unbelievingly at the unexploded round. Clyde, seldom at a loss for words, found it a little difficult to speak but when he did, he asked with a quivering voice,

"Permission to speak, sir?"

But Lieutenant McNerney, appearing as if he'd just awakened from having a bad dream, hesitated, not answering right away. When he did, his reply was nothing more than an unintelligible grunt.

Clyde continued,

"Ah think Ah need a little shot a Red Eye but first, if you don't mind sir, Ah think we outta get the hell away from this here thing real quick?"

Still speechless, the lieutenant could only nod in agreement. But because they'd suffered an alarming shock, they found their legs too weak and rubbery to stand. So, like two inchworms, they crawled away. It took several minutes for them to regain their composure and enough strength to walk upright. If North Korean infantrymen had attacked at that particular moment, Clyde and the Lieutenant would have had to fight them from their knees.

Remnants of War

In the debris that was strewn about, I found a damaged Browning automatic rifle. As I grasped the weapon in my hands, I wondered what had happened to the man who had carried it, if he were still alive. From the condition of the weapon, I was quite certain the guy must have put up a *helluva* fight. The barrel was warped, the stock shattered and, for the most part, the weapon was useless. Trying to forget about the fate of the previous owner, I quickly set about stripping the good parts from it believing they might come in handy some day. And they certainly did. I eventually used most of them to repair other automatic rifles in the battalion.

As we left the area, a branch from a bush that had been burned by a napalm bomb brushed across Clyde's cheek, leaving a smudge of charcoal. For weeks after, even though Clyde bathed and shaved whenever he could, he always seemed to miss scrubbing the smudge from his homely mug. It matched perfectly the color of his black hair and dark Indian eyes.

Attempting to return to the Company by a different route, we patrolled single file into a low area and then climbed a small rise that was covered with thick, chest-high brush. I was the point man, and even though the area was quite dense with thick foliage and unlikely to be mined, I still had to be concerned about them. Normally when I was the point man, I carried my BAR sideways with the barrel and front sight pointed at a forty-five degree angle to my left. The theory was that if someone unpleasant popped up in front of me, I could squeeze off a full magazine and the recoil would cause the rifle to sweep from left to right spraying everything in front of me. But this stuff was so thick I had to hold my BAR at high port to keep it from catching in the brush.

We knew there was a road in the vicinity, one that would lead us to camp. I was searching for it. What I didn't know was that we were standing darned near on top of it, right above it in fact. Bulling my way through brush that had grown out over a bank above the road, I suddenly disappeared from sight, falling through space. I fell, tumbling perhaps fifteen feet to the roadbed, suffering a cut to the palm of my hand and a sprained wrist. I felt like an idiot, but I'd done my job and found the road.

We passed a South Korean military unit sitting beside the road eating a meal of rice and dried fish, seasoned with a hefty dose of garlic. This seemed to be common fare for the Korean people but not in any way appetizing to us. The odor of the mixture was unpleasant and it attracted swarms of pesky, voracious flies. We were quite thankful that we didn't have to eat their food and they were probably just as thankful they didn't have to eat any of our c-rations.

The Crow

Another new lieutenant accompanied our squad on yet another reconnaissance patrol while in reserve. Every patrol was risky business, even those behind our lines. We always had to watch out for mines and booby traps although an area might have been cleared and checked several times. Infiltrators took every opportunity to booby-trap paths and trails that were well used or appeared innocent.

Working our way along an old farm path bordering a large stream, we patrolled for some distance, checking burned out huts and, occasionally, old abandoned bunkers. Usually J. J. Miller, armed with a shotgun, did the physical checking while I covered him from nearby with the BAR and the rest of the squad deployed behind us, covering our flanks and rear.

We had achieved our objective and were returning to camp when the lieutenant halted the patrol, asking J. J. for the shotgun. He took the weapon and, without explaining why he wanted it or what he was going to do, began crossing the creek, stepping from rock to rock. Midway, he lost his balance and stumbled into the water but it was barely shinbone deep. Not seeming to care, he waded the rest of the way to the far side as all of us watched with a gnawing curiosity. He crept along an ancient rock wall that paralleled the creek and as he neared a large, dead tree, we saw what he was after; a big black crow perched high on a bare limb. The lieutenant rested the shotgun on the wall, took careful aim at the crow, and pulled the trigger. We heard a *click* but no shot. He jacked the slide back to seat a round in the chamber and again aimed and pulled the trigger. Again it went *click* and again no shot. He stood up, waded back across the creek, and walked up to Miller. Not saying a word to the lieutenant, J. J. held out his hand holding the shotgun shells. He'd unloaded the weapon just moments before the lieutenant had asked for it.

His face aflame with embarrassment, our leader said something like,

"Bend over Miller. I'm gonna give this shotgun back to you."

To a man, we bellowed with laughter. Our new lieutenant turned out to be a pretty darned good Joe and even he, reflecting on what had happened, thought the incident amusing.

Chapter VII

November 1951

In November we were on the move back into those miserable hills to the front lines, occupying defensive positions on or near Hill 812. By this time I'd acquired a pack-board, a piece of equipment that every infantry Marine desired because they saved us considerable discomfort, replacing the cumbersome haversack packs. Properly adjusted, it rode high on ones back, providing excellent balance and thus made the heavy load manageable. With the exception of my weapon, grenades and ammunition, I stowed everything I owned in a rubber-coated, waterproof bag and bound it to the pack-board with a heavy cord.

Moving out from our staging area, we passed a compound of Korean huts that were occupied by a tank crew. One of those tankers carelessly left his Thompson machine gun leaning against the outside wall of a hut. None of the crew was standing about so…what could I do? I took the gun like any red-blooded Jarhead would do. But too late did I realize the blasted thing wasn't the lightest firearm in the world. For its size, it was very, very heavy and had I known about its weight beforehand,

The author, holding a Thompson .45 caliber submachine gun

I might not have filched it. But, to me, packing a Thompson into combat was like some farm kid driving a Jaguar in a drag race.

As we climbed upward into the hills, I spotted a North Korean rifle lying just beside the trail. Like an idiot, I picked it up also, thinking what a dandy souvenir it would make. Another Marine probably had the same thought I did before he dumped it there. We referred to this particular kind of weapon as a Long Tom rifle because of its extraordinary length.

I now had my Browning automatic rifle, a Thompson machine gun and a North Korean Long Tom rifle, not to mention extra, fully loaded BAR magazines, an extra bandolier of thirty-caliber ammunition, six to eight hand grenades, and all of my personal gear. The load on my back had to weigh well over one hundred pounds. After a few hours of backbreaking agony, climbing and crawling up a treacherous mountain trail, I got smart and dumped the Long Tom rifle for some other poor sap to claim. By day's end I no longer packed the Thompson either, giving it to some other misguided fool.

I often wondered how many guys picked up, carried, and eventually dumped that Long Tom Rifle before I did, and how many picked it up after I had discarded it, thinking, as I did, that it would be a wonderful souvenir.

Chapter VII

Defensive Tactics

Tactics had changed since the attack on Hills 749 and 673. Instead of attacking hill after hill, the United Nations Forces began building static defensive positions, preferring to hold territory while negotiating with the Communists to end the war. Defensive tactics were not at all what the Marines were trained for, but nonetheless these tactics were still deadly and we sure as hell continued to fight. Enemy artillery barrages intensified and were expected every day and enemy probes were anticipated every night. Patrols, behind and in front of the lines, became more frequent as well as night ambushes and taking prisoners, a primary objective for both sides. We did our best to keep the enemy guessing and off balance and, likewise, the enemy did everything it could to keep us guessing and off balance.

Building defensive fortifications, preparing good fields of fire, stringing concertina wire and setting booby traps were hard work. And it was done as we endured artillery barrages and sniping. We dug a trench from which we could move without being detected and from which we could fight if attacked. The trench was our Main Line of Resistance and stretched for miles possibly across the width of Korea. At strategic places, bunkers were incorporated into the system by digging out the back of the trench and putting a roof over it, buttressed by logs and sandbags. The bunkers became our living quarters, fighting holes and, for some, our graves. Ponchos draped over the open ends of the bunkers hopefully prevented light inside them from being seen outside and, if attacked, we could move along the trench and through each other's bunker without exposing ourselves to the enemy. In areas of particular concern, outposts and listening posts were established in front of the lines.

Sound power telephones had not been installed in each bunker in this area and communicating with men who were not immediately adjacent to our positions was not always possible. We seldom knew what was going on with the other platoons in the Company and I often found, only after going into reserve, that someone whom I knew had been killed, wounded, or had rotated home.

The barrier of coiled, tangled and barbed concertina wire, erected several yards in front of the trench and bunkers, probably stretched continuously across the width of Korea, as did the trench. The wire maze was in some instances ten yards deep. We hoped it was sufficient enough to thwart an enemy banzai charge and discourage infiltrators from trying to sneak up on us. Empty c-ration cans were our burglar alarms. They were tied to the barbed wire in such a way that they'd rattle if someone messed with the wire, trying to get through. Some defenders anchored c-ration cans within the concertina maze and put armed hand grenades inside them. With trip wires attached, they became excellent booby traps. If an enemy soldier tripped over the wire, the armed grenade, pulled from the can, would detonate in a few seconds.

Bouncing-Betty mines, very similar in shape to the Bouncing-Betty flares, were planted in areas not close enough to cause us harm but very likely to cause the Communists considerable misery. The mine propelled an explosive package upward some eight to fifteen feet before detonating, shredding any nearby life form with shrapnel. It was instantaneous, effective, and it was deadly.

Even though we prepared well, our defenses were really very thin. Usually just two men defended each position. Depending on the terrain and the availability of supporting fire, some bunkers were built as far apart as one hundred feet. It was quite possible for a platoon of forty men to be spread out over a distance of 600 to 700 yards. If a sizeable enemy force concentrated an attack, it was conceivable that only six to ten men would be in position to defend the area at the onset.

Lou-Lou

Louie Caruso was again assigned as my bunker mate—maybe because no one else wanted to put up with the nut. Continually working on some scheme or project, he'd scrounged up pieces and parts of an old radio, intending to assemble the junk to make a working receiver. After a few days of wiring, splicing and taping things together, he hooked a battery to his creation and, lo and behold, the darned thing worked. But the stations he received were either Korean or Chinese, certainly nothing that we could understand. But Louie wanted more, convinced that by attaching a larger antenna to his radio, he'd pick up additional stations, hoping some of them would be in English. But he was perplexed wondering where in the world he could find the materials needed to build such an antenna.

Pondering the problem, a few nights passed when he suddenly got a brilliant idea. He asked me to alert the men in the adjacent bunkers that he was going down to the concertina wire and not to get excited and flip a grenade his way. He fixed one end of a communications wire to the antennae terminal of his makeshift radio and attached the other end to the barbed wire maze in front of our bunkers. Amazing! To my surprise, he received several additional stations, some as clear as a bell, and some of the commentators spoke English, sounding as if they were Australian. But, very interestingly, the voice on one station spoke a language that sounded quite like Russian but sometimes spoke English. The barbed wire maze stretched nearly continuously across the breadth of Korea, making it perhaps the largest radio antennae in the world. My crazy buddy—the guy was a genius.

Louie received a package that contained a Polaroid camera and a few film packs. The Polaroid was new on the market and something we'd never seen before. Like magic, within seconds after taking a picture, it produced a developed photo. But they weren't the best of quality, not nearly as clear as the conventionally developed photos. To preserve them, one had to coat them with some kind of chemical paste. But Louie was so captivated by the camera that he wanted to buy stock in the company, convinced that it would be a sound and wise investment. He'd heard that stock could be purchased for fifty cents a share and figured to invest one hundred dollars. When he asked if I, too, wanted to buy some, I thought he was nuts and told him so.

"Look at those pictures, Louie. They're ugly, yellow and brown and streaked. Only a nut would buy a camera like that."

Mulling over my comments and scanning the brown pictures, Louie finally took my advice and decided against it. It's probably the only time he ever really listened to me. And do you realize what happened to Polaroid stock…? Its value skyrocketed. If he'd purchased the amount he wanted, it would now be worth tens of thousands of dollars and he'd be very well off. Louie has never forgiven me for talking him out of it and I've never forgiven myself for not buying in with him.

One day, we received word to test-fire our weapons at a designated time and to continue firing for a specified number of minutes. When the time came, we opened up right on cue and made one horrible, deafening racket. We had fun just spraying the brush in front of us. Later, we heard that the Marines tied in on our flanks thought a major enemy offensive had been launched against our lines. Jittery and on edge, they figured they were about to become involved in one hell of a fight. I never heard why we did the test fire but Louie surmised that it was to let the North Koreans know that we had plenty of firepower and not to mess with us.

With the exception of the platoon leader, platoon sergeant, corpsman and runner, nearly every man in the platoon stayed on the forward slope at night on fifty percent watch. Because the nights had grown so cold, most of us stood watch in our sleeping bags to keep warm. This wasn't the most intelligent thing to do because being warm made us too comfortable and being comfortable made us sleepy. And who could be wary and alert when sleepy?

Daydreams

Most nights prior to one of us hitting the sack, Louie and I stood watch together for the first few hours. We talked about home, our girls, and our families and sometimes about the kind of work we wanted to do when we got out of the

Chapter VII

Marines. But most of the time we just stood together watching in silence.

I wanted to be a rancher. Not a farmer, but a rancher. I even drew a layout of my dream ranch. I knew exactly where I wanted the barn and the sheds to be built in relation to the house. I even knew what I wanted my home to look like, the kitchen, the living room and even a covered porch. But no chickens! I absolutely didn't want any stinking chickens dropping poop all over the place. I even had plans for a baseball field. I wanted every kid who lived anywhere near my dream ranch to have a place to play baseball.

There were nights that Louie and I talked about stupid, inane things too.

"Louie, do you remember when we were at Camp Pendleton in Advanced Infantry Training, when those instructors told us that it took six men to back up one man on the line? Well, where in the hell do you suppose my six guys are anyway? I haven't seen one of them since we've been here in Korea. You got six of them, too—somewhere. If we put your six guys and my six together, we could have another squad of guys up here to help us stand watch."

But most of the time we just stood in the trench together, near our bunker, gazing out into the dark, daydreaming in silence. Sooner or later, one of us crawled into the bunker to sleep while the other began the nightly routine. Two-hour watches were the norm. We kept track of time using Louie's wristwatch. I had no watch of my own and his was a sorry thing. The wristband was loose and sloppy and to keep it working, I sometimes gave it a little rap against the stock of my Browning. But it had to do because it was the only timepiece we had.

What was a guy supposed to do at night while on guard in combat? He was supposed to be alert—hyper alert at all times. All of his senses needed to be employed at the highest level to give himself the best possible chance of survival. But that really wasn't possible. Boredom and loneliness were a reality. Daydreaming was a tool that I employed to fight off boredom and loneliness and I daydreamed constantly. I was good at it. I dreamed about a lot of things but mostly about my mom and dad, my family and of Maggie and my friends.

Occasionally, my trance was interrupted by the sound of a dry twig snapping, leaves rustling, a movement or an odd feeling that something was amiss. Most of the time the wind was the culprit, causing movement or noise and after satisfying myself that everything was normal, it didn't take long before I'd slipped back to thinking about the people that I loved and cherished.

But sometimes I couldn't immediately identify the reason I'd become concerned. When that happened goose bumps rose on my arms, my heartbeat increased and the pulse pounding in my ears was deafening. Sometimes, hardly breathing for minutes and standing motionless, I listened for the slightest noise and watched for the slightest movement. The only parts of my body that moved were my eyes, searching the dreary, cold blackness for something that shouldn't be there. A wary enemy watches for little telltale signs to pinpoint his quarry: the glow from a cigarette, the smell of smoke, hushed whispering, the rattle of a canteen, the steam from exhaled breath. Our enemy loved to catch us unaware just as we loved to catch them unaware.

I could never relax completely because I never knew with absolute certainty that they were not there: a sniper waiting to strike or a snatch team after a prisoner. The Communist Army most likely sent ten times the number of patrols to probe our lines as we sent to probe theirs. Most of the time, when they were close, we heard them or sensed their presence. But I have no doubt there were many times that they were very close and I never knew it. Had I not been as dumb as a stump, I'd have worried myself to death.

I wondered about them; what they had on their minds, what they thought of us, what they felt, and if they daydreamed about their families, homes, girlfriends. I wondered if they were lonely, if their families missed them. But thinking of them like that meant they were human and that was dangerous. It's easier to fight and kill an enemy if you considered him as something less than human. From all of the reports I'd heard, they didn't

Chapter VII

relish going against us. Because of the yellow canvas leggings we Marines wore, they referred to us as *yellow legs*. What we Marines called *them* wasn't near as nice.

During daylight hours, when we weren't improving our defenses, I busied myself with little projects. Besides drawing house-plans, I tried to trisect an angle. Challenged by my high school mathematics teacher to find an easy way to trisect an angle, I was never satisfied that I'd done my best and continued trying. Using a forked branch from a bush, I made a primitive compass and attempted many times to solve the problem but, alas, I never succeeded. However, the challenge took my mind off the cold and the war and made me feel like I was doing something constructive and useful.

During the day when visibility was good and we felt it safe, two or three men were selected from each squad to remain on the line to keep watch while the rest of us gathered on the reverse slope in a large thermal tent equipped with a small stove. It was a relief to get warm after being chilled all night and to be able to talk to the other guys and relax. The tent was also a handy place to get our mail and c-rations and to find out if we were scheduled for a lousy patrol or ambush.

W. J. Miller received some interesting mail from his folks one day. After reading for a moment, he murmured something incoherent and then blurted out a comment that got our attention because it was so humorous.

> "Well for........! Would ya get a load of this horse crap! I've been drafted! My dad wrote that I've been drafted into the stinkin' Army. Now, ain't that a buncha B. S.? Those damned cruds....! What the hell am I supposed to do now?"

A draft notice arrived in the mail at the Miller home for W. J. but his dad nonchalantly threw it in the garbage, believing the government would eventually come to its senses and realize his son was already in the military. Then, follow up notices came and they too were tossed. Because there was no response, two government officials were dispatched to the Miller home to arrest W. J. as a draft dodger. His father, angry that they refused to believe Jon was already in the Marines and in Korea, told them to get the hell off his property. But then, realizing the joke was on them, he gleefully told them that his son would gladly surrender himself to them if they'd only go to Korea to get him.

I hungered for mail from home, always hoping that some would contain pictures. Mom's letters were the best, always written with light-hearted humor. She kept me informed of every event that occurred around home and the neighborhood. She wrote so well that, sometimes, I almost felt as if I were there with her. Some of the other men, having read many of Mom's letters, began corresponding with her themselves and continued to do so even after I left Korea.

Maggie and I wrote frequently to each other, too. She penned lovely letters and, unfortunately, I tried to read more into them than she intended. All of us did that sort of thing because we were starved to be with our girls. My breast pocket was so full of mail and photographs from Maggie and my family that had I been shot in the heart, the bullet would have had to penetrate three inches of paper. To me, the letters and photographs were my most important possessions and never was I without them with one exception—when I went on a patrol or ambush. We didn't dare take anything personal in the event we were captured because the Communist bastards were damned good at using personal mementos to pressure their prisoners into talking. But the very first thing I did when I returned from a patrol was to return my precious memories to my breast pocket.

Moosan

Our battalion faced a formidable hill situated a few miles to our front. Someone told me it was called Moosan and there had to be at least a division of enemy troops defending it. Every day, the Navy pasted the hell out of the place using 16-inch guns on their battleships. And when the Navy took a break, the Air Force took over with relentless bombings and strafing. But with all of the bombardment leveled on them, when there was a lull in the action, they went right back to work reinforcing their defenses just like a colony of ants.

Rumors circulated that our Regiment was going to attack and take Moosan. Apparently capturing it would give us a great deal of control over Wonsan Harbor, a strategic port farther north. Rumors were always flying around but this one filled me with dread. If they were true and we attacked it, there was little doubt in my mind that we'd suffer a horrendous number of casualties. The place was like a massive fortress, a huge maze of bunkers, trenches, and machine gun emplacements. Taking it away from those little bastards would take an incredible effort on our part and every time I looked toward it I felt uneasy and almost sick to my stomach.

With one exception, there seemed to be no live vegetation remaining. That one exception was a tree growing on the side of the hill about two-thirds of the way to the top. It, too, was nearly barren of foliage. A few withered limbs were barely hanging on but yet there was still some life in it.

Using binoculars, I think I studied Moosan's terrain as much as anyone. I used the lone tree as a point of reference, locating bunker emplacements where I was reasonably certain that machine-gun squads would surely be lurking. The tree, in my estimation, was the only thing on Moosan worth looking at. It was a symbol of survival. One day, the Navy began its systematic bombardment of the hill. A round exploded right at the base of *my* tree, obscuring the scene with dust and debris. When the air cleared, I could see that it was gone—obliterated—my tree blown to hell by the U. S. Navy.

I bellowed like a wounded buffalo,

"Those rotten bastards! Those stinking rotten bastards!"

Louie, hearing my tirade and hoping nothing bad was about to happen, came scrambling out of our bunker with his rifle in hand. His eyes darted back and forth along the wire in front of our position, searching for the reason for my sudden outburst. Continuing my verbal assault on the Navy, I pointed toward Moosan,

> "Look there, Louie! Those stinkin' swab jockeys just shot the hell out of my tree."

When my words sunk in and he realized we weren't about to be annihilated by a screaming horde of North Koreans, he cocked his head to one side and unleashed some of his own words on my poor sensitive ears.

> "Pledge! What the hell's the matter wit youse? Don't youse do that to me again or I'm gonna stick that BAR of yers up yer back-end. That lousy tree! Ory-gone nut, youse!"

> "Its pronounced, Ory-gun, Louie, Ory-gun."

> "Ory-gone, my butt! Ya know what, Pledge? Yer nuts!"

With that, Louie crawled back into our hole to finish writing to one of his sweethearts back home. He seldom used foul language but he'd come very close to it. But I hadn't, continuing to mumble obscenities at the Navy, but under my breath. In a very short time, every remnant of the tree was gone, used by the North Koreans to repair and reinforce their bunkers. It was probably just a matter of time anyway before they'd have cut it down.

About a half hour later, it was our turn to take a pasting. The North Koreans opened up with artillery and blasted the hell out of our section of the line, some rounds hitting only yards away from our bunker. Louie and I curled up in fetal positions in the back of our hole clutching our weapons and clenching our teeth; wincing and cringing with every impact, hoping and praying they wouldn't get a direct hit on us. We were as helpless and defenseless as newborn babies. Early into the shelling, tough-acting Louie, asked,

> "What the hell did youse do to those Koreans to make 'em so mad at us?"

Hearing him talk was disconcerting and, needing every ounce of concentration to cope, I just wanted him to shut up. Mercilessly, they shelled our section of the lines for thirty minutes, doing their best to ruin what was left of our day.

At noontime on November 10, 1951, the Communist cruds got paid back, a little gift from our guys. Marine Corps artillery and the big guns of the Navy opened up with everything they had, pouring devastating barrages on the enemy forces occupying Moosan. You might say it was gift giving in reverse because November 10th was the Marine Corps birthday.

Winter Gear and Cold Weather

Those of us who had not yet experienced a winter in Korea had no idea what was in store for us. I could never have imagined any place on this earth to be as miserable and unbearable as the frozen hills of Korea. Once it got cold, we got cold and we were never able to warm ourselves sufficiently to the point that we were comfortable. The cold knifed through even the best of winter gear and lingered in our bodies well into the following spring.

The nights were chillingly cold, especially when the wind blew. Snow flurries fell frequently by late November. It accumulated in the hills and drifted deep in the gullies. Our summer sleeping bags had become insufficient to keep us warm but the good old Corps finally came through, not letting us down. We each received an issue of cold weather gear that consisted of a cap with earflaps, a parka jacket with a fur-lined hood, thermal boots and a feather-down sleeping bag. In addition, whenever we went on ambushes or patrols, we were provided with thin white hooded uniforms that covered our regular dungaree clothing to help us hide in the snow. Even though all of this new gear kept us warmer, it was also more weight to carry on our backs.

The thermal boots were bulky, black in color and just flat ugly. Because of their odd, bulbous shape, we nicknamed them *Mickey Mouse Boots*. The old shoepack footwear, a boot used during the previous winter, had done little to prevent severe frostbite to the feet of the men who wore them. The thermal boot, developed to replace the shoepacks, was purported to prevent frostbite if the wearer took certain precautions like changing to clean socks daily. Therefore, we were warned that if anyone suffered frostbite to the feet, he would receive a court-martial. We found the boots did a good job keeping our feet warm but only if we kept moving. But once movement ceased for any length of time, the heat faded and our feet got cold, sometimes freezing.

Ambushes were troublesome because we had to remain motionless, lying quite still in the snow, often three to five hours at a time. Fearing that we would give our positions away, we couldn't move our feet enough to generate sufficient heat in the boots to keep them warm. Merely wriggling our toes didn't help much either and neither did wearing clean, dry socks under those circumstances. Unfortunately, many of us still suffered some frostbite but few dared report the painful condition for fear of a court-martial. Regardless, though, they were still a tremendous improvement over the old shoepacks.

It was reported too that a few Marines who were wearing them had stepped on shoe-mines but, because of the boots' construction, had suffered nothing more than a few broken bones or sprains. That was welcome news indeed.

The cold weather caused other problems too. For instance, writing letters. Those few men who carried fountain pens had difficulty preventing the ink from freezing. One fellow tried thawing his by putting it under his arm. The ink cartridge ruptured and turned his armpit dark blue. Pencils were affected also. The lead became brittle and easily broke.

Most of us sported moustaches because shaving in the blistering cold weather was tough on our faces. But sporting a moustache caused us problems too. Breathing through our noses, especially at night when it was freezing, the moisture in our breath froze on them, forming tiny icicles under our noses.

Except for my shoes, I slept fully dressed in my winter sleeping bag. If something happened, good or bad, I figured it was best to be dressed. My shoes or boots went under my head for two reasons: to act as a pillow and to keep them as warm as possible. My feet were always cold. For added protection and warmth, I cut the bottom eighteen inches from a summer sleeping bag, put it in the bottom of my winter bag and slid my feet into it. But, no matter how many layers of clothing I wore and how much extra protection I employed for warmth, the cold still penetrated.

Clyde Bridge had warned me when I first joined the company that the Korean winters were brutally cold. He said that during the previous winter it was so cold that he had to goose himself just to pee. We made small stoves out of c-ration cans, filling them with dirt and soaking the dirt with fuel oil. The dirt acted like a wick, but when lit, the stoves smoked like a foundry in Pennsylvania. As a result, our gear, our clothing, our faces and our bunkers were coated with thick, grimy, black soot.

The Veep

"Remember when we were at Camp Pendleton, Louie, and trainin' in a hundred ten degree heat and walkin' in sand? Well, I wished the hell we had some of that sun now."

Thanksgiving Dinner

Headquarters Marine Corps managed to feed us a hot turkey dinner on Thanksgiving Day. The amount of planning and work required to bring hot meals to us on the front line must have been overwhelming. We filled our mess kits, and any other containers that we could find, with food. Still with the company, Lieutenant Jack Lilley gnawed on a huge turkey drumstick as a Marine Corps photographer took his picture. Luckily, I managed to scrounge a copy of the picture and still have it today.

While involved in a casual, friendly chat, Lieutenant Lilley told me a few stories about what had happened to him prior to becoming our platoon leader. As a newly commissioned second lieutenant, he joined Easy Company and was initially assigned to the third platoon. Being new, he worried that his men might not respect his leadership.

During his first combat action, Jack's platoon was held in reserve as other platoons began an assault on a hill defended by North Koreans. When the men of the first platoon became embroiled in a furious firefight, Jack was informed by radio to be ready to move his platoon forward to engage the enemy. As he waited for orders to attack, he tried to relax but worried about his leadership, about making good decisions, and about sending his men into harm's way. One of the veterans packed a guitar with him and when he began strumming on it and singing quietly to himself, Jack became a little irritated and concerned that the guy wasn't mentally preparing himself for the battle to come. But then he realized the music had a calm-

Thanksgiving dinner,
Lieutenant Jack Lilley eating turkey

Chapter VII

ing effect on him and on the others around him. His men *were* ready and, for the moment, he was learning from them, learning how to relieve the tension and how to cope with stress.

Jack's platoon attacked a series of bunkers with small arms, grenades and flamethrowers. Believing all of the bunkers had been neutralized they continued the attack pushing through the complex. But one North Korean had survived the firefight by hiding in a concealed hole behind one of the bunkers. After Jack passed by him, the North Korean popped up and fired a burst from his burp gun at him. One of the bullets knocked Jack down but he rolled over and came up firing his carbine, killing his assailant. His head ringing, he thought he'd been hit in the back of the neck. By a stroke of luck, the projectile that surely would have killed him had struck the blade of a small hatchet fastened to his pack. The hatchet directed the bullet upward, knocking the helmet off his head. Luckily, Jack was only stunned, and suffered nothing more than a headache and a trembling fright.

Not many days later, Jack suffered a leg wound in another skirmish and was sent to a rear area field hospital. Nearly fully recovered from his injury, he was sitting beside a road when a truck, driven by an old friend, stopped in front of him. His friend invited Jack to go for a short drive and to share a few bottles of beer. Never one to turn down a free beer and, since there was nothing else to do, Jack joined his friend and off they went. They had so much fun that they lost all track of time and distance traveled and before they realized it, it had become too dark to return to the hospital. They were forced to camp out because it was forbidden to use vehicle lights. At daylight, Jack went into the brush to relieve himself and, not having any toilet paper, he used a handful of leaves. But those leaves proved not to be kind to him. Returning to the field hospital a few hours later, he found his doctor infuriated with him. The doctor informed Jack that since he was capable of wandering around all night drinking booze then he was certainly fit for duty. Jack reported back to Easy Company but before the day had ended, he'd come down with a horrible, itching rash on his hands and backside. Squirming and scratching something awful, he had to grin and bear it, knowing full well he'd receive little sympathy from that doctor if he dared return to the hospital for treatment.

Our lieutenant told several stories on himself but he was never one to crow about his achievements. Not many knew that he'd received a silver star for his bravery and excellent leadership during the earlier spring offensive. And he was concerned early on that he might not be good enough. Well, he was. He proved that he was one of the finest. Just ask one of us who served with him.

Lieutenant John "Jack" Lilley, getting warm

Chapter VIII

Squad Leader Miller

Some of the old timers, including Larry Pressley, were gone having rotated home. Jerry Miller was now our squad leader. A new replacement joining our ranks was a very nervous individual by the name of Eddie Newman, a reserve corporal from Chicago. He quickly earned the nickname, Chicago Eddie. The Gods were not kind to him though because Jerry assigned him to bunk in with Jack Mills for the first two nights in Korea.

Jack's nonchalant way of handling firearms was just a little bit scary, even for those who knew him well. Preparing to hit the sack and without saying a word to prepare Eddie, he hauled out his pistol and, with one shot, extinguished the candle. Eddie, now inside a pitch-black bunker, screamed bloody murder believing he'd just been shot to death. Before he'd spent a full day on line, the poor guy was ready for the loony bin.

One of the things that Louie and I did, to Eddie's consternation, was to count the number of artillery rounds discharged by enemy guns and the number of those rounds impacting on our hill. We were curious to know how many rounds we were receiving compared to the total number of rounds being fired. Eddie thought we were insane and asked what good it did to know.

Without thinking, and almost in unison, our reply to the confused corporal was,

"If we're getting more than our share of incoming, we're gonna complain."

Late one night, J. J. led our squad on a recon patrol into a rugged, snow-covered area of No-Man's-Land. Not only did we have to be concerned with mines and booby-traps, we had to put up with the numbing freezing cold, struggling every inch of the way, plowing through drifts up to our butts. Fortunately, we encountered no enemy probably because they had sense enough to stay put in their holes. Reaching our objective, near the bottom of a wooded valley, we formed a temporary

Eddie Newman next to his bunker

defensive perimeter and hunkered down, resting a few minutes before beginning the exhausting trek back uphill to our lines. Using a hand-held radio, an authentic piece of junk, J. J. called our Company Command Center to report our status. Failing to get an answer, he tried again, practically bellowing and causing me, and likely the rest of us, considerable nerve-wracking concern. But before receiving a response, some Army fellow cut in with a transmission. J. J., infuriated, told the guy to get the hell off the air, that he needed to send an urgent message. In a split second, the two were engaged in a war of filthy words, cursing each other's ancestry.

Thankfully the soldier gave up. After a few more attempts, my fuming squad leader made contact, reporting that everything was okay and that our patrol was about to return to the lines. Then he asked for a time-check.

But before the command center could respond, the Army guy piped in again,

"For Pete's sake, fella, I could'a told ya that."

Enemy Probe

Now that the weather was considerably colder, the North Koreans came more often, mostly at night, probing and searching for weaknesses in our defenses. They had a reputation for trying to infiltrate our lines to take prisoners and, unfortunately, they sometimes succeeded. They were very patient and lay motionless, concealed in the snow all day within view of our bunkers, waiting until dark to move in closer. Being taken prisoner was one of my biggest fears and you can bet that any unexplainable movement or noise in front of me, especially at night, immediately drew a grenade.

It was early in the morning but still dark when I sensed that something was amiss near the wire in front of our position. The hair stood up on my neck and arms as a shivering chill swept over me. I had a bad feeling and I was certain that it was not just the gentle wind sweeping over the ridges and through the trees that caused it. Somehow, I knew that an enemy patrol was there, probing our defenses. I could almost smell them. Perhaps I did and didn't realize it.

Louie was sleeping only a few feet from me but I was afraid to take the few seconds needed to crawl into the bunker to wake him fearing that would be the very moment they would attack. I had to hope that when the shooting started, he would wake up and get his butt outside with me. Standing motionless in the trench, I peered into the darkness, my BAR lying ready on the parapet and a grenade in my hand. Then, for some reason, I knew it was time to lob the grenade. My body trembled almost uncontrollably in anticipation as I removed the pin and chucked it as hard as I could, trying to throw it into the area where I was certain the enemy was hidden. Something else sailed down the hill as well as the grenade. For just a split-second I was stumped but then I discovered that it was Louie's watch. It had come off my wrist.

When the grenade exploded, all hell broke loose. A few rifle shots and a burst of automatic fire from a burp gun shredded the crisp night air. The men in adjacent bunkers retaliated, flinging more grenades toward enemy gun flashes. After the echo of the explosions died in the distant hills, it became deathly quiet, the exchange occurring in mere seconds.

Louie woke and soon scrambled out of the bunker with his rifle in one hand and the other clutching his helmet trying to keep it on his head. As he slouched down in the trench beside me, he asked in a tense, almost inaudible, whisper,

"What the hell's going on?"

Pointing toward the wire, my voice hoarse and quivering, I told him the North Koreans were out there and that they'd shot at us. Louie grabbed a couple of hand grenades and went through the bunker to watch from the other side. Having him close by was a relief and made me feel much more secure, but I couldn't stop trembling.

Mortar flares, drifting slowly back to earth, lit up the area with an eerie light. Shadows slipped across the landscape but nothing human could be detected. No movement, no shoot-

Chapter VIII

ing, no noise, nothing. The enemy had retreated back down the hill leaving us on edge and jittery, leaving us to wait and watch for the remainder of the night, wondering if they'd be back.

As daylight began to break in the east, Louie rejoined me on my side of the bunker and, after a short discussion about the probe, asked for his watch. I had to confess that I no longer had it, that it flew off my wrist when I threw the grenade, and that I thought it was somewhere down near the wire. Louie damned near had a cow and, by the way he carried on, one would have thought the watch was an heirloom or some precious chronometer given him by the King of England.

"Youse trew my watch at those gooks? Youse big ox! Go get my watch. Now!"

"Now? I'm not goin' down there, Louie. No way! Not until it gets really light."

At mid-morning, a patrol searched the area in front of the wire but found nothing, only tracks in the snow. They came in the dark like ghosts and they left the same way. I found Louie's wristwatch about twenty feet in front of our hole. The darned thing was still ticking too. Louie examined it carefully and by the way he handled it, one would have thought it were a fine, jeweled timepiece. From that night on when I stood watch, following Louie's orders, I kept his crummy watch in my pocket.

Not many nights later while on watch, I again heard a noise in the wire in front of our bunker. Again, the hair stood up on the back of my neck and goose bumps popped up on my arms as I strained to see movement. I heard it a second time, as if one of the cans tied to the wire was being jostled. I thought it strange because there was just too much noise. The North Koreans weren't that careless when they came snooping. I took one of the fragmentation grenades we had lined up on the parapet, removed the pin, and lofted it down into the wire. When it went off, I knew the explosion brought everyone nearby to full alert and I hoped it woke Louie as well. After several tense seconds, hearing only my pulse beating in my ears, I again heard a sound in the wire.

To my relief, Louie came bursting out of the bunker just as he'd done a few nights before. I told him that something was in the wire, that I'd heard noises, thrown one grenade and, just before he emerged, heard the noise again. Whispering to each other, we questioned whether the men in the bunker to our right had heard it, too. One of them was a tall kid from New York named Richard Vandenburg, whom we'd nicknamed *Hoyt* after the famous Air Force general. Louie, straining to see if he could see anything around his bunker, saw a movement in the dim light of the night sky, followed immediately by another tinkling sound in the wire. It was Hoyt. He was throwing pebbles into the wire, playing a devious trick on us. His little prank succeeded, too, scaring the hell out of us. Louie was as mad as a disturbed nest of hornets and, although I couldn't see him in the dark, I just knew his chest and neck were swelling up like a puff adder. Determined to retaliate, he wanted to toss something in front of Vandenburg's bunker, to put a little fear in him.

"Maybe a grenade will teach the dope a lesson."

Tossing a grenade wasn't a very smart idea but I agreed that we should do something, like toss a rock, to at least let him know that we were on to his can of B.S. Making a faint rustling sound when it hit, it apparently caught his attention because he stopped messing with us and behaved the remainder of the night, tinkling our cans no more.

For defensive purposes, the company had set up a fifty-caliber machine gun several hundred yards to the east of our bunker. This thing could fire accurately for, I suppose, three thousand yards and fifty caliber rounds could penetrate several inches of wood and dirt. Marines occupying positions adjacent to the machine gun used it for sniping at enemy emplacements, bunker gun ports, and trails. Pre-selecting a target before hitting the sack, they occasionally squeezed off a few short bursts during the night. It was very effective and it had to keep the North Koreans on edge. I could only imagine how terribly frightening it had to be for them, not knowing when a burst of fifty caliber bullets would rake their positions. The gun was certainly a morale booster for us and, at the same time, I'll bet it put theirs in the toilet.

Animals

With my sleeping bag pulled up over my shoulders to keep me warm, I had taken the first watch and had already become too complacent and relaxed, daydreaming about home. It was just getting dark when an unexpected darting movement gave me a chilling start. A rat had suddenly scurried by me along the top of the trench parapet. My first reaction when I saw the movement was to grab for my BAR but the sleeping bag, wrapped about me, momentarily restricted my arms. I knew having the bag pulled over me was dangerous and every split-second lost shedding it was a disadvantage. But I did have a choice: try to endure the freezing temperatures or wrap the bag around me and take the chance that I could free myself in time to defend myself should I suddenly be attacked. It was a gamble that nearly every one of us took.

I pulled the bag around me again hoping nothing more than a rat would come visiting. Feeling warm and comfortable, I recalled a story that I'd heard about another Marine who was captured while in his bag. Two North Koreans slipped up on him while he was sleeping, grabbed the bottom of his bag, and ran downhill dragging him behind them. By the time he came to his senses and realized what was happening, his captors had dragged him beyond help from his squad. He was barely able to unzip his bag before they stopped and turned on him. With no weapon to defend himself, he should have been defenseless—so thought the North Koreans. He was wearing his dungaree shirt and in the pencil pocket he carried an *itiwa* spoon. Grasping the spade part of his spoon, he jabbed one of his attackers in the stomach with the slender spoon handle and then struck out at the other, sticking him in the arm. The surprised enemy suddenly realized that they were the ones being hurt and quickly fled into the dark. Except for a cut across the palm of his hand, the Marine was unharmed and able to crawl back to his hole, shaken but safe.

With the same suddenness as before, the rat scooted by me again. I nearly jumped out of my skin. A dumb rodent had given this dumb kid a very serious case of the jitters and something had to be done. If I didn't eliminate it, I would become a nervous wreck by morning. So, I declared war on the rat and planned my attack.

"If it comes by again, I'll stab it with my K-Bar knife."

The varmint zipped by a third time appearing and running by so quickly that I couldn't react fast enough. My stab missed. Twice more it darted by and twice more I futilely chopped away, not even coming close to whacking it. Then, it scurried down into the trench to my right and stopped, remaining motionless. A change in tactics was needed. I took a fragmentation grenade, crimped the pin back so that it wouldn't detonate, and threw it like a rock at the rat. But I missed. Instead, the grenade bounced down the trench, went under the poncho covering the entry to Vandenburg's bunker, and stopped in the middle of a four-man poker game, resting smack dab atop a pile of ante money. A split second later, four men burst out of the bunker, two out of each end, tearing away the ponchos covering the entries. When the card players saw the grenade, they reacted instinctively, as if they'd been shot from a cannon. No need to say that they were furious, mad as hell at me, and wanted a piece of my hide. Try as I might, they just wouldn't buy it that it was an accident and that I was just trying to kill a rat. With a few rotten words thrown in, they told me they were also going to kill a rat, but it was of the two-legged Italian variety.

O'Malley watched nervously as something moved toward his position, something like a man crawling in the snow. It was the middle of the night and he couldn't see well enough to determine what it was. Finally, getting too close for comfort, John took a shot at it. It bounded away like a huge cat, running parallel to the line of bunkers. The next day, trying to determine what John had shot at, Captain Maxson and some of the men ventured down in front of O'Malley's bunker and discovered large paw prints in the snow. Although it was difficult to believe, we heard later that someone down the line had killed a monstrous cat that they thought was a snow leopard. It was likely the same animal that wanted to make lunch out of O'Malley.

During the time we were in this area, Henry Brinlee, one of our machine gunners, had been standing watch and, relieved by his bunkmate, was preparing to sleep for a couple of hours. He slipped into his bunker, pulled his shoes off, and slid down into his sleeping bag. As he pulled the zipper up, he discovered he wasn't the only thing in it. His feet touched something hairy and it was moving. It was a rat, a big one. Struggling to unzip the bag, he let out a horrible blood-curdling shriek that scared the hell out of his bunkmate and the men in adjacent bunkers. The rat made a charge for freedom running up Hank's chest, over his face and out of the bunker. From that night on, no matter how sleepy Henry had become, he literally hit the sack, pounding and beating the hell out of it with a stick before crawling in and even then, he slept with it zipped no more than half way.

Big Guns

One shivering cold day, several of us had gathered in the warm-up-tent on the reverse slope and were engaged in conversation with Lieutenant Lilley when the entire ridge was violently shaken by three gigantic explosions. Large explosive projectiles had struck the hill on the forward slope, and even though we were on the reverse side, the enormity of the blasts stunned and confused us. Lieutenant Lilley immediately began shouting orders to the men and one of them was directed at me.

> "Get up on the ridge, Veep, and find out what they're shootin' and where it's comin' from."

That sure as hell was the last place I wanted to go at that particular moment. Obediently and quite nervously, I worked my way to the top, peeked over, and saw a gigantic smoking crater some distance in front of the wire. I stayed but a very, very, very short time before doing my *crawdaddy* crawl back down the hill to make my report.

A deep basement-like hole had been blasted into the frozen earth in front of our bunkers and two more smoldering craters could be seen farther down the line. The tops of several bunkers had been damaged just by the concussion and, although none of our men had been killed or severely injured, some of them suffered bloody noses. The first thing to cross our minds was that the North Koreans had fired at us with something comparable to our eight-inch artillery piece. If they had that kind of weaponry with that kind of destructive power and were so close that they could shoot directly into our lines, we were in for a heap of trouble. But, thank goodness, it wasn't so. We learned shortly afterwards that one of our battleships had fired a battery of three 16-inch projectiles into our positions by mistake.

"The Navy? They're supposed to be shootin' at Moosan, not at us. How the hell can those deck apes make a mistake like that?"

The men directed some stinging, sarcastic remarks toward the Navy such as: mayonnaise from their ham and cheese sandwiches got smeared on their firing orders, a new ensign was allowed to plot the firing coordinates, and so on. Whatever the reason, we had a small taste of what the North Koreans on Moosan were putting up with every day.

Men from the Deep South were quite adept at setting up stills, any time, any place, under most any circumstance. They scrounged raisins, potato peelings, apples, and anything else they could find to make a little moonshine, a little liquid fire. And the finished product was like unstable nitro. Stored in five-gallon water cans whenever the cans were available, it caused the enameled paint inside the cans

Chapter VIII

to peel. Sometimes these liquor stills went bad and blew up or caught fire. Jack Lilley was one person who could attest to that.

A few nights after the snow leopard incident, I heard a commotion down the line and could see someone trying to extinguish a fire by beating on it with an empty sand bag. As the fire intensified, I heard a few muffled explosions and saw sparks fly. I thought perhaps another liquor still had gone bad setting someone's bunker afire. If the truth were known, we probably lost more bunkers from stills blowing up than from enemy artillery. The North Koreans also saw the flames and pounded us with artillery for the remainder of the night.

The next day I went down the trench line to see what had happened. It was John O'Malley's bunker and it was still smoldering. The fire was caused when a homemade stove was accidentally overturned. Nearly everything inside had been destroyed including ammunition. But no one was injured.

John, covered with soot and dirt, was sitting in the ashes, eating pork and beans from ruptured c-ration cans. He loved that crap and he'd accumulated several cans. Taking advantage of it being hot, he decided to chow down rather than let

O'Malley and Schaus

the food go to waste. I could see at least six empty cans in the bottom of the hole that had once been his living quarters.

"Havin' beans for chow today, John?"

"Yeah! How'd you guess?"

"Oh, I kinda got wind of it."

John, no doubt, was going to be one giant gas bubble by evening and I wondered what poor unfortunate soul had been chosen to bunk up with him.

2nd squad, O'Malley (partially hidden), Chief Brightman, Name forgotten, Evans, Louie Racca, Squad Leader Butch Schaus, Pavelcik in front of Schaus, Name forgotten, and Roy Phillips

On the way back to my bunker, enemy artillery pounded us again with a dozen more rounds, catching me in the open. Fortunately, I was down in the trench and it afforded some cover but I was still afraid a round might hit a tree and detonate above me. It was *hang-on-tight-time* and all I could do was grit my teeth and eat dirt. Some of the rounds impacted so close that the ground heaved violently, so much so that I got bounced around. The concussion from them made me grunt and whimper. Either the enemy gunners had seen me or they were firing at John's bunker again. Only after the barrage ceased did I realize that I'd been buried under several inches of dirt, rocks and tree limbs. My ears rang and my nostrils and mouth were filled with soil, but otherwise I was unharmed, just scared *spitless*.

Unlike Mortar Valley, where we received daily barrages of mortar fire, here we were subjected to daily bombardments from large enemy artillery pieces. Some volleys consisted of only a few rounds while others were absolutely brutal, lasting for what seemed like an eternity. We endured so much *incoming mail* that it's a wonder my teeth weren't ground down to the gums. As long as the impacts weren't too close, we were able to deal with it. Seldom did one ever strike a bunker. Because the shelling had become so frequent, I could tell if a round was going over us or if it was going to impact the hill.

Silk and Srebroski

We obtained precious drinking water any way we could. Even though the Chiggy Bearers tried, there were not enough of them to haul all the water we needed. Fresh snow was a quick source but the top of the ridge where we were entrenched had been shelled so often that most of the snowfield was covered with dirt and debris. A tiny spring, out of sight from our positions hidden by brush and small scrubby trees, was discovered in a ravine a hundred plus yards below our defenses. Two or three men from each platoon routinely gathered up canteens, making the five-minute trek to the spring to fetch water. One man kept watch while the other filled the canteens.

Early in December 1951, during a light afternoon snowfall, Lehman Brightman and Louis Racca gathered canteens for their squad and went through the wire down the hill to get water. As they approached the area of the spring, Brightman began to feel uncomfortable, certain that something was amiss. He told Racca that he was troubled but couldn't give any reason for his anxiety. They surveyed the area but saw nothing suspicious, no footprints in the snow, no noises, nothing. But Brightman continued to feel distressed. So, instead of standing by Racca at the stream, he smartly positioned himself some distance back up the trail with his weapon at the ready.

As he filled the canteens, Racca too began to feel uneasy—as if he were being watched. Finished with their chore, they backed out of the area with their rifles pointed toward the stream and went back up the trail to the lines. On the way they met James Silk and Joseph Srebroski coming down the hill. Assigned to the Company's sixty-mortar

Near the spring

section, it was their turn to make the water-run. Conversing with the two for a moment, Brightman told them of his uneasiness at the spring and cautioned them to be alert and on their guard. The two mortar-men continued on their errand, their weapons still slung on their shoulders.

Men in the mortar section became alarmed when their two buddies hadn't returned from their errand within a reasonable time. They reported their concerns to their lieutenant and, in less than two hours after they were last seen, a squad was dispatched to the spring. Searching the area, they found only snow-covered tracks but no trace of the missing men and soon returned to the lines to make their report.

Little doubt remained in our minds that the North Koreans had taken them prisoner. Our cunning enemy probably found signs that we had been getting water from the spring and laid a trap knowing some of us would return. The word spread quickly from one man to another, up and down the line, of what had happened. Certain of the fate that had befallen our two mates, everybody went on watch. There would be no more letters written, no more improving our defenses, no more drawing house plans, nothing, not until we'd exhausted all means of retrieving them, alive if possible. Before it was totally dark, a combat team was dispatched into No-Man's Land and in no time they got into a brisk firefight. And throughout the evening, incoming mail pounded our section of the lines. It was like they'd poked us in the eye and were telling us to go to hell.

Several patrols went into the ravines and down to the valley floor below our lines to search. Whenever a patrol left, the remaining men on the line filled in the vacated positions and went on one hundred percent watch. Our squad went out too. We were hoping to find something, some trace of them, but after searching for hours, we too returned to our lines, tired and empty-handed. Finally, one of the patrols spotted a body frozen in ice in the river far below our positions. But they also spotted the North Koreans lying in ambush nearby ready to strike. Maneuvering around behind them, they surprised the would-be bushwhackers, killing several before driving the survivors away.

A couple of our men crawled to where the body lay. It was James Silk. He'd been stripped of most of his clothing, his hands tied behind his back, and executed by his captors. As the members of the patrol tried to remove his body, they were again fired upon. After another brief but heated exchange of rifle fire, the enemy was driven off once more. Several hours passed and more snow fell as men, exhausted and chilled to the bone, worked to free Silk's body from the ice while under sniper fire. Using picks, they finally completed their mission. Strapping him to a stretcher, they began the treacherous ascent up the steep, snow-covered hill toward our lines. Falling snow made visibility difficult for both sides but it presented our enemy a chance to move into ambush positions without being

Winter patrol

detected. To thwart that possibility, our mortars fired supporting rounds into the valley behind the patrol and our machine gunners kept up a steady volley of fire to the flanks of their return path hoping to discourage the enemy from following. We weren't privy to everything that had happened during the two-day rescue effort but we did hear that several of the enemy had been killed in the firefights.

Still wearing their white camouflage uniforms, some of the exhausted men returning from the patrol passed me like ghosts, appearing out of the bleak darkness making no sound. They moved in grim silence carrying and still protecting Jim Silk's poncho-covered body.

Being assigned to mortars was considered to be a safer assignment than being assigned to one of the rifle platoons. Yet, out of the dozens of men that made the water run, these two were the ones to be taken. What irony! How many times had those little Communist bastards watched me as I was filling canteens at the spring? The thought was chilling.

Sadly, this wasn't the first time that United Nations Soldiers had been executed after being captured by the Communists. Many had been found bound hand and foot and shot in the head. The older veterans told a chilling story of an incident that had occurred earlier in the year, involving several dozen Negro soldiers who were thought to have been Army truck drivers. The entire lot of them had been captured and executed, some of them also bound hand and foot.

What would I have done if faced with fighting to the death or surrendering? That was a question I'd asked myself many times and it was probably a question every man in combat had asked himself at one time or another. I really don't know, but the chances are I would have chosen to go down fighting, realizing I'd likely be killed anyway if I did surrender. If they wanted me, they would have to pay a price. It wasn't being heroic. It was just being realistic.

Joseph Srebroski never returned home. He reportedly died while in captivity. Most likely he, too, was executed.

The PRC-Six Radio

The platoon received two new PRC-Six hand-held radios. We nicknamed this particular type of radio the Prick-Six. The old radios, held together by tape and wire, had limited range and just weren't at all reliable. We sorely needed the new equipment.

Butch Schaus, now acting as our platoon sergeant, was dug in on the reverse slope with Lieutenant John Carella, our platoon leader. Butch and J. J. Miller arranged to test the new radios at a pre-arranged time that night but something happened and the radios failed to work. Not receiving any communication, J. J. walked from his position on the forward slope over the ridge to Butch's bunker. Butch was standing on the trail just outside his bunker with his back to the ridge still trying to make contact as J. J. quietly approached him from behind. Jerry, trying to be careful, accidentally slipped on the frozen, snow-covered path and slid into the back of Butch's legs. Startled and believing he was being attacked, Butch instinctively whirled about and, with the only weapon at hand, smashed the new radio over Jerry's head. His skull would have been crushed had he not been wearing his helmet. Now, one of the new radios was as worthless as the old ones.

Church On Line

Most of us, particularly those of us who'd seen combat, attended religious services whenever possible. Fortunately, our chaplains came up to the front lines whenever they could to visit and give us their blessings. It mattered not to us their faith: Baptist, Catholic, Jewish, Methodist; we were just glad to see them. Our faith didn't matter to them either; they accommodated everyone.

One of the chaplains, a Catholic priest, had come up to the lines and, after finishing the service, was having casual conversations with some of the men, one of them Louie Caruso who was a Catholic. The priest asked Louie what he did to make

Chapter VIII

his life a little more bearable considering the weather was so terribly cold. Louie, in all innocence, told the priest that he'd scrounged a few things like a pocket warmer and a sweater from some other outfit.

The priest was curious and pressed him,

"Well, Louie...did you not think that it was wrong to steal those things?"

Louie straightened up, answering,

"Oh, Fodder! I didn't steal nuttin'. I just scrounged 'em. Scroungin' ain't stealin'." Scroungin' is—uh—well, it's just scroungin'."

Louie Racca, who was also a Catholic, decided to say Mass one Sunday for the Catholics in our platoon. Several of us gathered on the reverse slope and, somehow, we muddled through it as best we could remember. It was nice to see that so many of the guys came to be involved. Then I began to realize something.

"There are a heck of a lot of Catholics in our platoon. How come?"

Several of the men who'd remained on the forward slope to stand watch were also Catholics, adding to a number I thought was already too large. Whimsically, I began mulling this over in my mind.

"Why is the platoon composed mostly of Catholics? I wonder if some Baptist or Methodist assigned to Division Headquarters is sending all of us to the front line and keeping the others safe and secure in reserve areas? Or is this just coincidental?"

"Another thing! Several of us in the company and even the platoon have last names beginning with the letter "P", such as Pavelcik, Plick, Prevost, Proietti, Pileggi, Pompeo and Phillips."

I wondered if someone had a grudge against people with a last name beginning with the letter "P"? And then there was Caruso. Did they throw that little monkey into the mix just to torture the rest of us? Or was it because the jerk was a Catholic?"

The Captain and The Gunnery Sergeant

Captain Embree Maxson, our company commander, was a large, compassionate man with a great smile and large, searching eyes. The junior officers referred to him as *Bigfoot* but we troops referred to him fondly as the *Old Man,* even though he wasn't much older than the rest of us. He definitely had our respect because he was an enlisted man's officer and understood our problems. He was truly one of those people who cared about the men under his command.

The death of our new lieutenant in Mortar Valley a few months back forever haunted Captain Maxson. He'd allowed the lieutenant, who volunteered but who had just joined the Company a few hours earlier, to lead the patrol. After that incident, the Captain vowed that, if at all possible, his new officers with no combat experience would not be thrust into dangerous situations until they got their feet wet. He took every man's death and injury personally, something that he should have shrugged off but couldn't.

Gunnery Sergeant Morris Virili was all Marine Corps. Even when he was on line for weeks at a time, his dungarees appeared to be freshly washed, starched and pressed. No one could figure out how he managed it. He sported a beautiful, well-manicured handlebar mustache equal to none and always carried a swagger stick. He wasn't large in stature, but when he barked an order, everyone paid attention—even the junior officers.

As I was fetching my c-rations one morning, the entire line began receiving enemy artillery. A few rounds hit close to us, but most were missing the top of the hill by mere feet, as usual, and crashing into the valley somewhere behind. Sergeant Virili, waving his swagger stick, positioned himself atop his bunker at the onset and yelled at us *kids* to take cover. Only when he knew every man was safely inside a bunker did he too seek shelter.

Bill Poutz, machine guns. He was over 6'5" in height. To his chagrin, we were seldom in position long enough for him to finish digging a foxhole deep enough to accommodate his large stature

Checking an abandoned Korean house

Chapter IX

Christmas at Camp Tripoli

It was Mid-December when we were relieved from front-line duty. Plodding out of the hills to a staging area, we boarded Marine Corps trucks and were transported some distance to the rear to a place called Camp Tripoli. It was a cold ride but it sure beat the hell out of walking. Large tents had been erected to house us and we slept on canvas cots—beautiful canvas cots. Compared to sleeping on the cold damp dirt floor in our bunkers, the cots were as welcome as feather mattresses. We ate hot food, took hot showers, and we were able to get clean clothing. But the best of all luxuries was getting warm. It wasn't the Ritz but it was nonetheless wonderful. The accommodations were fantastic, considering we were still in a war zone. And what a relief it was to no longer worry about assaulting Moosan.

A bundle of letters arrived from home, three of them from Maggie and the others from Mom. Mom wrote that my brother Tom had been chosen to be Li'l Abner at the annual high school Sadie Hawkins Day Dance. Dick mashed his thumb working on the tractor and Dad and the boys had filled the barn with hay for the winter. Dad had gotten a few more geese and, MacTavish, one of our dogs had died. The letters were filled with news about high school sports, the neighbors and about my mischievous little sister Charla. Had I been home, most of this would have been boring to read but being so far away, I absorbed every word, every little detail. Even though Dad never wrote to me, I knew from Mom's letters that he was deeply concerned about my safety. My old man tried to act tough but he was really just a big softy at heart.

All I wanted to do was eat and sleep, but Camp Tripoli was not all rest and relaxation. We continued to train and to keep ourselves in fighting condition. The weather was cold and, occasionally, snow fell even though we were now at a lower elevation.

During a training exercise a few days before Christmas, we took a company hike up into the hills. Several hours of trudging through snow was tiring, and required that we take an occasional rest. During the first break I tried to get as comfortable as I could on the cold, snowy ground.

I had lain back on my elbows when I spotted something that sent a shivering chill up my spine. Sticking up just above the snow were three metal prongs. It was a Bouncing-Betty mine, and my left elbow was just a few inches from it. If I hadn't been so cold, I would have broken out into a nervous sweat. Even though we were in a reserve area, we were still in extreme danger—and this was a good reminder for us to stay alert. We marked this one for the engineers and gingerly left the area.

After several hours, we began our return to Camp Tripoli by a different route, moving single file plodding along a snow-covered ridge that dropped down to a small hidden ravine. The ravine emptied out onto the valley floor and from there it was only a half hour's walk back to camp.

Our squad was in the lead and Louie was the point man. The Company took a break for fifteen minutes before descending the hill. We had no knowledge of the terrain in front of us and couldn't see into the small ravine. As we rested, Louie took it upon himself to make a trail for us, sliding down the hill on his rump, stopping at the edge of the ravine. The little

Chapter IX

imp saw what lay ahead and knew what would happen if we slid past him.

The hillside gave way to a nearly perpendicular bank that dropped twenty feet to the bottom of the ravine that had become filled with drifted snow at least five feet deep. Perhaps the others in the squad sensed the same thing that I did, that Louie was up to some kind of mischief as he waved for the rest of us to slide down. Five or six of us scooted down to Louie but stopped just short of where he stood, feeling certain that he had something up his sleeve. By then, the trail had become really slick with packed snow.

Louie waved for the next bunch of troops to slide down to him. It was great fun. The next guy shot down the slope as though he were riding a toboggan, and went sailing by us out into space and into the ravine. One after another they came with the same result, until seven or eight guys had gone over the edge and disappeared from sight. By then, the rest of the

Willie Schlei and his squad leader Butch Schaus at Camp Tripoli.
Willie never looked old enought to smoke.

company knew something was up and made their own trail down the slope, staying off Louie's snow slide.

Instead of being back in camp, we spent another hour finding weapons, gear and digging out the unfortunate ones who had fallen into Louie's trap. As usual, he was in a heap of trouble because most of the guys who went over the edge were from our squad and he knew that, sooner or later, they'd find a way to get even.

The company commander found out that one of his young Marines owned a bugle, had it in his possession, and professed an ability to play it. Instead of having the platoon sergeants roust their men out of bed in the morning, he thought it would

Camp Tripoli. Left to right: Norm Wagner, Bob Urban, Jack Mills, Lieutenant Lilley, Jimmy Richardson, "Hoyt" Vandenburg, and Charles Creel (squatting)

be better to have this kid blow reveille. It was a bad idea, a very bad idea. Whoever told that kid he was musical was nuts. The noises he made were absolutely excruciating to hear and it made all of us mad as hell. Marines were supposed to be fighters, not horn tooters. The guys voiced their displeasure but it continued. After several mornings of being shook out of our sleep by sour notes, J. J. Miller decided it was time to do something. So, he and half-a-dozen Marines planned an ambush. In the midst of a note, they came from nowhere, charging the poor kid from all directions, surprising the crap out of him. We heard through the grapevine that he put up a good fight but that they wrestled the bugle away from him and straightened it out like an Alpenhorn. Nary a note was played thereafter and everyone slept soundly like a litter of kittens.

Prevost and Proietti

Two crazy unforgettable characters assigned to Easy Company were Edward Prevost and Danny Proietti, both from upstate New York. They were assigned to the company's

Back, L to R: L. Blackwater, C. Snyder. Dan Proietti and Ed Prevost. Front, L to R: J. Nichols and Carl Radwanski (note MG muzzle)

machine gun platoon. Prevost, the taller of the two, was a constant talker while Proietti, on the other hand, was quiet—but only some of the time. Both were jokers. Nearly inseparable, they reminded me of the cartoon characters, Mutt and Jeff. Wherever Prevost went, so went Proietti. Wherever Proietti went, so went Prevost. It mattered not if it was to the showers, to the mess tent, or to get a haircut.

Prevost's hair was light in color but there was a natural white spot, the size of a half dollar, right on the very top of his head. With a mischievous grin, Prioetti gleefully made a point of telling us that the white spot was the doings of a pigeon; that it left its droppings there and his friend never bothered to bathe. He told the story so many times that we began to believe it, that his buddy was truly nothing but a crud. Prevost, in retaliation, told everyone that Proietti was a substitute, albeit a poor one, for Charlie McCarthy, the wooden dummy belonging to ventriloquist Edgar Bergen. Both were goofy individuals and could easily have performed comedy on stage. Their good-natured comical bantering with each other was as fun to watch as a U. S. O. show and when they were around, my spirits were uplifted.

Christmas

Christmas trees appeared in nearly every tent at Camp Tripoli. The trees looked somewhat like our Oregon shore pines and while they were not the most beautiful trees in the world, they fit our needs well. We decorated them with strips of red and clear cellophane from cigarette packages, tin can lids, corks, tin foil and any other miscellaneous items that looked colorful and cheery. I also made a bell from the shell of the upper half of a spent hand-illumination grenade and hung it on the tent flap so that it would ring whenever someone entered. It made a beautiful tinkling sound. Our new platoon leader liked it very much, maybe too much. It mysteriously disappeared right after Christmas.

Jimmie and Mikey were little Korean kids orphaned by the war. Like so many Korean youngsters, they survived the best

Chapter IX

way they could by going from camp to camp washing clothes and running errands for the troops in exchange for food and clothing. During our stay in Camp Tripoli, they became our *washy-washy boys*, Jimmie living with us in our tent and Mikey with another squad in the next tent.

Jimmie

Jimmie liked Louie and Louie liked Jimmie. In fact, Louie wanted to adopt him, a heartbreaking impossibility for an enlisted man. Sooner or later we were going back into the lines, and Jimmie certainly wouldn't be allowed to go with us.

This was probably Jimmie's first Christmas experience. Some of us received packages from home and whenever possible, the men shared their good fortune with their friends. A new replacement, a corporal was not a particularly popular person with many of us because of his haughty attitude toward the Koreans and, in particular, Jimmie. A package came for him just before Christmas that contained a harmonica and a yo-yo, strange gifts to be given an adult. Jimmie was curious and very innocently picked up the yo-yo to examine it. When the corporal saw his toy in Jimmie's hand, he snatched it away and slapped the kid's face. Instantly in a rage, Louie came off his rack like he'd been stung in the butt and charged with fists clenched, ready to do battle. Grabbing my feisty buddy, we held him back but it would have been easier stuffing an angry wildcat in a burlap sack. His intense anger and especially his use of vulgarity was a complete shock to me. Seldom had I ever heard him say anything as off-color as he did at that moment, yelling at the corporal. I did a lot of fast-talking and so did everyone else trying to cool his temper.

It wasn't easy and even though Louie was a foot shorter, he was damned capable of getting the bigger fellow's hide. The corporal, also stunned by Louie's outburst, did the right thing by keeping his mouth shut and by keeping his distance. Ultimately realizing that the rest of us in the tent were just as incensed as Louie by what he'd done, he apologized to everyone: Louie, Jimmie and the rest of us. But Louie never forgot nor forgave him.

The corporal didn't stay with us long. He transferred out of the platoon. Maybe he asked to be moved but, whatever the reason, it was most likely for the best, not only for him but for us too. One reason was the guy couldn't walk quietly, stumbling and bumping into things. What would he have been like on a patrol? Even walking in deep snow, he made noise.

Christmas was a solemn and tranquil day, at least for those of us in rear areas. We had the day off: no patrols, no inspections and no special details other than a few men on sentry and mess duty. Church services were held in the morning and we ate a very welcome hot Christmas dinner later in the afternoon. For the most part, though, the men were quiet, hanging around their tents, probably thinking of home. I know I was. I was extremely homesick. Except for our sentries, everyone went to bed early. I lay on my cot thinking about Maggie, Mom and Dad and home, wondering if I'd make it through the rest of this war in one piece, wondering if I'd be home for next Christmas. I fell asleep listening to the mournful music of someone playing a harmonica, probably someone who was also thinking of loved ones and a place far, far away.

Before we left Camp Tripoli, an ugly incident occurred in the camp. Discarded artillery ammunition casings, opened at both ends and partially buried vertically in the ground were used as urinals. We referred to them as *piss tubes*. One night someone tacked a rebel flag to a stick and flew it from one of the piss-tubes. The boys from the Deep South took issue, being deeply insulted by the act. Arguments broke out among the men and some were punctuated by fistfights. As the day wore on, fights became more frequent and eventually it got out of

Chapter IX

hand. It all began as a disagreement between the North and the South but it turned into a free-for-all with nearly everyone involved. Being from the West Coast, I figured that the entire fracas was plain stupid. I was determined to stay out of it. We had enough problems with the current war and getting the crap beat out of me re-fighting an old one wasn't my idea of having a good time.

That same night, we realized Jerry Miller hadn't been seen for some time. Searching around the camp, we found him draped over a wooden pole, limp as a wet dishrag. He was okay—just tanked out of his ever lovin' mind. Jerry had gotten into some rotgut, drank too much, wandered off and passed out. He was a sorry sight, and smelled just awful. Louie wanted to strip his trousers off and leave him hanging over the pole. Truthfully, I gave it some thought but I knew that if he ever found out I had a hand in it, my life wouldn't be worth a plugged nickel. We hauled his sorry ass to our tent and put him to bed like a mother would her infant child…but with one exception. We didn't kiss the big bow-legged ape goodnight.

One of the new replacements to join the company was my new fire team leader, Corporal Albert Jerome (Jerry) Rogalla. He was a reservist and this was his first combat assignment. Rogalla, a pretty big fellow with a great big mischievous grin, was from Minnesota. I traded one Jerry from Minnesota for another Jerry from Minnesota. I was lucky. Rogalla was a happy, congenial and pleasant fellow and it was easy getting to know him. I thought to myself,

Piss tube

"Just wait! He'll change! When he's been here for two or three months, especially when we go back into the lines where it's nasty assed cold, he'll get bitchy and pissy just like the rest of us."

He and his wife, Donna, had married only a few days before he shipped out for Korea. Seldom did an hour pass without him mentioning her. He loved his new bride very much and there was no doubt about his missing her. Our families, our friends and our homes became the most favored topic of our conversations. We soon knew each other's past life as well as we knew our own.

Camp Tripoli. Jerry Rogalla, Hoyt Hutchinson, Charles Long; Jimmie, our washy-washy boy, and Louie Caruso

Chapter X

Helicopter Lift

It was time to go back into the dreaded front lines. I hated the thought of it. But one intriguing bit of information we received was that we would be transported there in helicopters. This was going to be a new experience because not one of us in the squad had ever before flown in one. Some of us, including me, were undoubtedly a little apprehensive but it certainly seemed better to fly to our positions than spend two or three days walking on muddy roads and climbing mountains to get there.

But, we had to walk to the lift site—four stinking miles. Don Young seldom talked much but, until we reached the helicopter pads, he never let up, bellyaching about everything under the sun. He wasn't happy about walking, about riding in a chopper, about the weather; he wasn't happy about anything. Everything irked him. The rest of us couldn't help but grin, tickled by his grousing. But we wisely kept our mouths shut, all of us but Jerry Miller. He just had to say something to rile Don even more and Young was quick to snap back at him.

> *"Ya know, J. J.? I never really noticed before but you walk kinda funny, like a baggy-assed ape."*
>
> *"Well, let me tell you somethin' you red-headed turd. You'd walk funny, too, if you had the Veep following right behind you all the time with that damned BAR of his stuck up yer ass. One of these days, I'm gonna grab that feather-merchant by the stackin' swivel and pitch his butt over a cliff."*

His comment drew chuckles from everyone within earshot, even from Young. But not me: I took the hint and dropped back a few paces—but only for the time being.

As we trudged along in two columns, a couple of Army jeeps passed through our formation and, as usual, each carried four soldiers. A chorus of hoots and insults rose from our ranks and a few of the guys barked at our dogface comrades including my new and normally reserved fire team leader, Jerry Rogalla. Seeing the Army riding in vehicles gave Young that much more reason to gripe, carping on and on that we seldom got to ride when we were on the move.

> *"We never get to ride anywhere unless command wants us there in an awful big hurry. And ridin' in a helicopter means they want us there damned quick. And when they want us there quick like that, it's usually someplace we don't wanna be."*

His remarks were prophetic.

Depending on the amount of equipment to be hauled, each chopper carried four to six men. As soon as one left with a load of Marines, another landed, the rotation well organized, quick and efficient. But there were so many men that it still took some time to transport everyone. We had to wait our turn to be airlifted and that gave us time to do a little requisitioning—in other words, scrounging.

Any outfit that had erected tents was usually easy pickings for a bunch of thieving Marines and an artillery unit camped in the vicinity was the target. It's an historical fact that Marines, in particular those who spent time in combat, were proficient

Chapter X

scroungers and, immediately, some of the guys began looking for anything worth taking, especially food.

Rogalla's pack was not overly large when we arrived at the departure area but when it was our turn to leave, I noticed as we climbed aboard the helicopter that it had become mysteriously enormous. Louie's pack had also gained some size, as had a few others. They'd draped ponchos over their packs, a common practice to keep things dry, so whatever was beneath couldn't be seen. They'd found something they thought worth taking but I had no inkling what it was. They weren't talking and I wasn't asking.

Once we boarded the helicopters, it took little time to lift us up into the cold, snowy front lines. The ride actually turned out to be fun. It was where we were going that wasn't going to be fun. It was a cold, gloomy, dismal-looking place. Everything appeared gray and bleak. As soon as I set foot on the hill, I felt a terrible foreboding, a deep fear, sensing that we would have a terrible time here. And I was right in my assessment.

Sikorsky helicopter

Hell Frozen Over

It was late in the day when we arrived. I think the place was referred to as Hill 884 although I was never certain. To be truthful, at the time I really didn't give a rat's rear-end what it was called. Our helicopter put down on a makeshift landing-pad constructed on the reverse slope, just out of sight of enemy-held positions. Quickly, we jumped out and just as quickly Marines who were being relieved climbed in. As our helicopter was leaving, another one was coming in with more troops. There was little noise other than the *chop-chop-chop* sound of the helicopter rotor blades and the hushed whispers of non-commissioned officers giving orders. We were escorted, quickly but quietly, to bunkers on the forward slope. The men whom we replaced were glad to see us and spent little time visiting except to tell us a little about the terrain, the location of booby traps and what problems to expect. They wanted to get to the reverse slope as quickly as possible to catch a ride to hot chow, cots, and warm showers.

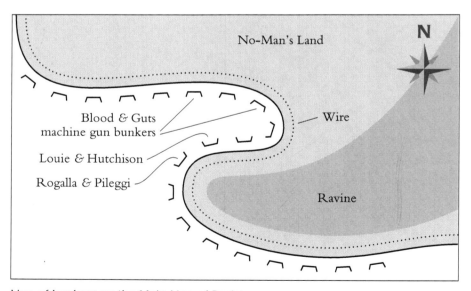

Line of bunkers on the Main Line of Resistance

Chapter X

Rogalla and I were assigned to a small bunker in a sheltered part of the lines. The line of bunkers running from west to east curved around in the shape of an inverted "S", the top of "S" facing north. Our bunker was located in the inner curve of the lower end of the "S" and was facing in an easterly direction. It was nearly impossible to approach because of the steep terrain and because it was surrounded on three sides by bunkers manned by other troops. Louie was bunked up to our left with an old China Marine, a new replacement named Hoyt Hutchison.

Winter scene

Stolen Heat

At last Rogalla removed the poncho from his pack, revealing his loot. I was dumbstruck. He had swiped a small pot-bellied stove from the artillery unit. I asked him what he was going to use for fuel and where he thought he could get it. He told me that Louie had taken a five-gallon can of fuel oil and someone else had filched a couple of stovepipes. I was absolutely amazed…but probably not nearly as surprised as those artillery men when they returned to their tent and found their stove missing. Rogalla was new to Korea but he'd already learned a little about surviving and how to scrounge. And I'd have bet my last dollar that Louie Caruso, my little buddy and the master of all scroungers, had a hand in his training. Without a doubt, Marines are the biggest scroungers in the world but few could hold a candle to these chaps.

If the Marines needed something, they requisitioned it. If they couldn't get it that way, they simply stole it—usually from the Army. The Army always seemed to have plenty of everything while the Marines seemed to have plenty of nothing. It wasn't unusual to see a jeep or a truck with the yellow letters "USMC" stenciled directly over white "USA" lettering. We even put captured Russian trucks to good use, painting out the Communist red star and replacing it with the letters "USMC".

W. J. Miller told me that a friend of his, who was with a Marine motor transport company, *requisitioned* an Army truck, believing it was loaded with beer. But he had no time to inspect the vehicle's cargo before heisting it to confirm his hunch. Upon arrival at Easy Company's position, he and a lot of disappointed Marine friends discovered the truck wasn't loaded with beer but with socks, hundreds and hundreds of pairs of socks. Even though it was somewhat of a letdown and they couldn't tie one on, the men welcomed the clean socks and took as many pairs as they wanted. Hoping to make the truck look as if it had always belonged to the Marines, Miller's buddy obliterated the Army identification lettering with paint, dirt and grease and it too was added to a motor pool of select vehicles.

Chapter X

Caruso and Hutchison's bunker was out of sight of the enemy lines and considered nearly inaccessible to infiltration. So, we selected it to install the stove and made it the squad's warm-up bunker. Within a few days, we'd enlarged the structure enough that it comfortably accommodated six to eight men at one time.

Blood and Guts

Two machine guns were emplaced in bunkers to cover a small ridge jutting to the north toward Hill 601. Even though the last one hundred fifty yards from the ridge up to the bunkers was steep and difficult to climb, previous units had experienced several probes coming from it. The east side of the ridge was steep but the terrain on the west side was gently

1st Squad machine guns. Standing L to R: Brinlee, Hurt, Phillips, Pompeo, and Sommerhoff. Kneeling L to R: Poutz, Blackburn, Jones, and Bingaman

sloped and easily traversed. An up-thrust of rock several hundred yards out was a problem too because it provided concealment for enemy snipers.

The code names for the two guns were Blood and Guts. As in Mortar Valley, just about every bunker was equipped with a sound power telephone providing us with good communications. Using their code names, during the night the machine gunners reported hourly to some PFC at the company command post. The sound power phones were meant for emergencies and not for fun but it didn't take many nights before some of our machine gunners began cracking a few jokes when they checked in. Then late one quiet night, one of the jerks hammed it up with ghoulish laughter and wolf-like howling. No one would have thought that a lieutenant would be listening in on the phone but one was and the machine gunners caught all kinds of hell for improper use of their equipment. For days, they acted like spanked children and spoke to no one except when it was absolutely necessary.

Two of them, Paul Caltry and Earl Fank, shared the same bunkered-hole flanking one of the gun bunkers. They not

The ridge in front of Blood and Guts

Chapter X

only shared the same hole, they shared their food and water, their socks and a well-used toothbrush.

One bleak, cold night, Caltry was standing watch with his sleeping bag pulled over the top of his head and zipped up to his neck to keep warm. It was dead quiet. Peering into the darkness, he suddenly realized someone was standing directly in front of his bunker. He couldn't see the man's eyes but he was certain the guy was staring directly into the darkened gun

Dan Proietti, machine guns

port. From the outline of the uniform, he was certain it was a North Korean soldier but he couldn't determine if the man was armed or not. A frightening chill swept over him, his body quivering, as he quietly began to unzip his bag with numbed trembling fingers. To Paul's horror, the sleeping bag zipper became stuck, bound tight by the bag's fabric. He was frantic and he was helpless, as helpless as if he were in a straitjacket, and he knew that he'd have no chance at all if the Korean pitched a grenade through the port. After several tense seconds the enemy soldier turned and, for some unknown reason, made his way back down the icy slope away from Paul's bunker, soon disappearing out of sight. Finally freed of the bag, he woke Fank and told him what had just happened. Neither slept the remainder of the night keeping watch together expecting the North Korean to return with some of his comrades. Discussing the incident and the strange way the enemy combatant had acted, they eventually came to the conclusion that the fellow might have wanted to give up fighting but couldn't find anyone to whom he could surrender.

Sergeant James Osborn and PFC Troy Watson, a new replacement who had just joined the company, manned another bunker that flanked Blood and Guts. Not many nights after Caltry's harrowing experience, Watson was awakened by a slight rustling noise, like dirt falling on a poncho. Rubbing the sleep from his eyes, he could see that dawn was fast approaching and wondered why Osborn hadn't shaken him out to take his turn at being on watch. His eyes clearing, he could see the sergeant had fallen into an exhausted sleep and he could also see beyond Osborn through the gun port, the outline of a person. It was an enemy soldier, squatting down and peering into the dark gun port. Just as Caltry had experienced, a North Korean had crawled up to the bunker. But, instead of this guy backtracking, he had reached into the bunker and was shaking Osborn, determined to get his attention.

Front line bunkers on Hill 884

Chapter X

With a lump in his throat and his eyes glued to the Korean, Watson unzipped his sleeping bag and gave Osborn a sharp kick. The sergeant came to life and feeling someone touching him, raised his head. When the cobwebs cleared, he was alarmed realizing that a North Korean soldier was right in front of him and had hands on him. Instinctively, Osborn drove the butt of a rifle into the enemy soldier's stomach, knocking him backwards, down the embankment. Rising to his knees and frantically jabbering, the enemy combatant threw up his hands, gesturing that he wanted to surrender to the two dumbstruck Marines. Had Watson not yelled that he thought the guy was trying to surrender, Osborn might have killed him. The Korean was armed with a fully loaded burp gun and hand grenades but he wanted no more of the war.

Conversing with Osborn and Watson later in the day, Caltry wondered if this was the same individual who had approached his bunker a few nights before. From that night on, everyone in our sector stood watch with churning, uneasy stomachs.

Building bunkers

Johnny Pompeo holding a thirty caliber M.G.

Curiosity about the two incidents was killing Louie. He'd heard bits and pieces of conversation about it over the sound power but he wasn't satisfied and was determined to find out all the details. When he asked me if I wanted to go with him to visit Caltry, I should have known better and remained in my hole. But, no, I just had to listen to the nut and went with him, plowing our way through the snow and right into a work detail.

After two hours of hauling bunker logs and freezing our butts off, we skinned out and made our way to one of the gun bunkers. We found it manned by Johnny Pompeo, another one of our Italian buddies, all bundled up like an Eskimo in his winter parka. To ward off the cold wind, he'd also draped a few empty sand bags and a poncho over his head. He looked like a frozen mummy, just sitting there behind his machine gun staring out at the drab dreary landscape that lay before him.

"*Hey, Pompey! How you doin? Got any scoop?*"

Without looking our way or giving us a nod of recognition or anything, he just began talking,

"*Naw, crap! There ain't nuthin' goin' on. But, how the hell would I know. Nobody tells me anything, anyway, fer*

Chapter X

cryin' out loud. Ya know, I been sittin' here in this stinkin' hole just thinkin' that this wouldn't be too bad a war except for one thing. It's not the mortars or the stinking artillery or snipers or mines or anything like that. It's the damned cold. It's cold enough to freeze the toes off a brass monkey. Fer cryin' out loud! The cold makes this fracas one really lousy war."

Pausing for just a moment, he finally looked at us.

"Ya know—when I get out of the Marines, I'm gonna buy me the biggest heatin' stove ever made and I'm gonna build a helluva fire in it. And then I'm gonna plant my ass right on top of that damned thing and I ain't never gonna be cold again. No sir! Not ever! Geez, I'm hungry. You guys got any extra chow?"

Winter on the front lines, January 1952

"Hell, Pompey, that's why we're over here. We're scroungin' for some extra grub too."

Pompey returned his attention to the snowy hills before him and fell silent, falling back into a trance. He always went into a kind of dream-state when thinking of food. We gave up and went on our way back to our own bunkers.

"That nut! I'll bet he's dreamin' about spaghetti with clam sauce. Hell, there's no sense tryin' to talk to him when he's like that. He's like a damned zombie."

Hollywood Louie

Louie continued to amaze me with his antics, his pranks and his resourcefulness. Even though we had been bunkmates most of the time in Korea and had become good friends, it was difficult to read his mind. He was absolutely unpredictable. Some folks are not difficult to read and you almost know what they're thinking. Not so with Louie. He wasn't aloof but still he sometimes seemed a little distant.

One snowy day he crawled out of his bunker with a big grin on his mug, cleanly shaved and wearing, of all things, dark sunglasses. My jaw must have dropped to my knees in amazement. He looked like a movie star going out for a stroll in the beautiful, scenic, snowy hills of Korea. I had no idea when or where he had obtained the sunglasses. I only knew that he was wearing them here in the middle of a war. I had to take his picture as evidence because I knew that at some time in the distant future I would tell disbelieving people about this peculiar nut and this particular incident.

Some of the men took the strangest things with them into combat. One fellow carried a guitar. He was the fellow Jack Lilley had told us about. Another guy had a pet crow that perched on his shoulder and then there was the guy who wore a black derby hat. Then there were the guys from the Deep South who carried Confederate flags, some proudly displayed, draped over their packs. Yet another Marine carried a red flag that we

Chapter X

referred to as *Maggie's Drawers*.

When Marines fired for qualification on the rifle range, a red flag, or *Maggie's Drawers*, was waved to indicate to a shooter that he'd missed his target. This particular fellow who carried the flag sometimes waved it at the enemy when they took a shot at him. It mattered not if the shot was from artillery, mortars or from a rifle. The North Koreans probably knew exactly what the flag indicated and I'm sure it infuriated the hell out of them because every time he waved that damned thing, they threw more junk our way.

Pet crow

Louie's Love

Louie wrote love letters simultaneously to two young ladies who lived near his home in Brooklyn. The letters were absolutely identical. If a person put them together and held them up to a bright light, the letters would have looked as if they'd been traced. The names of the two girls were the only difference. The girls just happened to be friends, they worked in the same office, and they compared their letters. How in the world he got away with something like that was mystifying as all get out but he did. And what's stranger, after being discharged from the Marine Corps, he actually married one of them, a sweet lady named Dolores. They're still married and, believe it or not, they had six boys.

Standing: Joe Caffiero and Leo Plick
Squatting: Louie Caruso (with sunglasses) and Hoyt Hutchinson

Chapter XI

Patrols and Ambushes

Our commanders continually planned squad-sized patrols and ambushes in an effort to confuse our enemy and to keep him guessing. Unfortunately, we poor *ground-pounders* had to carry out those missions, causing us nearly as much grief as it did the enemy. It was grim and deadly business, going beyond the Main Line of Resistance into No-Man's-Land, particularly at night. There were times when we ventured two or three miles into unknown territory and because everything blended together in the dark, it was darned easy to get lost. After crossing over the wire, we paid close attention to every foot of terrain around us, memorizing every tree, rock and bush so we could find our way back. Mines and booby traps weren't easy to detect during the daytime but at night they were downright impossible to spot. Every step we took posed a terrible risk.

After settling into an ambush, we counted the stumps, boulders and trees. If, during the night, an extra stump appeared, it got shot. And we too could stumble into an ambush ourselves while returning from one. The trickiest and most dangerous feat was finding the correct re-entry point back into our lines in the dark. Each re-entry was prearranged, and if we approached the lines at the wrong point, we were certain to draw fire in the form of hand grenades and mortars from our own men. And another thing...every time we returned, the patrol leader visually checked the face of each man to make certain he wasn't an enemy soldier who had infiltrated the column in the dark, trying to sneak into our positions.

The North Koreans were well aware that our patrols most often returned to the same point in the lines from which they had exited. If they spotted one coming through, they'd take up positions near the departure point and wait in ambush themselves. Not only would the patrol come under enemy fire when it returned, our own men manning positions near the re-entry would also fire on them, not taking any chances that it might be an enemy probe.

Winter combat patrol

Butch Schaus took his squad into No-Man's-Land to set up a night ambush on a trail believed used by the North Koreans to approach our positions. The moon was not yet full but with snow on the ground and

Chapter XI

the night sky cloudless, there was enough light to see some distance. The trail, lined with thick brush, meandered in serpentine fashion from a valley uphill toward our lines. The men were put into positions above the trail with a good field of fire. Otto Pavelcik took the most vulnerable and dangerous position farthest down the path beside a small tree. It was dead quiet, it was cold and it was miserable.

After four hours of trying to keep warm and drifting in and out of daydreaming trances, Otto became

Otto Pavelcik

alarmingly aware of the strong odor of garlic. He knew that enemy soldiers were very close but, staring down the hill watching for movement, he had no idea where they were. Alert but on edge and shivering, he steeled himself for a firefight, concerned though that he wouldn't be able to move fast enough because his legs had stiffened from the cold. Nonetheless, hoping not to give his position away, he flexed and moved them until he felt he could stand. As he slowly pushed himself up to get a better view of the trail below, he heard a plopping noise in the snow nearby. Immediately, a blast bowled him over, knocking him a few yards down the hill into a thicket of bushes. Obviously, the North Koreans knew someone was there and had thrown a concussion grenade his way. Regaining his senses and unharmed, he remained motionless and could actually hear them talking with hushed voices only yards below him. Wondering if they thought he was dead or if they even knew where he was lying, he suddenly got an answer. One of them cut the brush above him with a burst from a burp gun. There were no doubts that it was time for him to vamoose out of there. Clinging to his rifle and crab-walking on his hands and numbed feet, Otto scrambled up the icy hill as fast as he could, screaming at the troops above him to throw grenades. He was frantic and in a mighty big heap of trouble. His biggest concern wasn't being hit with grenade shrapnel but being captured.

When the other men of the squad heard the grenade and burp gun fire, they had already readied themselves for a fight. Hearing Otto's panicked request, they heaved grenade after grenade into the vicinity where they thought the enemy were positioned. Gasping for air, Otto rejoined his squad thanking the good Lord that he'd escaped unscathed. After a brief encounter and riddling the hillside with gunfire, both patrols gave up and withdrew to the safety of their own lines. It was a narrow escape for Otto but to hear him tell it, it was just another night in the life of a combat Marine.

One frigid night our squad was assigned to set up an ambush several hundred yards in front of and below our lines. We were to stay in position, motionless, for five hours, unless the enemy was unfortunate enough to venture into our trap. Because snow covered everything and because we wore white camouflage uniforms, it was horribly difficult to maintain sight of each other en route to the ambush site. By the time we arrived, my fingers had become numb from the icy wind, my trousers stuck to my thighs, and my neck and chin felt like a block of ice. Even though I wriggled my toes inside my Mickey Mouse boots, my feet soon became numb too. The icy weather was more than horrible. It was unbearable.

The wind was blowing but nothing moved—every limb, blade of grass and leaf probably frozen solid. Almost everything was blanketed with snow, making it easy to see a dark, moving object. We had been there nearly three hours when suddenly

Chapter XI

I was jolted by a rifle shot right next to me. Every thought of being cold instantly disappeared as I tensed up, waiting for return fire from an unseen enemy.

Like everyone else, Louie had become fed up with the freezing cold and had fired his rifle at a stump, exposing our positions. Since he'd compromised our ambush, we had to pull back into the lines. Our bodies aching and our feet numb without feeling, we stumbled and staggered like drunken sots back through the wire.

Louie didn't have a chance. Don Greenlaw, the platoon sergeant, set upon him like a red-tailed hawk after a baby chick, chewing him out for ruining the ambush. Louie's explanation to the sergeant was that he thought he saw something move. No one could argue about that because that kind of thing had happened before but, nonetheless, Louie still received a stern warning to be darned certain what he was shooting at next time. When he returned to his bunker, I asked him why he'd fired his weapon, knowing full well he'd done it on purpose.

"A butt-chewin' beats hell out of layin' out there in the snow and freezin' to death."

I couldn't have agreed more. Every one of us owed him one.

It seemed as if it took days but when I finally got warm, my left heel burned, hurting something awful, causing me to believe that I'd suffered frostbite. It was painful and stung for several days and, for months after, I endured oozing sores on my thighs and under my chin. To this day when I get sick, my left heel turns bright red, and after several weeks, the skin peels like a snake shedding its skin.

Many of the men had trouble with their feet, caused by the cold weather and W. J. Miller was no exception. Oozing puss, the big toes on his feet turned black and, eventually, the toenails loosened and fell off. He was another man too stubborn to check in with a corpsman. Limping from pain, to this day he's still suffering from foot problems.

I cannot imagine how the men who went through the previous winter fighting their way out of the Chosin Reservoir were able to survive. They not only had to endure one of the coldest winters, they had to fight off hordes of Chinese in horrendous firefights.

Snowing continuously the night following our ambush, conditions worsened as the wind blew and snow swirled around in the hills. When daylight came, the sky was a grayish-white. The wind had stopped blowing and nothing moved. It was deathly quiet. Everything was covered with snow and not one thing had any definition to it. Trees, communication wire, ridge tops, trails, bunkers, not one thing had an outline. We couldn't determine where the earth ended and the sky began. It was called a *whiteout* and it was dangerous to venture far from our bunkers for fear of becoming disoriented and lost. It remained like that for a couple of days before the snow began falling off of things, exposing some detail of the terrain.

Korean prisoners

Chapter XI

Dreadful Loss

A week later, we again donned white camouflage uniforms and pulled another ambush, setting up on the low ridge in front of Blood and Guts. We used a knotted rope, tied to a tree stump in front of the machine gun bunkers, to help us scale the steep, slippery part of the slope. It was a dark, dreary, ugly night. Trees, bushes and other objects could be seen for a distance of perhaps a hundred yards, but beyond that everything faded into a drab darkness. The cold wind, blowing over the snowfield, drove sleet into our faces like ice picks. Cautiously, we made our way along the narrow ridge until we had moved several hundred yards below our defensive positions into No-Man's-Land. A natural ground formation shaped like a cup was our destination. A few other ambushes had been set there in the past without results and I personally hoped this one would end the same way. Two men with a roll of communications wire laid a line for a sound power telephone so we would have contact with the lines. Some one hundred yards beyond this position was the up-thrust of rock that an enemy could use as concealment to approach our positions.

Ebb Daughtery covered the narrow trail behind us, the trail that we would use to return to our bunkers. I was placed in the right front of the cup formation, facing forward with my BAR. On my right, the terrain was incredibly steep and covered with snow. On my left, where Louie and the others were located, the slope of the ground was much more gentle. Rogalla laid crossways on his stomach 20-feet in front of me and slightly to my left, facing to the left beside a huge, car-sized, boulder. From my position, I could see past his feet and the right end of the boulder, straight down the ridge towards the rocky up-thrust and trees. Except for Daughtery who faced to the rear and me facing to the front, everyone else faced to the left on line. The right side of the cup was not defended because we were quite certain the enemy could not climb the sheer cliff-like hillside.

It was well past midnight when the enemy appeared. Three North Koreans, walking abreast from the direction of our lines on the narrow trail, quietly approached our positions. Like us, they wore white camouflage uniforms and were nearly on top of Daughtery before he realized they were there. He fired three quick successive rifle shots into the middle figure. The other two grabbed their stricken comrade and leaped over the precipitous side of the slope, tumbling out of sight. To our complete surprise, enemy riflemen were all around us. Immediately, all hell broke loose. We engaged each other in a deadly firefight for the next two or three minutes. Bullets pinged off the large boulder where Rogalla was lying. Jerry Miller fired at two enemy soldiers who popped up in the snowfield, momentarily firing their burp guns at us. Then I saw a movement in front of me. One of them was slowly working his way around the huge, snow-covered boulder, coming up behind Rogalla. I zeroed in and squeezed the trigger of my Browning. The mechanism in my BAR was frozen and only one round fired, failing to seat another one. I manually cranked the bolt into position and almost immediately another figure appeared. This time I got off a short burst. Then more figures came and I fired more short, precise bursts. Muzzle flashes very briefly pinpointed where the enemy was lying. I knew some of their rounds were striking close because pieces of rock and chunks of frozen dirt pelted me like bee stings. Because of their white uniforms, I couldn't tell if I'd downed any of them. In the bleak darkness I caught glimpses of figures darting about, firing whenever I thought I had a target. Then all shooting stopped and it became as quiet as the inside of a tomb. They were gone. In just seconds, I'd shot over two magazines of ammunition at fleeting shadowy figures, not knowing if I had hit any of them

    J. J. began calling to each one of us in a hushed voice to see if we were okay. When he called Rogalla's name, he didn't answer. Suddenly filled with dread and without thinking, I hurtled myself over the rocks, dirt and snow to where he lay. He was dead, shot in the temple just below the helmet brim by one round from a burp gun. I knew it was useless but nonetheless I hovered over his lifeless body, protecting him. At that moment, nothing but Rogalla's life mattered to me. Grief and remorse so utterly filled my soul that I was ready to die myself.

We put Jerry's body on a stretcher and carried him back along the narrow ridge-trail to our lines. We passed the machine gun bunkers knowing the men inside were watching and wondering who had become the casualty. Covering his body with a poncho, we laid him next to the platoon command post and the men dispersed, moving back to their positions. But I couldn't bring myself to leave my fire team leader, my good friend, hoping with all my heart that somehow he was still alive. Greenlaw and J. J. finally convinced me that it was senseless to remain and that I should leave. Alone and distraught, I returned to my hole and like a small child, I sobbed uncontrollably for the remainder of the night. We had lost other men in the company but none that had affected me so much. Jerry and I had become close friends and this one really hurt. Our chats about families, about growing up and his recent marriage all came back to me like a flood. On January 18, 1952, it all ended for Jerry Rogalla and for the wife he dearly loved, out there on that miserable point of land somewhere in Korea.

I now know in my own mind that we, as young men, never gave the North Koreans or Chinese much respect or credit for being intelligent warriors. We were all too damned *gung ho* and thought of ourselves as invincible. The North Koreans knew we were out there to ambush them that night. They were probably all around us as we left our lines. They simply found our communications wire and followed it to where we lay in wait. We got ambushed ourselves because of a simple, stupid mistake. We had no idea how many we had killed but that didn't matter to me. Losing Jerry was the only thing I cared about.

Two days later, J. J. moved me into the warm-up bunker occupied by Louie and Hutchison. It helped being with someone, especially Louie, because I'd slipped into a deep depression and everyone knew it. For years, I was haunted and tormented by Jerry's death and even though I know I couldn't have prevented it, I nonetheless felt guilt and shame. I felt guilt because I was still alive and he was dead. So, I swore a vow to God that

I would never forget Albert Jerome Rogalla, my friend from Minnesota.

Corned-Beef Hash

I knew very little about Hoyt Hutchison but I did know that he and Louie *duked* it out a few times. Both had fiery tempers and acted like two Bantam roosters, circling each other before tangling. Most of their disagreements were over stupid things and their bow-necked posturing tickled the heck out of me. I tried to hold them apart by putting my hands on their heads to keep them from swinging at each other, their fists barely grazing my sides. But that only angered them more and soon I became the target. Eventually when I tired of being pummeled myself, I just gave up and let them go at it.

    A box of c-rations contained three meals, plastic eating utensils, toilet paper, cigarettes, and a can of fruit. Each meal consisted of a can of food to be heated and a can with crackers, jam, powdered cocoa and the like. The cake of cocoa, supposedly in powder form, looked like a brown hockey puck and was equally as hard. The guys joked that if we ever ran out of grenades, we could always throw the cocoa cakes; they were certain to maim anyone who got hit. To make a cup of hot chocolate, one put the hard cake of cocoa into a canteen cup or an empty can and beat the hell out of it with the butt end of a K-Bar knife handle until it was once more powder. Lucky Strike cigarettes were the most desired cigarette and sliced peaches the most favored fruit. Since I didn't smoke, Louie got all of my cigarettes but not my peaches. The foulest tasting and most unappetizing of all the c-rations, nicknamed the big three, were corned-beef hash, meat and noodles, and meat and beans. The meat and beans were a bit greasy but not too bad. The noodles were pasty and tasteless, but the corned-beef hash was just outright ghastly. Hutchison was the only guy I ever knew who liked corned-beef hash and he liked it best when it was burned to a crisp. Needless to say, Hutch got all of my hash even if he had nothing to offer in return.

Chapter XI

It took less time to heat food in an unopened can and it was simpler and cleaner, no messy pots to clean afterwards. After heating the sealed can for a few moments, it was removed and shaken vigorously and then the opposite end placed on the fire. The process was repeated two or three times to assure that the contents were thoroughly heated before the can was opened. One had to be careful, though, not to leave it on the fire too long because it would rupture—sometimes with a vengeance.

Early one night, instead of tending to business, the three of us were playing a game of cards by candlelight. One of us should have been on watch at the bunker port but it was early in the evening and, because of the steepness of the terrain in front of our bunker, we figured that the chance of an infiltrator trying to sneak up on us was zero.

Hutchison became hungry during the course of the game and put a can of hash on the pot-bellied stove. When the game became interesting, he completely forgot about it and the damned thing exploded, extinguishing the candle, the only light we had in the bunker. Boiling hot corned-beef hash spewed all over the place. But it wasn't the hash that we thought had exploded. The three of us figured the same thing at the same instant—hand grenade. My face burned like fire and grasping my forehead, I thought it had been chopped to pieces by shrapnel. If an enemy soldier had pitched a grenade into our bunker, his next move might be to get inside. Somehow, Louie found Hutchison's BAR in the dark and, yelling at us to hit-the-deck, he emptied a full magazine toward the bunker entrance. It was then that I realized it was the corned-beef hash.

We found and lit the candle, discovering that dirt was pouring out of the sandbags forming one wall, the stovepipe nearly shot in half, and smoke filling the bunker. At the same time, J. J. Miller was screaming on the sound power, wanting to know who was shooting and what the hell was going on. What a mess we had. Not only did we have to do some quick emergency repairs on the stovepipe and the sand bags, we also had to clean hash from everything we owned. And for being foul-ups, Louie, Hutchison and I were sent on a work detail the following morning. I had indeed fallen in with bad company, bunkered up with two legitimate lunatics.

Winter Replacements

A new second lieutenant joining Easy Company made quite an impression on the battalion commander, on his platoon sergeant and on some of the troops. But it wasn't the kind of impression he intended. Jim VanAirsdale, who was from the state of Washington, was understandably nervous because this was his first combat assignment.

From a staging area behind the lines, he and a few other men began the long, tedious climb up into the mountains to our positions. Lumbering under their heavy packs, they trudged, crawled and worked their way up the steep, rocky slopes, taking frequent breaks to catch their breath. On one occasion sitting off the side of the trail to regain some strength, a supply train of Chiggy Bearers caught up and passed them, going in the same direction. The Chiggy Bearers were carrying heavy loads of equipment, ammunition and food, but instead of plodding along as the Marine replacements had been doing, they were trotting—uphill.

Second Lieutenant James VanAirsdale, Winter 1952

Chapter XI

Delivering their load of supplies and returning down the hill, the Chiggy Bearers passed the small band of struggling Marines two hours later. After another hour of torturous climbing, Jim and his fellow replacements reached Easy Company positions, encountering a Marine guarding the trail down the reverse slope. Asking where the company's command post was located, the guy pointed down an icy, snow-covered pathway and told them to walk straight on for about seventy-five yards until they saw an arm protruding above the snow just off the trail to the left.

The arm

"Then take the path immediately to the right and walk about fifty yards. You can't miss it, Lieutenant. The captain's tent is down in a sheltered area on the reverse slope where the North Koreans can't see it."

Jim was puzzled, quizzing the Marine.

"What are you talking about? An arm sticking out of the snow?"

"Yes, sir! A dead North Korean was buried there in a shallow grave, and for some reason his arm popped up out of the snow. It's stickin' straight up like a frozen post. I guess the rest of him is still underground. You can't miss it. Just turn to the right at the arm, sir."

Jim, leading the other replacements, trudged down the path, believing the Marine to be a wise guy who was screwing around with him. But sure enough, by a small, broken tree, there was a human's arm, visible from the elbow up, sticking out of the snow just off the trail. It was a grizzly sight. Jim wondered as he turned down the trail to the right as the Marine had instructed,

> "Why don't they re-bury that guy? That's a helluva thing for anyone to see. Maybe I'll do something about it after I get settled."

The arm was, indeed, a ghoulish sight and Jim couldn't get away from it fast enough, relieved to finally arrive at the company command post. The battalion commander, the captain and the first sergeant were waiting for them.

Addressing the boot lieutenant, the battalion commander commented,

> "You've just set a new record for climbing this hill, Lieutenant."

Jim, his chest swelling with pride, almost grinned but the battalion commander continued speaking, bursting the lieutenant's bubble.

> "Never has it taken anyone else as long to get here as it's taken you."

After receiving instructions and orders, the humbled lieutenant was given directions to his new quarters, a bunker built just off the crest of the hill on the reverse slope where his sergeant and some of his men were waiting. His platoon sergeant, according to the captain, was a grizzled old veteran named Harvey Wright.

> "He knows more about the Marine Corps and warfare than most officers."

Jim took the comment as a hint that it was best to listen and learn and not be too gung ho. With his bulky pack and weapon strapped to his back, he began negotiating a dozen treacherous, icy steps cut into the hillside to his bunker. He hoped that he'd at least appear to be a competent leader to his men even though he hadn't given that impression to the battalion commander. A few steps away from the bunker doorway, he slipped and fell on his backside, tumbling into the bunker and landing prostrate at the feet of a few startled Marines and Staff Sergeant Wright. The men, recognizing that Jim was their new platoon leader, helped him to his feet and removed his pack. Sliding into the bunker on his butt was the last thing he intended to do and, naturally, his ungentlemanly entrance embarrassed the hell out of him but with a straight face he introduced himself. Sergeant Wright, sizing up his new platoon leader, spoke with tongue in cheek.

"Welcome, Lieutenant, and may I say, sir, that was a heck of a landing. Are you by any chance one of them pilots that washed out of flight trainin'?"

Taking his sergeant's comment in good humor even though his pride had been somewhat ruffled, Jim managed a grin. The entire day had been the pits for him and he hoped his commanders, his salty sergeant, and his men would soon forget about it. As he unpacked, he and his men became better acquainted and during their conversation, Sergeant Wright informed Jim of something he didn't particularly want to hear,

"You know, Lieutenant? You are my sixth platoon leader since I've been here."

Not at all anxious to know what had happened to the previous five lieutenants, he wished to hell that Sergeant Wright hadn't given him that little piece of information.

After a few weeks with the company, Jim had earned the reputation for being a fine officer and an excellent leader, the pratfall into the bunker just a humorous memory. Adapting to the crummy conditions of front-line duty, he came to realize why no one had bothered to re-bury the dead North Korean soldier whose arm was sticking out of the snow. The men, weary and cold and miserable put up with the shelling, snipers, cold chow, patrols and ambushes because that was their job and they expected it. But otherwise, they just wanted to be left alone. Digging a hole in the frozen earth just to re-bury a body that was nearly completely buried anyway just didn't seem to make sense to anyone.

The General and The Bunker Rat

We were alerted that a Marine General, accompanied by some of his staff, would be conducting an inspection of the lines to check our conditions and talk with some of the men. Everyone was admonished to bathe, to be clean-shaven, to wear the cleanest clothing we had on hand, and to look like Marines and not like a bunch of hopeless, homeless bums.

Washing and shaving in the freezing weather was not a comfortable chore. There were no handy springs on this hill, so melting snow was the most convenient way for us to get water. Even though most of the men grumbled and carped, every one of us washed, shaved and cleaned ourselves as we were told, save one person—Louie Caruso. Louie probably thought no general on earth was going to venture onto the frozen forward slope in this war just to talk to him. How wrong he was.

General Franklin Hart, accompanied by his aides, the company commander and the gunnery sergeant, went from bunker to bunker, occasionally stopping to ask the inhabitants questions about the chow, their health, if their gear was in good condition, and so forth. Everything went well and the men, for the most part, looked decent. But when the general and his entourage arrived at our bunker, our Company Commander was shocked and damned embarrassed by what they found. Coated with soot from our bullet-riddled stove and the candles we burned at night, Louie crawled from our bunker like a hobo crawling from under a bridge. His hair was shaggy dirty, he smelled absolutely awful as if he'd been sleeping in a pile of camel dung, he was unshaven, and he looked as if he'd worn his clothes for months without changing them. Louie had all the appearance of a typical bunker rat.

Later that afternoon, my little buddy was "escorted" to the company command post and given a bath. Yes, like a small boy being bathed by his mother, he was scrubbed from head to toe. Our company executive officer, First Lieutenant Tim O'Reilly, a very irritated man, was the *scrubber* and he wasn't exactly gentle with poor Louie's ears. When my buddy returned to the bunker, he was baby-butt-pink. I had a hell of a

Chapter XI

time stifling my mirth because I knew he'd whale the tar out of me if he saw even a trace of a grin on my mug. Seldom was there a reason to giggle like a bunch of school kids but Louie provided one. And it served the nut right.

Left to right: Gunnery Sargeant Morris Virili, Captain Embree Maxson, Lt. General Franklin A. Hart, Lt. Colonel Kirgil, and the assistant Battalion Commander. Winter 1952

Charles Creel and Lt. Tim O'Reilly

Chapter XII

Clam Up

High Command conceived an idea to trick the North Koreans into thinking we had pulled out of our positions and had moved to another range of hills several miles to our rear. They hoped enemy patrols would come snooping and stumble into a gigantic ambush.

In early February 1952, operation *Clam Up* was implemented. Instructed to pack all of our gear, we left our bunkers in broad daylight making no effort to conceal our movement and moved over to the reverse slope. Most of us knew little of the plan but once out of sight of enemy lines, we gathered into our platoons, receiving additional instructions and a five-day issue of c-rations. We were told that after dark, we'd reoccupy our bunkers and remain cloistered in them for the next five days. Open fires and nighttime smoking were forbidden and that meant we couldn't fire up our pot-bellied stove. And absolute silence was necessary. Unless attacked, we were not to reveal ourselves for any reason. Only at night could we step outside our bunkers and then only for a few minutes to relieve ourselves. With that, we hunkered down and waited for nightfall.

Not permitted to talk, roam about, or smoke, we sat quietly freezing our butts off until well after dark. Stealthily, we returned to our positions but crawling into our holes was a bit nerve-wracking because we had no way of knowing if the North Koreans had already come to investigate and were waiting for us. I wondered if the big brass had considered that possibility.

Sometime around midnight, Louie startled Hutchison and me with an alarming announcement. He told us he was leaving for a few days. He wanted to sneak down the reverse slope to see if he could find an outfit with some grub. At first, I thought he was just joking but when he strapped his ammo belt on and donned his helmet, I knew he was damned serious. Hutchison and I, in a near panic, asked the same question almost in unison,

"My God, Louie! Are you out of your mind?"

We thought he'd really lost it. Pulling a stunt like this could get him hung. Not only hung, but drawn and quartered as well. That is, if he got away with it without being shot by one of our own men. Now that we'd buttoned up, it was a damned dangerous time for anyone to be moving about in the dark.

"Why in the hell now, Louie? Why not go during a time when everything's normal? These guys'll shoot anything moving, no matter if you're behind the lines or in front. You've got to be nuts! And, if you get back without anybody shootin' you, you'll probably get court-martialed. You know, some general put a lot of thought into this clam-up thing and if you go screwin' it up, they'll stand you up against a wall and blow your stupid brains out. And what about us? They'll prob'ly shoot us too because we let you go without kickin' yer dumb ass."

He'd planned this venture in just a few hours, defying all logic and common sense.

"We've got five days with nobody checking up on us and I want somethin' more to eat than these lousy c-rations. Don't youse worry 'cause nobody's gonna find out."

Chapter XII

Don't worry! Nobody's going to find out! I think the dumb goofball wanted to pull this stunt just to prove that he could. We continued trying to reason with him but our pleadings fell on deaf ears.

> "Any outfit that's got food other than c-rations has to be miles behind the lines. It'll take a couple of days to do this, Louie. And you'll have to come back up to our lines, and that's probably more dangerous than leaving."

We couldn't talk him out of it and soon he left us, crawling out of the bunker. I was certain that I'd never see him alive again and told Hutchison that if he got killed, it would serve him right. I wasn't about to worry. But I did.

> "I should have shot the idiot in the foot or something. What happens if we have another whiteout? He'll probably get lost and wind up on some other mountain, and we'll never know what the hell happened to him. The hell with him! I'm finished worrying about the dumb jerk."

Hutch, even though he and Louie often fought with each other, was just as concerned about him as I was.

> "I'm gonna smack him in the mouth when he gets back, Veep. I owe him one. You just hold him for me so I can land a good, hard punch on his kisser."

The remainder of the night was quiet and uneventful. Fretting and angry, Hutch and I were more concerned about Louie than about a curious enemy who might come calling on us.

Louie returned before midnight on the third night. We didn't see him but we heard his voice, alerting us that he was coming in. He scooted through the bunker port, carrying a sandbag containing a dozen eggs, a few onions and a large can of Spam. With a stupid grin on his ugly mug, he asked,

> "Hey Pledge, Hutch! Youse guys miss me?"

No one will ever know the relief I felt when I heard him speak his Brooklyn version of English. I'd just lost one great friend and I didn't want to lose another. Kicking his lousy butt would have given me some pleasure but all I could do

Vito Pileggi. Weight: Under 150 pounds. February 1952

was marvel that he'd pulled this stunt off without getting caught, without getting hurt.

Louie told us about his fantastic venture. He'd found a small artillery or four-deuce mortar outfit and raided their pantry. Those guys posted guards too but they probably weren't as alert as the line outfits. Lucky Louie had pulled off an amazing stunt and not another soul other than Hutchison and I ever knew he was gone. His daring provided us with a banquet for the next two days. The food was great, particularly the onions, but I was still miffed at him for putting us through the ordeal and hoped he wouldn't think up another stupid stunt to pull.

The North Koreans finally came snooping, realizing that we'd done something but not really certain what it was. Their patrols probed along the wire but our troops were disciplined and remained hidden, holding their fire. Several enemy soldiers finally came through at a few points along the line and the fight was on. Our machine gunners on Blood and Guts and some of the riflemen and BAR men, on the opposite side of the hill from us, got into brisk but brief firefights. No enemy came up the steep slope that we were watching. At

Chapter XII

least, no one came that we could see.

Farther down the line, one machine gunner was said to have killed an entire North Korean squad. We heard that a few made it to the top of his bunker but he killed them with hand grenades.

The following night, our little neighbors from the north came calling again and they got the same results. When Clam Up ended, we came out of our bunkers to assess the damage we had inflicted on them. Near one of the machine gun positions, the body of a North Korean soldier lay frozen in the wire. Some of the guys propped the body against the wire in a sitting position with his frozen arms outstretched, and left him sitting there with dead, un-seeing eyes staring down the hill. The corpse gently rocked back and forth in the wind, making a gruesome scene to view. After a few nights, we were ordered to dispose of the body, to bury it someplace.

Dead North Korean

Were we becoming too calloused and hardened at the sight of death? Maybe! But, if anything, it was their deaths that we had become calloused to, not ours.

Non-Commissioned Officers

Hutchison returned to our bunker, after getting some supplies and mail from the Company Command Post, with surprising news.

"Ya oughta see all the staff NCOs I just seen. They got three or four new master sergeants and a bunch more tech and staff sergeants just sittin' there at the Company CP. I wonder what the hell's goin' on and what they got planned for us."

That was puzzling information. Why, all of a sudden, do we have all of these staff non-commissioned officers? The Company was normally staffed with just a few of them. As far as most of us were concerned, Top-Sergeant Foster needed no help running things. He ran the Company like a clock.

Responding to Hutchison's comments,

"Well, whatever the reason, Hutch, I'm staying clear of the CP. You go up there and run into one of those guys and the next thing you know, you're on a work detail. If we need something, we'll con Louie into going."

Louie was a master at squirming out of work details. Once a non-com told Louie that he had something for him to do but he found someone else after Louie's response.

"Do you want me to do it now, Sarge, or wait until after finishing the detail the lieutenant asked me to do?"

"Forget it. I'll get someone else."

We heard later that Headquarters Marine Corps had erroneously received information that some line companies were dreadfully short of Staff Non-Commissioned Officers. So, being efficient, thoughtful commanders, they rounded up a horde of these folks and sent them to us. Now, we had Staff NCOs coming out of our ears.

The Milkman Cometh

Headquarters gave some of the men, who had been through rough times, a week of Rest and Relaxation (R & R) in Japan or somewhere in South Korea, out of harm's way. Don Young was picked from our platoon for one of those R & R

Chapter XII

breaks. If anyone deserved to be away from the misery of front-line duty, it was he.

Returning a week later, he brought a surprising gift for his bunkmate, Butch Schaus. It was a quart bottle of fresh milk. Curiosity was killing us.

"Where in the world did he find fresh milk?"

We had forgotten how it tasted or, for that matter, what it looked like. It was like staring at a pot of gold. Even in reserve, we were given a mixture of water and powdered milk but never fresh milk. The word about it spread like a desert wildfire and soon a horde of us descended on their bunker. Young, staring at us menacingly, sat on the parapet with an M1 rifle across his lap. He intended that Butch be left alone, so that he could enjoy the milk, and warned us rather sternly not to come closer and not to try stealing it. Steal his milk? Why, hell, we would never have thought of doing a thing like that.

A letter came addressed to me with a Minnesota postmark. It was from Jerry Rogalla's wife. I didn't want to open it certain that she was going to ask me if the report of Jerry's death had been a colossal mistake. I must have looked at the envelope dozens of times over the next two days, knowing that eventually I had to read what she'd written. The return address was smeared and I guessed that one of her tears had fallen there causing the ink

The author and our Korean interpreter, Charlie

to run. With a lot of agonizing and tearing at my heart, I eventually gave in and opened it to read the words that I knew would make me weep again.

> *Pfc Vito Pileggi*
>
> *I hope you may be able to help me. My husband is Cpl. Albert J. Rogalla. He sent home his Xmas menu with some of his buddies' signatures. You were one of them. He's in the 14th draft.*
>
> *I received a telegram saying he was killed in action on Jan. 18. Do you know if this is true & if so, how it happened? If he's alive & you see him, please don't let him know about this cause then he'll worry.*
>
> *Thank you so very much for any help you can give.*
>
> *Sincerely,*
>
> *Mrs. A. J. Rogalla*

Guilt and despair engulfed me again as it had the night Jerry died. What could I ever write to this woman to console her, to comfort her? I had no words and I felt utterly helpless. Not having the courage to tell her that her husband was indeed dead, I tucked the letter away, intending to write something later, not wanting to add to her grief, to her agony. But I kept delaying writing a response until it was too late, until too many weeks had passed. I added her letter to the other precious mail I kept in my breast pocket. I still have it, saved with my mementos, not as a war souvenir, but as a reminder of a very special friend.

Relieved But Not Out Of It

Sometime in March 1952, we were relieved from the front lines and moved to the rear. We bunker rats were miserable, we were tired and we were cold. In addition to enduring the coldest months of the winter under the harshest of conditions, Easy Company had lost several good men, wounded and killed.

Chapter XII

It was dark when we arrived at a campsite carved out of the steep, reverse slope of some hill. Tents had been erected, each one capable of housing several Marines. And each tent contained folding cots but nothing else. At least it was dry. A security perimeter was established around the camp, requiring a few reluctant men from each platoon to stand guard. The rest of us threw our sleeping bags on the cots and crawled into them like numbed zombies, soon drifting off into a deep sleep. No one bothered to tell us that an artillery unit was positioned in the valley directly below us, the muzzles of their large-bore guns pointing right over the tops of our heads. In the very early morning hours, the artillery unit fired a salvo that literally shook our tents, scaring the ever lovin' crap out of us. Wide awake but completely dumbfounded, we had no idea what had happened, whether the blasts were from incoming rounds or from bombs. Most of us dove under our cots, not that they would have helped.

When we found out what it was, everyone wanted to strangle the sadist who chose this particular spot for us to bivouac. Being in front of a big gun when it shoots is almost as nerve-wracking and agonizing as receiving incoming. And we never knew when they were going to shoot.

Bullock, a *short-timer* and due for rotation, was leaving the company. For weeks, just like other short-timers had done before him, he fretted and agonized fearing he'd become a casualty before he could get out of Korea. Physically, he was worn out and his feet were like W. J. Miller's, cracked and bleeding. The freezing conditions of the past winter were not kind to any of us. But now that we were in reserve and he was close to rotating home, his spirits had picked up. Wanting to give me a gift before he left, in his Mississippi drawl, he offered,

> "*Veep! Do yuh want muh socks? They're dang near new. Ah'll leave 'em here fer yuh if ah kin jest peel em off muh sorry feet.*"

New socks were most welcome but not those, not even if I boiled the stinking things in a vat of lye. I didn't want to hurt his feelings but I didn't want him leaving them either.

"Hey Bullock! That's all right, partner. I've got an extra pair."

Bullock was one of 16 Marine reservists from Meridian, Mississippi that had been activated and sent to Korea. A few days prior to leaving their companies and returning home, they got together and, purchasing 16 cases of beer, held one whale of a raucous reunion. After consuming six or seven bottles of the brew, Bullock got the bright idea to swipe Easy Company's banner and take it home as a souvenir. So, in broad daylight, he climbed up the hill one more time to the command post and, sure enough, there it was hanging in front of the captain's tent, his for the taking. But, just as he was about to snatch it, Captain Maxson stepped out of the tent right in front of him. Thinking fast, Bullock came to attention, saluted and said,

Thomas "Ed" Bullock. Fixin' to go home.

"Howdy, captain! Ah jest came to wish you good luck, sir, and to say goodbye."

After returning his salute, Captain Maxson shook Bullock's hand and thanked him for his courtesy. Even though the Old Man said nothing, Bullock knew his commanding officer was wise to his shenanigans.

We remained camped there for several days, being shocked out of our skivvies with frequent and unexpected volleys of artillery shoots that rocked the hillside. The weather didn't seem any warmer but the ground was beginning to thaw. We were permitted to build campfires during the day to keep warm and to heat our food. We were also informed that the area where we were camped had at one time been mined.

Exclaimed one Marine,

"That's just great! They bed us down in a damned shootin' gallery. Then they tell us we're sleepin' in an ole minefield."

There was always a chance that a mine could have been missed when a minefield had been cleared. We were lucky not to find one.

Easy Company Command Post, March 1952

Before we moved from the area, the artillery unit below us received *incoming mail* from the enemy. Several rounds exploded in their compound, destroying tents, supplies, and a truck. The remnants of the truck caught fire and blew up and we could see the men who had been manning the big guns running for cover. Because of the suddenness, accuracy, and intensity of the barrage, there had to be casualties. Most of our company gathered and sat on the side of the hill to witness the bombardment, as if we were spectators watching a duel in a Grecian amphitheater. Some of us would have punched it out with the artillerymen for keeping us on edge but we sure as hell didn't want this to happen to them. They really caught hell.

Some of us speculated that a North Korean infiltrator was probably hiding out in the nearby hills and had radioed the coordinates of the artillery unit's position to his comrades. Someone in command of the artillery unit must have arrived at the same conclusion because four or five squad-sized patrols were dispatched into the hills only a few hours later.

Captured Russian truck

Chapter XIII

Go West, Young Man

The entire division moved to the west coast of Korea. Every conceivable kind of conveyance, including captured Russian trucks, was used for transportation. None of us knew, at least not at the platoon level, where we were going. There were as many rumors as there were men in the division. Some speculated that the Chinese were going to make a big push with tanks and air power down the west coast and that only the Marines could be expected to hold them back. It was just the kind of crap that I didn't want to hear.

Even though spring was coming, the weather was still cold and rainy and the ride, for the most part, was horribly miserable. But, someone in higher command had a little compassion for us and allowed the caravan to pause for a few hours to give us a break and eat some good hot chow. When our battalion stopped in a rocky river-bottom, we poured out of the trucks glad that we could stretch our legs and it wasn't long before we figured a way to have a little fun and raise some hell.

Two dozen of the biggest and most gruesome-looking Marines imaginable obtained a large length of rope for a tug of war. Twelve men on each end anchored themselves in the rocks and boulders of the river bottom and began to pull like they were pulling a barge through the Erie Canal. A rag had been tied to the middle of the rope so that all could see who was gaining the upper hand.

Suddenly appearing on the scene was my little buddy, Louie. Something was up because he had that devilish look on his dumb mug. He walked up to the center of the rope where the rag was tied, holding a large corn knife concealed behind his back. With one overhead stroke, he sliced the rope in half like an executioner severing some poor soul's head from his body. The men tugging on the rope bowled over each other, trying their best to stay upright and not kill themselves on the rocks. They were stunned and bewildered for just a moment. Without a second's hesitation, Louie was off and running like an African gazelle, bounding through the throng of onlookers, seeking a place to hide. When the very angry, bruised and bleeding Marines recovered their senses, they went after him, passing by me like a thundering herd of buffalo. They never caught my little buddy, thank goodness, or they would have been pounded him into paste. Caruso had struck again—and survived again.

Honey Buckets and A-Frames

As we rode westward, the terrain began to change from high, rugged, snowy mountains to gentle rolling hills. We began to see many more rice paddies, more Korean civilians, and more villages. We seldom saw a Korean civilian on the eastern side of the peninsula, except for a few washy-washy boys who hung around the rear area camps. The farther west we traveled, the more civilization we encountered. The villages became towns and the towns became cities. Then we came to Seoul, the metropolis capital of South Korea.

As our truck convoy snaked slowly through Seoul's ancient streets, everyone in the trucks craned their necks looking at the buildings, the people and especially the pretty girls. It was obvious that the city had endured horrendous battles. Most factory

Chapter XIII

chimneys had been destroyed by tank fire to eliminate snipers and artillery spotters. Many beautiful and historic buildings had been damaged or demolished. Even though much of the city had suffered some devastation, it was still filled with throngs of people, hundreds of thousands of them.

The Korean people, although small in stature, could carry incredibly heavy loads on their backs. I saw old men with homemade A-frame pack-boards carrying huge bundles of wood, building materials and even piles of brush. Instead of walking with these hefty loads on their backs, they trotted. Women carried large bundles of clothing or water containers balanced on their heads and, at the same time, carried things in each hand while packing an infant on their backs. Many people, including women and children, carried wooden shoulder yokes with *honey buckets* tied to each end. They transported human waste to the fields to be used as fertilizer. Nothing went to waste in this poor country. Anything discarded by us was immediately scavenged and put to use.

The convoy stopped frequently, sometimes pausing several minutes before resuming. When we halted, groups of children appeared out of nowhere, surrounding the trucks to beg for food, cigarettes and candy. During one of the stops, an oversexed yard bird riding in the truck in front of ours leaped out and darted into a crowd of

Korean family

women, trying to grab one. The NCOs in his truck stood and threatened him with brig time if he didn't immediately return to his seat. I was certainly no prude and I liked seeing the pretty girls as much as any other man. But sometimes I felt shame and discomfort because of our demeanor. It went against my grain to treat women as if they were common whores. If a young woman happened to be too near our slow-moving trucks, she drew a chorus of solicitations and if she dared look up, the amorous gestures, comments and whistles escalated, every man trying to draw her attention. A couple of guys in our truck who knew some of the vulgar Korean language continuously called to the Korean women, asking them if they wanted to make a few dollars. By the way they hung their heads and stared at the ground, it was obvious they felt humiliation and embarrassment. Fortunately, most of us behaved—most of the time—thanks to a few older, wiser veterans who were able to maintain some control.

Our New Home

Our temporary home for the next few weeks was not too distant from the west coast of Korea. From there, we were going to occupy positions referred to as the Secondary Line of Defense. Entering the encampment on trucks, the men craned their necks eyeing the tents that had been erected for us. One of the tents caught everyone's attention generating some very happy grins. A sign was posted at the entrance with the word "Shower" painted on it. It was as if we were checking into the Waldorf Astoria.

The road, bordered by our tents, circled around in a large teardrop loop. Inside the loop was a landmass of perhaps six to ten acres surrounded by a fence. Triangular signs attached to the fence warned us that it was a minefield that had yet to be cleared. More damned shoe-mines. It seemed we were always bivouacking in or near a minefield.

I was looking forward to sleeping somewhere other than in a hole in the ground and, maybe, getting some hot food. But first, and more than anything else, I wanted to take a hot shower and get some clean clothing. We had little chance and no facilities to clean up since we came off-line and I was filthy dirty, probably stunk horribly, and I definitely needed to change clothes because everything I wore was baggy, worn and cruddy.

As soon as we got settled in, the entire company headed for the showers. Just knowing we were going to be clean sent our morale soaring through the roof. Thank goodness there was plenty of hot water because the guys took their sweet time bathing and who could blame them. After living in a frozen hole for nearly three months, nothing could describe how soothing and wonderful and luxurious the warm showers felt.

John O'Malley; a haircut, a shave, and a shower; now for a can of pork and beans.

Grown Old

Someone had actually found and put up a real mirror for our use. I was shocked when I looked at my reflection and for a fleeting moment I thought it was the image of some other poor jerk.

I almost uttered the words out loud.

"My God, I've grown old."

My face was pale and thin and my eyes were tired and appeared to have sunk into dark holes in my face. Some of my teeth were loose and my gums bled easily. I had lost about forty pounds, and I had the same old looking, gaunt appearance that Miller and Doc Kees and Daughtery and Bullock and the others had had just before they went home.

I murmured to myself,

"I'm not a kid anymore. I'm an old man."

The underside of my chin was a mass of running sores, probably caused by exposure to months of freezing weather, and it made a clean shave extremely difficult. I was a mess, but I wasn't the only one. Taking a long, hot shower boosted my morale and made me feel a lot better.

Old, worn and dirty clothes were thrown into a pile as we entered one side of the shower and clean clothes, piled in neat stacks, awaited us on the other side, where we exited. After showering, I plowed through the piles, like a kid looking for a prize in a crackerjack box, until I found clothing that fit me properly. However the dungaree shirt that I'd selected had sergeant stripes stenciled on the sleeves. I was only a PFC but because it fit so well I kept it, figuring that beggars can't be choosers, and in combat it really didn't matter what a person wore.

The Minefield

Just before reveille, not many mornings after we had moved into the area, some idiot kid lofted several rocks into the minefield until he hit one. The explosion shook us out of a good sleep and sprayed the area with pieces of rock. At the time, Lieutenant Flores, the executive officer, was in the company commander's tent having a cup of morning coffee and eating crackers and jam. A piece of something zinged through the tent and sent everyone, including Lieutenant Flores, diving to the deck looking for cover. Even though he reacted without thinking, the lieutenant didn't let go of his precious food and, although he couldn't keep himself out of the dirt, he managed to keep his crackers and jam clean.

Another chunk of shrapnel or rock ripped into the old *four-holer,* hitting a sergeant in the rump. At the time, he was occupying the number one seat. His wound wasn't serious but everyone said he wanted to kill the kid for scaring the *crap* out of him.

Another tragic incident occurred involving the minefield. A young man, an office pinky or clerk typist not familiar with the area, stepped over the wire paying no attention to the warning signs. Before anyone could shout a warning, he stepped on one. It didn't kill him but it tore his legs to shreds. Top Sergeant Foster ordered everyone to stay back, that he'd go in after the injured man. Crossing over the wire, he inserted his hands into his back pockets, and stepping in the victim's footprints, walked boldly into the minefield. Scooping the kid up in his arms, he carefully retraced his steps, carrying the young man to safety.

Civilians

Other than the Chiggy Bearers and the washy-washy boys, we seldom saw a civilian and certainly no women on the east coast. But here on the west coast, it was quite different. There were many, many civilians: men, women and children. It was the kids who really got to us. There were always a few dozen of them huddled nearby, waiting for one of us to offer them candy or food. Some, being orphaned, lived in cardboard boxes and managed to survive under the most terrible of conditions. They were ragged little waifs with big sad eyes but somehow they always seemed to manage a big smile for us. A few of the children were missing fingers, arms and legs because they had picked up a box hoping to find food, only to be injured or maimed by an exploding booby-trap. No doubt many youngsters also died while scavenging. This war took a terrible toll on the civilian population and I was proud that we were here giving the survivors of this carnage a chance to live decent lives.

Most civilians who ventured near the camps offered us a variety of products and services. They sold souvenirs of every description: watches, jewelry, cameras and itiwa spoons. They provided services: barbering, mending and washing clothes and, of course, there were the prostitutes.

The majority of the Marines that I recall, especially the married men, stayed clear of the prostitutes, not wanting to chance catching a venereal disease. We were told that anyone who was found to have a venereal disease would likely face a court-martial and not be allowed to go home when their normal rotation came up. It would be a little difficult explaining to your loved ones that you had been hospitalized and couldn't come home because you had caught a bad case of something. In spite of the consequences, the temptation was there. It was easy to sneak out of the compound at night and there was always that ten percent who were willing to take the risk, spending two or three dollars on a lady of the evening.

Armed sentries patrolled the perimeter of our compound, not so much to keep the

Korean kids

guys in but to prevent sabotage by guerrillas and pilfering by civilians. Civilians were not supposed to be within the encampment. One night, one of the *girls* was caught wandering too close to the perimeter. A couple of the guys in Leo Plick's squad decided to use her to play a trick on him. Taking her to his tent, they shoved her in. Although he heard them approaching, he was still taken by complete surprise when a woman suddenly burst into his tent and fell on top of him. His first reaction was to draw back, not knowing what she was going to do. Then, realizing what his so-called friends had done and that she was a prostitute, Leo asked her,

"How much?"

She replied,

"Twenty dollah! No script money, please. Only American dollah."

He bellowed at the men he knew were outside,

"You guys, I know you're out there. Get her the hell outa here. I ain't payin' her no twenty dollars. What the hell does she think I am, a general?"

I noticed that men who didn't know me had been giving me a wide berth. Because I had showered and no longer smelled like a rank stable, I attributed their actions to the sergeant stripes stenciled on my sleeves. They probably thought I really was a sergeant and you can bet that I never bothered to let them know otherwise, either.

Two men, whom I didn't know, were propositioning a Korean woman while she was trying to do laundry for other Marines. It was obvious that she was distressed by their persistence so I intervened, telling them to leave her alone. They turned to see who had the audacity to interfere with their solicitations, saw the stenciled chevrons on my sleeves, and left the area without further comment.

I thought to myself,

"Ah yes.... At last, Veep, you have some real power."

Chosin Hotel

One of my favorite, all-time crazy people, Lehman Brightman, was sent back to Seoul for a week of Rest and Relaxation. He reported to a place referred to as the Chosin Hotel where men on R & R were housed. The place looked like a stockade to him and not a place for rest and relaxation. A solid, eight-foot-high wall topped with barbed wire surrounded the entire compound. Several other Marines on R & R were also housed there. Before they were allowed to go out on the town, they were given instructions and admonished not to drink any Korean liquor or bed down with their women. These instructions and advice did nothing more than whet their appetites, especially Lehman's. Everyone was reminded that they had to be back in their rooms by ten o'clock each night or they'd be in a heap of trouble. Ten o'clock seemed too early to return. That's when the fun started.

Brightman managed, without any difficulty, to do everything that he was told not to do. But somehow he managed to return to his room on time although he couldn't remember how he did it. Later that night, after bed check, he quietly sneaked out into the compound with the intention of going over the wall and back into town. Surveying the grounds, he noticed a tree growing next to the wall that he could climb. Once on top he figured he could leap over to the other side. But before he made a move, a guard appeared pausing directly under the tree. Patiently, he waited until the guard resumed patrolling and was out of sight. Sprinting to the tree, he was about to climb it when another Marine unexpectedly came out of the shadows. He wanted to get out, too. Asking Lehman if he intended to go over, Brightman nodded in the affirmative. Obviously, other Marines had done the same thing in the past because the tree trunk was well worn. They both climbed gaining the top of the wall and peered over but couldn't see anything on the other side but a black void. Brightman whispered to the other fellow that it was too dangerous to jump in the dark, not knowing where they might land. But the other Marine, murmuring that he was going anyway, jumped. He landed on his feet okay but, immediately, headlights from two Military police jeeps illuminated the area. Quite by accident, the fellow had nearly jumped into one that was parked nearly beneath them. He ran off down the road into the darkness with the two jeeps following in hot pursuit. Since they were chasing the other guy, Brightman figured he had it made in the shade and jumped.

That night, he got drunk, got caught and got thrown in jail. Several days later he got court-martialed, got busted, and found out that he'd caught a nasty dose of something.

Mail From Home

Mail came. Someone dropped a postcard in my lap. It was from my dad. I couldn't believe it. The old man had finally written to me. I'm quite certain my face had broken into a huge grin as I sat back to read the back of the card.

He wrote,

"Dear Teddy, Where did you put the crosscut saw the last time you used it? Dad."

I flipped the card over, looking for more. I checked the return address and my military address, trying to find something else but that was all there was to it. I read it again and flipped the card over again.

"Incredible! The old man wrote to me and all he wants to know is where I put the damned saw. I can't even remember the last time I used it. I've been gone for over a year."

Again I read the one sentence, but sure enough, there was nothing else to read. I wondered if he was sending me some kind of code or something. This was the one and only letter, card or telegram that I'd ever received from Pa. Mom always did the writing to me and she never failed to include comments from the family: Dad, the kids, and Grandma. But this was the first mail of any kind from Dad.

That night I wrote a letter to Mom, telling her the same old thing again—that I was okay and that I missed everyone very much. It was the truth but it was the same. I always tried to reassure her that I was quite safe and she shouldn't worry. At the end of the letter I added a P.S. and said,

"*Dad – Look in the shed. Your son.*"

Dear John

One of the few married men got a *Dear John* letter from his wife, informing him that she was filing for a divorce. With the letter clenched in his fist, he fell to his knees and screamed at the heavens in anguish and despair, his soul torn to shreds. This guy constantly bragged about his lovely wife, about how they had met, fallen in love, and married. Like most of us, he had a pocketful of pictures of her and their tiny family. It was obvious to all that he was head over heels in love with her. And he'd remained faithful to his wife, too, not wanting anything to do with the prostitutes. Her letter hit him harder than if he'd lost both legs and so devastated him that many of us were afraid he'd take a walk out into a minefield or that he'd intentionally expose himself to a sniper when we next went on line. He was due for rotation soon and many of us wondered why she chose to send the letter to him while he was still in Korea instead of waiting a few more weeks when he got home. Maybe she hoped he would do something stupid figuring to collect his $10,000.00 life insurance. Thankfully, the captain transferred him out of the company to a rear area unit. I often wondered if he and his wife were ever able to reconcile their marriage. Had he stayed with us, he would have been a big problem not only to himself but to the rest of us as well.

All too often, someone in the company received such a letter. Most of them took it extremely hard but they managed to work out the mental problems it caused. Some cried, some cursed and a few found a way to die. But most of them eventually accepted the bad news, electing to wait until they went home to settle affairs.

Chapter XIII

Every one of us studied our letters, reading them over and over again. Occasionally, someone would discover a clue that indicated something was amiss at home. Mom's letters were always upbeat and reassuring. I always found happiness in her writing, never a hint of despair. Maggie's letters were always sweet too and I loved getting them, but they seemed to lack something that left me wondering if she cared as much for me as I did for her, even though she always ended them with the words, *with love.*

It was rather ironic that a letter was circulating through the company about this same time. The fictitious letter was supposed to be humorous but it affected some of the men to the contrary. It struck a nerve. The letter was purportedly sent to a serviceman in Korea from a buddy at home in the U. S.

Dear Buddy,

Nothing much doing back here. I sure wish you were here but envy you in the thick of things. Bet you never have a dull moment.

I was over to see your wife last night and she let me read all your letters. They were a bit mushy but I don't blame you at all. Frances is a real swell girl. Wonderful figure, looks, personality. Guys still whistle at her when she walks down the street.

Your brother-in-law Smedley stopped in. He was wearing the brown suit you bought just before you left. Frances gave it to him as she thought it would be out of style when you got back. Several other couples came in and before you knew it, we killed two cases of beer. We wanted to chip in but Fran wouldn't let us. She said that you sent her ten or twenty bucks extra for her to spend as she wanted to. One of the guys is buying your new set of golf clubs. Paid $25.00 for them and will pick them up tomorrow. That's more than she got for your movie projector and camera.

Frances was the life of the party. I thought she'd be a little shaken up after the accident last week with the Chevvie, but you'd never know she had a head-on collision and smashed the other car along with your own to bits. The other driver is still in the hospital and threatens to sue. Too bad Fran forgot to pay the insurance but the funny thing is she doesn't seem a bit worried. We all admire her for her courage and nonchalance and especially her willingness to mortgage the house to the hilt to pay the bill. Good thing you gave her the power of attorney before you left. Smart girl!

To get back to the party, you should have seen Frances do an imitation of Gypsy Rose Lee. She was the life of the party. She was still going strong when we said good night to her and Claude.

Guess what? Claude is rooming at your house. It's nearer his work and he saves a lot of money and gas. He says Fran can cook the best bacon and eggs in the world and really does things to a steak.

Nothing new with me, except my wife got another raise. $100.00 a week now. So we do OK with the $90.00 I get from the office. It's getting late now old buddy so I better stop. I can see Frances and Claude having their night cap. He has on the smoking jacket you used to wear so often.

Well, buddy, I wish I could stop over there with you. Lucky guy. Give them commies hell.

Your pal, Lou

The Lighter Side

A reserve corporal from Alabama came to our encampment several times to visit an old friend. He was a gregarious sort of chap and soon he became acquainted with nearly everyone in the platoon. The fellow was very close to thirty years of age and, to my recollection, was one of the oldest corporals I had seen in Korea. To add to his age, the man was almost completely bald, a premature condition that somewhat aggravated him. No need to say that we found a few ways to needle him about his lack of hair. He was soon tagged with the name *Skins*. At first he was a little miffed by our constant referral to his smooth, shiny noggin but eventually he became accustomed to it and almost looked forward to the attention with some amusement.

It rained steadily one gloomy day, all day long, drenching everything. Skins donned his helmet, walked out of the tent into the rain, removed his helmet, and announced,

"You know, the rain makes the same sound hitting my helmet as it does hitting my bare head. The drops make beautiful musical pings as if someone were gently striking a bell."

He was so full of crap but like a bunch of curious school kids, we all gathered around him in the rain with our ears close to his head, as he took his helmet off and then replaced it three or four times. He was right. The sound was the same. But, it wasn't musical, not at all. It sounded more like someone thumping a melon.

Captain McGuire, our new company commander, had obtained another bugle but there was no one capable of blowing reveille. Lieutenant VanAirsdale, who had never tooted a horn in his life, offered to try it one morning. He managed to squawk out three or four notes, sounding something like a spastic goose, before the captain told him to stop it.

The captain, shaking his head, said,

"That was the worst noise I've ever heard in my life, Jim."

Jim, looking outside toward the Company Street said,

"I didn't claim to play it real pretty, Cap, but they are falling out, aren't they?"

The captain, still shaking his head as if to clear his ears of the ringing, countered,

"Only because they don't want to hear any more of that God-awful, frightful racket."

Our company commander authorized the construction of a large company logo in the shape of the letter "E" to be placed near the company command tent whenever Easy Company was in reserve. The very impressive "E", measuring five to six feet in height, was made of peeled wooden poles and suspended from a crossbar. And not one person asked any of us loggers from the Pacific Northwest to cut the timber, either.

Kimpo Line of Defense

Our company moved into positions forming a Secondary Line of Defense across a wide area somewhere north of Kimpo Air Base but still several miles south of the Main Line of Resistance. Because we were so far from the front lines, incoming mortars and artillery were not a concern. It was downright peaceful. Even though we weren't likely to be attacked by any sizeable force, we still dug a line of defensive fighting holes. We also had to be alert for infiltrators, maintaining at least a

Korean girl

twenty-five percent watch at night. When not on watch or in our fighting holes, we slept in our shelter half tents. During the day, we performed various work details, familiarized ourselves with our new surroundings and did search patrols looking for guerrillas. In other words, we kept busy.

Minefields were certainly more plentiful here in the west than in the eastern sector because the terrain was flatter and easier to traverse. The Chinese and North Koreans planted mines helter-skelter, as if they were sowing seeds in a field. Walking around in these low, rolling hills was like walking through a den of snakes.

Binoculars, seldom available to us on the east coast, were available here and surprisingly, they worked exceptionally well after dark. Sometimes out of curiosity we turned the field glasses on the company command post, a large tent, spying on our officers and staff NCOs.

The Commonwealth Division

A unit from the Commonwealth Division was tied in with our platoon on our company's right flank. Occasionally, some of their men came to visit us and we sometimes went to see them. Two British troops came to our tent one night with an M1 rifle, asking if we could spare a few rounds of ammunition. We gave them two bandoliers but they had no idea how to load the thing. So, we set about giving them instructions.

Loading an M1 rifle was a little tricky. If one weren't careful and quick, a thumb could be mashed by the sudden seating of the bolt. We referred to the painful injury as an *M1 thumb* and, in addition to hurting like hell, it usually left the victim with a nasty blood blister. We warned them beforehand that it could happen and it did. And the result was a blood blister, a real dandy one. After practicing the loading routine several times, the older of the two named Corporal Frank, peered down the barrel not convinced that a round was really seated in the chamber. The other man ducked away, shouting a warning,

"Look out! 'Ees going to blow 'is blinkeen 'ead off."

Both Brits were Cockneys. None of us had ever heard a Cockney accent before but, nevertheless, we had no trouble understanding them when they spoke to us. But when they conversed between themselves, it was a different matter and hilariously amusing, particularly when they seemed excited or disagreed about something. Their voices actually rose up a complete octave in pitch and I couldn't understand a thing they said, no matter how attentive I was.

Visiting the Commonwealth compound one day, I was escorted around the area by a proud Corporal Frank. He was in charge of supplies for his unit and knew all the men. Most of his mates, who pronounced his name as *Fronk,* warned me in jest to watch out for the old pickpocket and not to get into a card game with him, especially if the game involved money. Corporal Frank told me that he'd been in the British Army for well over eight years. Because of his comment, I wondered if rank was hard to come by in the British military.

As we walked through a large tent, I observed two rows of what I thought were sleeping cots made of boards and covered with khaki-colored blankets. I felt sorry for those poor fellows believing they had no mattresses. But soon, to my embarrassment, I discovered that we were in a mess tent and that the boards were tables, not beds. I felt stupid as hell. And then I discovered something else. Those Brits were actually eating hot meals, including steak dinners, while we chowed down on c-rations. Here I was feeling sorry for them when they should have been feeling sorry for me.

Corporal Frank, who had not been on the north slope of his unit's positions for some time decided to go visiting and explore the forward area one evening. He walked several hundred yards over a small knoll in search of their defensive positions. As he started down the slope looking for his comrades, he saw what he thought was a *piss-tube* and, needing to urinate, relieved himself into it. Just as he finished two Brits, armed with automatic weapons, came bounding out of a bunker beneath him. He was peeing into their stovepipe.

Chapter XIII

"Those blokes 'ad no sense of humor at all. They wanted to kill me. I 'ad to run fer me bleedin' life."

The Booze Runner

Not long after returning from his R & R, Lehman Brightman was transferred out of the company and assigned as a driver at regimental S-2. Little did anyone at S-2 know they had one of the world's most proficient scroungers and opportunists right in their midst. One of his first assignments was to drive an officer, who was going home, to the airport near Seoul. Before departing, Lehman learned about an Army Post Exchange in Seoul where one could buy beer rather inexpensively. Salivating at the thought of all that beer, he requisitioned a jeep with a trailer figuring to bring a load of booze back with him to drink and to sell. He delivered the officer to the airfield, found the Army Post Exchange, and purchased about twenty cases of beer. Returning to his unit and, after drinking a half case himself, he peddled the remainder for ten times the amount he paid, a pretty good way to make a quick buck.

Within a week he was ready to make another run to Seoul but this time the trip was not authorized. Lehman had somehow acquired a U. S. Army first lieutenant bar. Fastening it to his dungaree cap, he went to the motor pool, filled out a trip sheet, and got a jeep with a trailer. He set off for Seoul and again he purchased a load of beer. Anxious to get back to his unit, he wasn't paying attention to his speed and was driving much too fast. He hadn't noticed that another jeep had overtaken him, not until it pulled up beside him on his left, as if to pass. He glanced over at it and saw two Military Police Officers preparing to stop him. He knew he was in trouble because he drank several beers before leaving Seoul. And now he realized that he was driving much too fast also.

As he looked a second time, the two MP's saluted him. Momentarily, he was confused and wondered,

"Why in hell are they saluting me?"

Then he remembered that he was wearing the Army first lieutenant bar, another violation of military law. He returned their salute and they immediately dropped back behind him. He slowed the jeep to a reasonable speed and the MPs, apparently satisfied, turned their jeep around and drove away in the opposite direction.

Had they looked closely, they would have noticed that Brightman was wearing an Army first lieutenant bar on a Marine Corps dungaree cap, not a Marine first lieutenant bar. Army lieutenant bars are twice the size of Marine lieutenant bars. Brightman knew he'd just had a stroke of good luck. If he'd been caught, he could have spent considerable time in the brig for impersonating an officer, not to mention several other violations. After peddling his stock of beer, Lehman made a wise decision and retired from the booze-running business.

Short Timer Worries

I was becoming a *short-timer* with only a few months to go before rotation home. But Easy Company was scheduled to go back on line. That meant that I'd have to put up with mines, snipers and patrols one more time. The many stories I'd heard about men who, with only days remaining on their combat tour, had been wounded or killed kept coming back to mind. Most of them had become squad or fire team leaders and thus were more vulnerable to becoming a casualty. Like a bowstring ready to snap, I began to sink into a depression, worrying about my fate.

The day before we moved up, something disconcerting happened, causing me even more mental stress. With no warning, I suddenly became weak all over and my head began spinning like a top. In seconds, stumbling out of control, I passed out, falling into a ditch behind my tent. I don't know how long I lay there, perhaps four or five minutes. But when I regained consciousness, I found that I'd also vomited on myself. Weak as a kitten, I remained prone another 10 minutes before gaining enough strength to stand. The reason for keeling over was

Chapter XIII

a mystery to me but now I had something else to worry about, hoping that I hadn't caught some kind of bug that would require hospitalization. If that were true, it most certainly meant that I wouldn't be allowed to go home when I was due for rotation. I wanted to go home and even if it killed me, I wasn't going to let some lousy bug prevent me from seeing my family again. I was determined to get out of Korea—one way or another.

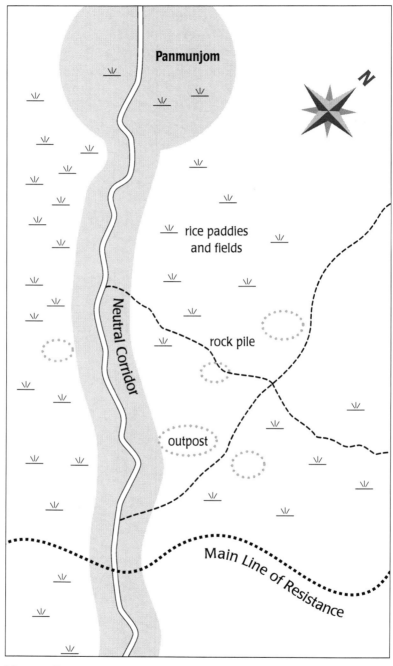

Move to Panmunjom

Chapter XIV

Move to Panmunjom

Our Company moved into front-line positions flanking both sides of a road that went out to the village of Panmunjom where the peace talks were being held between representatives of the United Nations and the Communist world. Panmunjom, in the middle of No-Man's-Land, was about four miles north of our lines and about the same distance south of the enemy's. The road and 200 meters on both sides of it formed a peace corridor that extended from our lines through the village to the enemy lines. It was absolutely taboo for either side in the conflict to shoot from it, through it, or over it. We could supposedly walk on it in sight of enemy observers without fear of being fired on. But, if one went out of the no-fire-zone by one meter, one had better find cover muy pronto.

Friendly outposts established from several hundred yards to a mile or so in front of our Main Line of Resistance were manned by units the size of a squad to a reinforced platoon. Outpost duty was quite harrowing because they could easily be surrounded, particularly at night. And if an all-out attack came, the outposts would be the first positions struck and that meant a fight to the death for the defenders.

Bunkers were incorporated into the fighting trench the same way they were in the Eastern Sector. Because the land was flatter and dotted with smelly rice paddies, there was little in the way of heavy timber and, thus, it was easier to see what lay in front of us. My bunker was about four hundred meters to the right, or east, of the Panmunjom Road and a hundred feet in front of an ornamental arched gate and several burial mounds. Just when I thought things were looking up a little, I found myself sleeping in a filthy hole near a graveyard.

Our company headquarters was positioned near the road and, because of the no-fire rule, was supposedly immune to attack. Nevertheless, it was situated well out of sight of the enemy lines. Whenever one of us had to go to the company CP, we stayed down in the trench until we were well inside the *no-fire-zone*. Presumably we could then pop up and mosey anywhere we desired. But, we had learned long ago not to trust that the Communist would hold to any bargains or keep their word. We relaxed a little but we continued to be vigilant and careful—mighty vigilant and mighty careful.

Relinquishing The BAR

All of the veterans who had been in the company when I arrived in Korea had gone home, most of them still in one piece. They had helped us, Caruso, O'Malley, Plick and me, to survive. But they were gone now and we were the old timers. We were the leaders and the new men joining our company looked upon us as the *Old Salts* whom they could depend on to guide and help them.

My lieutenant informed me that I was to be a fire team leader. I'd wriggled out of that job before because it meant giving up my Browning automatic rifle. Fire team leaders just didn't carry Brownings so I didn't want the promotion. I didn't want to be a leader of any kind. But the Lieutenant insisted and I had no choice.

Chapter XIV

My new BAR man, a fresh replacement from the States, was a young kid from Missouri whose name was Richard Haymon. I called him *Dickie* for short. He was a black kid not very tall but built like a rock. Handing the Browning to him, I felt the same reluctance giving it up as I'd felt giving up my M1 rifle for the BAR when I first joined the company. Taking his M1, I told him that I could help him carry it if he got tired. Could anyone fault me for helping my BAR man now and then? This way, I could get my hands on it, at least for short periods of time.

Morrisey and Oliver

Three other unique individuals also joined the squad. Bobby Oliver, a corporal who transferred from another unit within the company, took charge of our squad. He was from Ohio. Another new man, John Morrisey, who was from Philadelphia, joined the platoon about the same time, becoming good friends with Oliver. They were another Mutt and Jeff team, Oliver being the shorter of the two. They weren't as comical as Proietti and Prevost but they came close. Another black kid by the name of Brock joined Leo Plick's fire team. All three of them proved to be very interesting characters.

Another new replacement, that was an extremely excitable, nervous individual, reminded me quite a lot of Eddie Newman. He was a reserve corporal assigned to Lieutenant Jim VanAirsdale's platoon and bunked near the lieutenant's position. The very first day we were on the line, a salvo of enemy artillery dropped into our lines, but quite some distance from the new replacement's position.

Diving for his hole, shaken and nearly in a panic, the new corporal yelled a warning to Jim, who was sitting outside his bunker reading a magazine,

"They're shooting at us, Lieutenant. They're shooting at us."

VanAirsdale, continuing to read his magazine, very calmly replied,

"They're allowed to, corporal. They're allowed to."

At first, we put Dickie and Brock together in a bunker next to my position. But I felt uncomfortable without the BAR in my hole and, eventually, Dickie moved in with me. His laugh was infectious and it was fun having him in the fire team and we quickly became good friends. He was a happy-go-lucky kid. He had huge hands and his feet looked as large as a pair of surfboards. I wasn't accustomed to being around black people and I didn't know what to expect from him. Likewise, Dickie wasn't accustomed to being around guys with Italian names who loved slurping spaghetti and he didn't know what to expect from me. As time passed, however, we got along just fine and in the short time that we were together we formed a comfortably close friendship.

Haymon and Brock

I found that Dickie wasn't any different from the other guys. He had a family, he loved a girl, he had a God, and he was fighting for his country. When he grinned, his face seemed to split open to reveal a picket fence of sparkling white teeth and when he cried, his tears were as large and as real as anyone's tears. We shared our food, our water canteens, and our stories about our early youth. The Korean War far overshadowed any trivial thing like racial issues.

There was one thing about Dickie, however, that was not in the least normal. He snored. Not like any average human snores, not on your life. His snore sounded more like someone crushing cans in a garbage dump or a bull elk bellowing during rutting season. It was loud, so loud in fact that I feared if the Chinese were anywhere close to us, they could quite accurately pinpoint our bunkers. I sometimes tossed small pebbles at him trying to make him roll over hoping to quell the *snarks* and *horumps* that belched forth from our bunker.

The Birthmark

The summer of 1952 was upon us and the days were becoming warmer but the harsh and bitter winter that we had endured was still vivid in my mind. Moving from the snow-covered, mountainous region of eastern Korea to the low, rolling hills of the west coast was a welcome relief. Many of us in the platoon now went shirtless, soaking up as much sun as possible to drive the coldness from our bodies.

Sitting on the edge of my bunker, I dreamt of being home again with my mom and dad. The brown birthmark on the back of my left hand stood out in stark contrast to the paleness of my skin. Being with Dickie and looking at the birthmark reminded me of an incident that had occurred when I was only six years old.

My mother caught me one day taunting a teenaged black girl who lived in our neighborhood in southeast Portland. Mom was really furious with me and made me face the girl and apologize. I was so ashamed that I couldn't look her in the eyes; I just stared down at the ground. Mom also apologized to her and then she took me home to give me a good scolding and lecture.

She asked how I would feel if someone insulted her like I'd insulted the Negro girl. Then she told me something that I knew wasn't true. She told me she was part Negro. I already knew she was part American Indian and part Dutch and I wondered,

"How many parts could she be?"

Mom's best childhood friend, a girl named Bernice, was a Negro. Because Bernice was a black and Mom was half American Indian, they both endured a lot of misery during their youth. She pointed out the brown birthmark on the back of my hand and commented,

"You might be part Negro, yourself."

My mom was a good teacher and it was a lesson that I never forgot.

I was jolted back to the present by the sound of a bolt closing on a Browning automatic rifle. It was my bunker buddy. He was busy cleaning OUR weapon. Looking up, he began asking some of those touchy questions that the older guys didn't want asked.

"How many times have you been shot at? How many gooks have you killed? Whut's it like to shoot somebody?"

"I don't know, Dickie. I really don't know."

Then he made a comment that bothered me some.

"If I gets shot at, I know what I'm gonna do. You won't see me fer the dust b'cause I'm gonna shag-ass outa here."

I heard him say the same thing a few times to others in the company and I hoped it was just talk. But I wasn't really certain because he sounded so definite.

Chapter XIV

The Aerial Observer

On my way back from getting mail and my daily c-ration issue, I could see, off in the distance to the north, one of our aerial observer planes flying toward the Chinese lines. As it began a slow circular descent, the sky around it was suddenly filled with puffs of black smoke, an indication that Communist anti-aircraft gunners were shooting at it. The pilot, *pouring the coal* to his plane, made a straight beeline for our lines. I thought for certain that we would have to saddle-up and go fetch a downed pilot but he remained airborne. Passing low over our heads, seemingly no higher than a few hundred feet in altitude, I could see a lot fabric missing from the fuselage and I swear I could see the pilot's eyes, opened as wide as windows.

Patrols were still the order of the day but our unit never pulled any ambushes. I don't know if they were out of order here on the west coast or if our squad was just lucky not to pull one. The patrols, in most instances, were carried out during daylight hours, working their way out to one of our outposts before returning to the lines.

On several occasions, we went around or through ancient rice paddies. Sometimes we were forced to lie on our stomachs in those paddies and crawl through them when we came under fire. One day, one of our corpsmen reminded us, during a lecture about sanitation, that the Koreans fertilized the paddies with human waste. Granted, most of the places we'd wandered through smelled like poop but we'd grown accustomed to it. The corpsman, continuing his lecture, reminded us that whenever we used our *itiwa* spoons to eat, most of us habitually wiped them on our pant legs to remove dirt and grime before eating. Needless to say the lights blinked on in our skulls, illuminating the point he was trying to make. At that moment, probably every one of us, including me, wondered if we'd been infected with intestinal worms.

Brass Hats

Since our company straddled the *no-fire zone* and the road to Panmunjom, it was probably the safest place on the Main Line of Resistance. And because it was relatively safe, there always seemed to be a lot of the top brass around.

A special platoon was formed to extract the United Nations Representatives from the so-called peace talks in the event something horrible occurred. The unit, reinforced with tanks, was referred to as a *snatch platoon* and was constantly poised to make a dash into Panmunjom. Pyrotechnics—various colored signal flares—needed by the snatch unit if activated, were stored in two bunkers, one on each side of the road to Panmunjom and Easy Company positions. A colonel had come to the lines, one afternoon, to inspect the readiness of the snatch platoon and the availability of the equipment to execute the operation. As he scrutinized the placement of the two bunkers, he asked one young Marine what kind of pyrotechnics he kept inside.

The young man's reply was,

"Uh! Sir, I don't have nothin' like that in my bunker."

The colonel made a beeline for the company command tent and, confronting First Sergeant Foster, asked why the pyrotechnics hadn't been placed in the two assigned bunkers as ordered. The sergeant assured him they were but the colonel, needing more than his guarantee, suggested he accompany him to prove it. Returning to the bunker with the top soldier, the colonel repeated his question asking the young man if he had any pyrotechnics in his bunker. Again the Marine replied,

"Oh no, sir! We don't have anything like that, sir. It wouldn't be decent."

To the chagrin of Sergeant Foster, he realized the young Marine had misunderstood, confusing the word pyrotechnics with the word prophylactics, and clearing up the confusion, explained that the colonel wanted to know if there were signal flares in the bunker. Now the kid understood and with a big, sheepish grin, answered,

"Oh, flares! Yes, sir! Oh, hell, ah got so many in here, sir, that they're comin' outa my ass."

Jungle Jim

Jim VanAirsdale was leaning against his bunker, basking in the warm sun, browsing through a girly magazine and sipping on a beer, his shirt, flak jacket and helmet lying beside him. Hearing someone clear his throat, he casually glanced over to see a pair of shiny boots. Shiny boots? Up here on line? That caught his attention real quick. He looked up to see two men, one an older fellow wearing a red scarf and a general's star on his collar.

He quickly scrambled to his feet, murmuring to himself,

"Oh, crap! I'm in a kettle of hot water, now."

Brushing himself off, Jim introduced himself as one of Easy Company's platoon leaders, something the general already knew. After answering a few questions, Jim asked the general if he and his aide would like to inspect the area.

The general was emphatic, informing the nervous lieutenant,

"Yes, lieutenant, I would most definitely like to inspect the area. And, please, put your flak jacket and helmet on. And, lieutenant! Please, just for me, try to look professional and wear a shirt."

Jim dressed as he accompanied the general and his aide on a walk down the line of bunkers. He began to feel comfortable as he confidently disclosed the kind of weaponry and the number of men assigned to each position to the two command officers. Stopping at one bunker, he told them that it had contained an A-4 machine gun at one time but the bunker was now empty.

The aide, looking into the bunker, acted surprised and exclaimed,

"Oh!"

The general looked into the bunker and also exclaimed, somewhat surprised,

"*Oh!*"

Jim looked into the bunker and he, too, was surprised and quite embarrassed.

"*Oh, crapola!*"

To his utter amazement, it contained a machine gun, not an A-4 but an A-6. His sector was not authorized to have an A-6 and he had not the slightest idea where it came from or who had put it there. But there it was in a bunker that was supposed to be empty, a bunker that was in his charge.

After inspecting a few more positions, the general decided he'd seen enough. Conversing with Jim for a few minutes, he seemed satisfied with everything and announced that he and his aide were leaving the area.

"*I've seen enough, lieutenant. Carry on.*"

Breathing a sigh of relief and trying to appear as sharp as possible, he snapped a smart salute, and responded,

"*Aye, aye, Sir!*"

Forgetting that he was standing on the edge of the fighting trench, Jim did an about face and took an unexpected nose-dive into the bottom of the excavation, falling flat on his face. He was fortunate not to break his fool neck. Spitting dirt as he rolled over to a sitting position, he spotted some of his men down the trench line. They'd seen his ungainly swan dive and were rolling with laughter. Embarrassed and at the same time peeved he prayed to God the general hadn't seen what he'd done. But, alas, the general and his aide were standing on the edge of the trench looking down at him, both shaking their heads in disbelief. The general, rolling his eyes, turned to his aide and said,

"*Let's get the hell out of here before he does something to injure one of us.*"

Chapter XIV

It was a pitch-black night in May when Lieutenant VanAirsdale and Sergeant Harvey Wright led the First Platoon in a successful combat raid on enemy occupied Hill 67. Most of the men were armed with automatic weapons and, in addition, several carried explosive charges. They carefully worked their way through minefields, barbed wire mazes, and booby-trapped areas, sneaking up on the enemy's positions, catching them completely off-guard. During the first few minutes of the attack, they killed nearly every one of the estimated two platoons defending the hillock before receiving anything in the way of return fire. Only a few of the enemy escaped, if any at all. Before withdrawing, the patrol completely demolished most of the bunkered emplacements and destroyed a considerable amount of weaponry precious to the enemy. Just three members of the platoon suffered injuries, a couple of them hit by their own fire. All three, however, were able to return to the lines under their own power.

Corporal Sam Hillgrube, leading his squad in the attack, was one of the injured. Regrouping and preparing to withdraw, his men found that he'd been peppered with grenade shrapnel and had also suffered from a bullet wound in the shoulder. Later, while lying on a stretcher near the company command post awaiting evacuation, the first sergeant gave him a shot of whisky in a c-ration can. With blood pouring out of holes all over his body, an I.V. in one arm, and the shot of whisky in

West coast of the Korean Peninsula, May–June 1952

his good hand, he complained, not about the shrapnel in him, but about a small nick in one of his fingers, saying it hurt like hell.

One of the corpsmen attending to Hillgrube's wounds remarked,

> "He probably cut it on that damned c-ration can and if he thinks he's gettin' a purple heart for that, he's sadly mistaken."

Sam was decorated with a Silver Star and he got a purple heart for his wounds, too, but only for the legitimate ones of course.

Lieutenant VanAirsdale recounted another incident that involved Sam Hillgrube. Not many nights before executing the successful raid, Jim was leading a recon patrol into No-Man's-Land but this one only a squad in size. Just before crossing the wire leaving the Main Line of Resistance, he heard a hissing sound similar to the sound made by a beer can when the can is first opened. Even though they were still in friendly territory, moving in silence was necessary, and Jim, being quite concerned, didn't want this to occur again. Asking the men where the noise came from, each one merely gestured with his thumb pointing over his shoulder to the rear of the small column. The last man was Hillgrube and he was the guilty party. He'd taken a swig from his canteen, a canteen that he'd filled with beer instead of water. They were good friends but Jim ordered Sam to dump the remainder of it into the dirt, a torturous act that nearly brought tears to his eyes.

Moments of Sadness

The nights were still cool and sometimes downright chilly. Nevertheless, it was a sight better being on the west coast where it was warmer than in those ice-cold hills of the eastern sector. We were on fifty percent watch here, the same as in the east. Dickie and I often stood watch together for the first few hours before one of us hit the sack, just as Louie and I

Chapter XIV

had done so often. This night was no different. Our conversations were usually about family and friends back home. When I came out of the bunker to join him, I could see something glistening on his cheek in the dim light. There was no doubt in my mind that it was a tear. He'd been thinking about home and his family and he was feeling a terrible loneliness.

"Are you okay, Dickie?"

"Yeah, I'm alright, Veep. I was just thinking about my family. I wish I was back home with 'em right now. I don't like this here war."

I knew exactly how he felt and what he was going through. We stood silently for a time watching out front of our position. Eventually we began talking about sports and about football in particular. Dickie asked me,

"Did you have any colored boys playin' on your team in high school?"

"Naw, we didn't have any Negroes in our school. We played this one school that had a colored kid, though. He was big. I didn't want to block him because he was so damned big—like a mountain and we always heard that hittin' a Negro kid was like runnin' into a stump. I think his name was Sam. He played baseball, too. He pitched a double header against us one time. We won both games but the second game was close. Man! He threw faster and faster. The longer he pitched, the faster he got. The last time I got to bat, I could hardly see the ball."

Then in jest, I said,

"I suppose Whitehurst was probably the closest we had to a Negro in our school. He was red-headed and he had a bunch of brown freckles on him."

Dickie looked at me. Even in the dark, I could see that big grin spread across his face. He was feeling better and the loneliness that had engulfed him minutes before had now passed—at least, temporarily.

I was just about to go inside the bunker to sleep when we saw flares light up the sky over one of our outposts some distance in front of our lines. Almost immediately, we could hear the crackle of gunfire and the thunder of grenades and small mortars. We hoped that the outpost was just being probed but it seemed like a concentrated attack. Dickie and I said little to each other, just watched, leaning against the parapet of the fighting trench, glad that we weren't out there. After several minutes, the noise died down and it became quiet. A constant stream of flares continued to illuminate the area around the outpost with an eerie light. Minutes later, the silence was broken again by more rifle and machine gun fire and then again, silence. Flares continued to pop open above the outpost for some time but, thankfully, they suffered no more attacks during the remainder of the night.

Harry Levitt, May–June 1952

Dickie took the first watch as I crawled inside my sleeping bag. The firefight had been too intense; there had to be casualties. Hearing the news, friends of those killed would turn away in despair, their eyes closed tight to hold back the tears and their bodies rigid and knuckles white from squeezing their hands into tight fists. They'd go off somewhere to be by themselves. They always did. I'd experienced those desperate feelings myself. Worried and wondering if we

Chapter XIV

would be the next platoon to pull outpost duty, I fell into a restless, uneasy sleep.

We learned the following morning that the men on the outpost had successfully repelled the attackers but had indeed suffered a number of casualties, one of them Dick Schuckman. Manned for the first time overnight, it was defended by the third squad of the third platoon and Schuckman's machine gun squad.

Not long after dark, he, Harry Levitt and Troy Watson, manning the gun, overheard voices below their position. Watson put the weapon on full load as Schuckman tossed a hand-illuminating grenade. When the grenade popped open, the flare revealed a horde of Chinese soldiers, only forty to fifty feet down the hill below them. The fight was on. Chinese swarmed upon the outpost from all sides but they were repelled, suffering an untold number of casualties. After a short lull in the fighting, Schuckman told Watson to move the gun back to the outpost command center. They did, but they found the command center and all communications had been destroyed by a satchel charge killing one Marine.

The Chinese attacked again and mistakenly struck the position just vacated by the machine gunners. It cost them

Troy Watson with AC MG, May–June 1952

dearly. Several more enemy soldiers were gunned down and the remainder driven back down the hill. Then Schuckman and Watson returned the gun to the previous position. As they moved back to the hole, Schuckman was killed and Levitt and Watson wounded. Watson continued fighting off enemy probes and snipers until they'd had enough and withdrew.

I didn't know Schuckman or Levitt and the names of the other wounded and dead were not familiar either. But it didn't matter whether I knew them or not; they were still my guys. The constant attacks on our lines and outposts were grim reminders that the Communist forces were hateful, deadly enemies and that we were still trying to kill each other despite the peace talks.

> *"They're out there talking peace and we're still shooting the hell out of each other. Why? What the hell good is it doing?"*

Chapter XV

Another Damned Patrol

Every little thing irritated me as my nervousness intensified, worrying that I might get hit. Enemy probes, patrolling, and firefights had become more frequent and violent. Among the casualties were some of the men who were due to go home with me. Their luck had run out.

To add to my anxiety, ugly rumors began to circulate that our platoon had been picked for a tank patrol but the date had not yet been determined. Tank patrols were bad news for infantry. Whenever tanks rolled, you could be certain the enemy would uncork every piece of available artillery at them and being near a tank was suicidal. My stomach churned every time someone mentioned it and there were moments that I was on the verge of vomiting. It was the same sick, uneasy feeling that I'd had on the east coast when rumors persisted about assaulting Moosan. We'd heard there would be three tanks, one for each squad. So, I sweated it out hour-by-hour, day-by-day, trying to keep my food down.

The daytime temperatures had warmed considerably. To help boost our morale, command issued two bottles of Asahi

Beer to each of us. The bottles were large and wrapped in straw but the brew was too warm to drink. To cool it, we buried the bottles in empty, wet sandbags inside our bunkers with the intention of drinking the stout beer the next day.

Early the following morning before the thought of drinking beer had entered our minds, we got some unwelcome, unsettling news. Our squad had been picked to go on a combat patrol and we were leaving immediately, headed east of the outposts deep into No-Man's-Land. There wasn't anything out there but thousands of mines and a multitude of mad Chinese soldiers and we were going just to pick a fight. Another damned combat patrol—absolutely the last thing I needed to hear. My sanity and my luck were being pushed to the absolute limit.

"What if I get sick and pass out, like I did when we were in reserve? What if I pass out when we are out there in No-Man's-Land? God, I don't need this."

Dickie and the other new kids had never been on a combat patrol. For that matter, they had yet to experience an out-in-the-open firefight. They'd been on short recon patrols to the outposts and back but those weren't nearly as deadly as combat patrols. There was some consolation, however. At least this wasn't the dreaded tank patrol that we'd been hearing about but it was damned near as dangerous. We would be very fortunate, indeed, if we got back without suffering casualties.

We assembled in the trench and, preparing to go, checked our equipment. I complained to no one in particular but to anyone who would listen,

"What a bunch of happy horse crap this is! Why do we have to go on another lousy patrol? We can see nearly everything that needs to be seen within fifty miles of here."

Leo Plick's face also showed stress. The day was already warm and Leo, his chubby cheeks flushed red, was perspiring profusely. Half-heartedly and trying to bolster my own spirits, I told Leo that by the time we got back our beer would be nice and cool. His reply was filled with foreboding.

Chapter XV

"Yeah, It'll taste good if we ever get back from this one. I just hope some other jerk doesn't get to drink my beer because something's happened to me."

Leo undoubtedly felt the same dread and misgivings that I felt. His comment about the beer reminded me of the can of peaches I ate during the assault on Hill 749. I didn't want anyone else to get my peaches either, in the event that I died.

We walked down Panmunjom Road in plain sight of everyone, including the damned Chinese. I didn't like it one iota and I questioned in my mind the reasoning behind it. It was tough enough going on one of these patrols without giving the enemy the opportunity to see us coming. We left the main road, following a smaller dirt road in an easterly direction passing behind one of our outposts. It was on a small knoll, manned by a sizeable force of Marines, located well outside the *no-fire-zone* and had been attacked several times, including the night Dickie and I had been watching. One of the Marines assigned to the outpost was standing on the reverse slope and shouted some good-natured Marine vulgarity at us. A few of our men, acknowledging the guy, emphatically returned one-fingered salutes to him as we continued trudging eastward.

Cautiously, we patrolled in single file for some distance before climbing one of the many hillocks in the area. Bobby Oliver, the squad leader, led the patrol and I followed behind, keeping Haymon close to me—but not too close. Bobby crossed a cleared area of about an acre in size that was devoid of all vegetation. He paused at the brush line on the far side and signaled for the rest of the patrol to stop. Now, I was about midway across the clearing and none too thrilled about stopping in the open. The rest of the squad was still in the brush behind me and out of sight.

I squatted down in my tracks surveying the ground around me. The dirt was soft, as if it had been tilled for a garden. Then I noticed pocket depressions in the dirt. The hair stood up on the back of my neck because I knew I was smack dab in the middle of a minefield. Shoe-mines! They were planted thick as fleas on a dog's back, and upon closer examination I could even see the tops of a few of them. Bobby hadn't noticed anything peculiar when he walked across the clearing. It was just a miracle that he didn't step on one. The problem now was for me to get out of this predicament. In a cold sweat, I wondered if this was the end for me, if the last ounce of my luck had vanished. I scarcely breathed as I stepped in his footprints, walking forward out of the field. My heart was pounding like a racehorse at full gallop by the time I reached relative safety and sat down next to my lucky squad leader. I know I was shaking like a quaking aspen tree and I felt as weak as a newly born baby kitten.

Oliver could see that my face had turned ashen and asked,

"You're white as a sheet. You all right?"

I nodded and gulped a few times. Then, with a pretty weak voice, I said,

"Yeah! I did my best to lose fifty pounds, though, before I moved an inch. You're damned lucky you didn't step on one of those things, Ollie. They're thicker than hell. Crap! They're all over the damned place."

After a few more seconds and regaining some composure, I glared at him, barking a threat,

"If you do that to me again, Mister Ohio, I'll kick your lousy butt up over your shoulder."

Was I just lucky? You bet—many times over.

The rest of the squad carefully detoured around the edge of the open field joining us on the far side. After a short break, we resumed patrolling eastward until Oliver spotted something shiny on the side of a small, steep knoll a hundred yards to our front. Approaching from the south so we couldn't be seen from the enemy lines, we set up a temporary defensive line along a bank of ground at the base of the knoll. Ollie climbed up to the shiny object, a piece of metal sheeting, as Leo Plick crept past us and over a small rise to our right, taking up another defensive position just out of our sight.

Scanning the landscape before him, Ollie spotted six or seven Chinese soldiers creeping in behind a rock pile about a hundred yards farther east of us. He signaled John Morrisey, who was climbing up the knoll behind him, to get down. But it was too late; the enemy soldiers had seen John and opened fire with burp guns. He ducked down just in time and they missed. Only Leo was in a bad spot, the rest of us relatively safe, concealed behind the rise. Leo, hearing the shooting, realized that he was in extreme danger and made a beeline back toward us. But just as he was topping the rise of the embankment, the Chinese caught sight of him and tried downing him too with a volley of automatic fire. Puffs of dirt from bullet strikes hitting to his left made Leo run all the faster, crossing the rise at a torrid sprint to safety.

Brock, In the meantime, knew his fire team leader was in jeopardy and left his place of safety, running toward Leo to provide covering fire with his Browning. As Leo barreled over the rise, they nearly collided with each other. The BAR-man wanted to charge on to engage the enemy but Leo held him back, preventing him from un-necessarily exposing himself.

Oliver was in a good spot to observe them but not waiting for them to come at us, he radioed back to our lines, asking for supporting mortar fire. Within seconds the first round of an eighty-one mortar whistled over us and impacted. Oliver sent a range correction and another one sailed over us and impacted. Another correction put the next round right on the rock pile where the Chinese soldiers were believed to have concealed themselves. Several more rounds were fired on the target but one, referred to as a short round, impacted about 50 yards behind us. When it blew, shrapnel splattered the bank where we were lying but not one of us got hit.

Haymon, who lay to my left with his face buried in the dust just like the rest of us, had a death grip on the BAR with one hand and a handful of dirt clenched in the other. I wondered if he was thinking about shagging his ass out of here like he said he would. It was over a thousand yards back to friendly territory and it was all deadly space, completely saturated with mines and mazes of barbed wire. Lifting his head just a little, he grinned at me. He was nervous, uncertain, and scared, scared to death, but the kid was hanging in there. That's when I knew he wasn't about to shag-ass. It was all talk. I also knew at that very moment, that *my BAR* was in pretty darned good hands, and that I was never going to get my mitts on it again. It was his for keeps.

No longer able to see the enemy soldiers, Oliver called off the mortars. Then very carefully, we spent the better part of an hour checking the area around the rock-pile looking for wounded or dead. There were plenty of signs that they'd been there but during the mortar barrage they'd bugged out and had escaped.

Withdrawing through brushy terrain toward our lines, Oliver again took the lead taking another route down a ridge in a southerly direction toward a wagon road. We hadn't moved a hundred feet before he bumped into a trip wire, stopping just as it caught him across the chest. He was afraid to back up and he was afraid to cut it. Many of these booby traps exploded when the wire was tripped or when the pressure was released. Hardly breathing, he gambled and took a step backward. Actually, we all stopped breathing for the moment. Our luck was still holding. It didn't explode. None of us wanted to attempt disarming the thing and left it just the way it was.

But before we resumed our withdrawal, someone spotted a truck moving slowly to the east on another dirt road several hundred yards south of us. We squatted down and watched it for a few moments, wondering who they were. One person who looked like a Marine was walking in front of the truck and another person dressed in white was following behind. The outpost, responding to Oliver's radio call for status of the vehicle, had no information about it. If it was one of our trucks, it was headed into dangerous territory. We feared that if we yelled or fired a shot in the air to get their attention, they'd take a shot at us. We were stumped but there wasn't much we could do. The men on the outpost suggested we get the hell out of there.

As soon as the truck disappeared from our sight, we continued withdrawing toward the outpost that we'd passed nearly three hours earlier. Arriving at the base of the outpost some

Chapter XV

time later, we were warned that the truck was returning and, though it was out of our sight, was driving toward us. Running to get into position to stop it, we passed a Marine, whom I thought was a major that had just come down from the outpost to meet us.

As we hurried past him, I nodded and said,

"Hi, Major!"

We quickly got into prone positions along a dirt bank, weapons trained down the road at the approaching truck. Two members of the patrol stepped from cover and stopped it, discovering the occupants to be *friendlies*. Two regular infantry Marines, acting as guards, and two cooks riding in the truck were on their way to deliver food to the United Nations Representatives in Panmunjom when they became confused with directions and lost their way. One Marine, who had been walking ahead of the truck when we saw them earlier, had stepped on a mine. The others were returning with the wounded man, hoping to find their way back to friendly territory to get aid. The Marine's foot was badly mangled and the other leg had absorbed a lot of the blast. He'd gone into shock and from the looks of the poor kid I wouldn't have given a plugged nickel for his survival. A corpsman, stationed with the men manning the outpost, hurried down to give him aid and soon had him ready for transport back to an aid station.

As we gathered together ready to return to our lines, the Marine whom I had thought was a major, congratulated us for our quick thinking and efficiency, giving us a *well done*. I noticed then that he was not wearing the gold leaf of a major but the single silver star of a Brigadier General.

"God, I've stepped in it again. Boy, Veep! This time you've insulted a general."

We were hot, dirty, tired and quite relieved when we got back to our bunkers. That was one of the strangest patrols I'd ever been on. The Chinese knew we were out there and yet they didn't fire one single round of mortars or light artillery at us. Why? A lot of things happened that could have been disastrous. A lot of things didn't happen that should have. Why?

As I tried to rub the aches and pains out of my bare feet, I shivered thinking about how close I'd come to stepping on a mine earlier in the day. I wondered how many times I had nearly stepped on one since being in Korea, how many narrow misses I'd had with shrapnel and gunfire. Thinking about all of the close calls I'd had during the past year made me feel certain that there was nothing left in my bag of lucky charms. Some of my good fortune could be attributed to training, some to experience and some to determination, but most of it was just plain good luck.

Leo Plick was determined to drink his entire ration of beer that evening before something else happened to prevent him from enjoying it. These were not small bottles, either—not like the popular stubby-sized bottles at home. They were nearer quart size. Drinking one bottle was all I could handle because alcoholic beverages, no matter how tame, made me dizzy. Besides, beer went right through me. On the other hand, Leo downed his ration of beer in no time at all—including my remaining bottle. His ability to consume so much of it in so little time was mystifying. I could never understand how he could hold it all without peeing in his pants.

Chapter XVI

Farewell, My Brothers

A few days after the patrol, word came to me to report to the Company command post on the double. I wondered what the heck I'd done this time because I'd been behaving for a change. Then it hit me.

"Could it be how I'd addressed the general when I mistakenly called him major?"

The company commander, the top sergeant, and an office pinky were in the captain's tent when I entered. The captain told me to stand at ease as the top soldier handed a folder of papers to him that I assumed were about me.

Looking at them for a moment, he looked up and asked,

"How would you like to spend some time in the rear at Division?"

At first I thought he was referring to spending time in the brig but both men were grinning. As the captain continued to speak, I realized he was telling me that I was going to be transferred to the rear to safety. I heard the words he was saying but I could hardly believe them. Afraid that I would begin bawling like a baby, I could only nod in the affirmative. He told me to get my gear packed and be back in a half hour to catch a jeep south. My new assignment would be with the Public Information Office at Division Headquarters for the remainder of my time in Korea. I was getting out of the war. As I left the Captain's tent, the top sergeant whacked me on the rump giving me a final order.

"You got thirty minutes to get back here, Pileggi. Durin' that time, I want you to keep yer dumb ass down and don't get shot. I want you outa here in one piece."

Still not quite believing what I'd heard and a bit dazed, I asked myself,

"Do you realize what this means? No more patrols, no more ambushes, no more artillery, no more snipers and no more damned mines to worry about."

I was ecstatic and giddy, grinning like a Cheshire cat, feeling as if I'd been relieved of a huge burden. Then it hit me. What about Louie and Leo and O'Malley and Dickie and Ollie and all the others? I was leaving but they were remaining. My elation quickly faded and I began to feel guilt, as if I were running out on them, as if I were turning away from them when they needed me the most. I knew they would want me to go. If Louie had the chance to leave I'd want him to go, and as fast as he could.

Hurrying back to my bunker to pack my gear, I wondered if they could survive without me. Then I began wondering if I could survive without them. I knew I'd better pack or I might do something stupid like change my mind. This was my chance and I had to take it.

As I packed, I told Dickie that I was leaving, being transferred back to division. After stuffing a pair of clean socks into my pocket, I was ready to go. Dickie was just standing there, fiddling with a button on his jacket, staring dejectedly at the ground. I felt terrible, absolutely rotten, not knowing what to say. I wanted to see his face light up with that big grin just once more but it never came. Putting my arm around his shoulder, I gave him a big squeeze and said,

"*Keep yer butt down, buddy, watch the shadows and stay off the skyline.*"

Grabbing my pack and rifle, I forced out a choked farewell to my BAR man.

"*Goodbye, Dickie!*"

Within seconds I was going down the trench toward a waiting jeep. I found Leo on the way and presented him with the clean socks along with a lot of good-natured sass. Then Louie. Saying goodbye to this loveable, cagey little bastard was the toughest thing I ever did in my life. My eyes filled with tears and my lips quivered when I told him I was leaving. I tried to reassure myself that I would see him again on the ship when we sailed for the States. He, too, was struggling with his emotions but he was able to keep them under control. But I couldn't and I began to bawl. Trying to let me go the best way he could without breaking down himself, he said,

"*Youse don't be a big baby, now, Pledge.*"

He just had to show me that he was still a tough guy, but I wasn't about to let the jerk off that easy and managed to speak a few curt words.

"*Louie! Kiss my mangy butt!*"

Some kind of man-thing prevents young men from hugging each other and displaying their emotions. But, I didn't care. I loved Louie more than a brother and I wanted to say goodbye in my way with a hug. He nearly turned purple with embarrassment when I began putting my arms around him. Pushing against my chest with his hands, he asked with a voice reaching into the range of a soprano,

"*What the hell youse doin' Pledge?*"

"*Shut up, Louie!*"

This was one time that he had no choice and wasn't going to tell me what to do. I embraced him tightly, whispered goodbye to one hell of a friend and left. A few minutes later I was gone, slouched down in a jeep bouncing along on a dirt road, tears flowing unashamedly down my cheeks.

If I'd had the time, I would have hugged everyone in the company. I was so damned proud of those guys. Our souls were forever welded together in a mystical, almost spiritual bond that would never fade with time or age. The horrors and misery of war had done this. It forever united us as it had the men who survived countless other wars. I wondered,

"How many Easy Companies have existed over time?"

This was a joyous day for me in one sense but also a terribly sad one. I had survived nearly a year of this misery. But the guilt I felt for leaving my friends behind was overwhelming. I loved them, this family of unique individuals. They had become a huge part of my life. I was taking a little of them with me and leaving a little of me behind with them. I knew that it was time for me to go, and it was time for me to let go. Soon I'd be safe. No more tenseness, no more jangled nerves, no more fear. Now I could forget about looking for trip wires, diving into the dirt when a twig snapped or ducking merely because a bird flew by. I could look forward to living instead of dodging danger. I was going to safety and eventually I was going home.

The Little Corporal

The jeep ride to Division Headquarters seemed to take forever, probably because my mind swirled with every emotion imaginable. An hour ago, my mind was filled with worry and dreadful thoughts about the tank patrol and mines and firefights and now it was filled with relief and the knowledge that I was suddenly out of the war. All of these events were difficult to fully absorb in so short a time, and I must admit that I wasn't completely convinced that this transfer to the rear was something permanent, something real. But the appearance of increased vehicle traffic and more and more Korean civilians proved that I was indeed headed south away from that dreadful war.

We arrived at Division Headquarters, a huge compound of buildings, tents and semi-permanent huts. The place was a beehive of activity, Marines everywhere and every other one of them an officer. I never saw so much brass in one place. Other than the sentries and military police, no one wore a helmet and everyone was clean-shaven and wore clean uniforms. And here I was, a typical bunker rat, unshaven and dirty with a rifle slung on my shoulder wearing a dented helmet and clothing that undoubtedly stunk like it had been stored in a chicken coop. Feeling horribly out of place, I had no doubts whatsoever that military discipline was strictly enforced here just as if this was MCRD or Camp Pendleton.

The driver stopped and, pointing to a tent, told me to report inside. A couple of privates first class and a corporal were exiting as I was entering. They stopped dead in their tracks and just stared at me. I paused also, looking at them, because they appeared so incredibly young, so remarkably clean. I stopped in front of a desk occupied by a second lieutenant and came to attention. When the lieutenant looked up, I saluted and reported, handing my orders to him. He looked puzzled no doubt because of my scruffy, dirty, shaggy appearance. After reviewing my orders, he summoned a corporal, introduced him to me as Corporal Fox and informed me that the corporal would give me my daily assignments while stationed here. Then the lieutenant instructed the corporal to direct me to the nearest shower as soon as I'd dumped my gear in my new living quarters. Shower! What a beautiful word that was to my ears.

Corporal Fox had been in the Marine Corps all of eight or nine months and looked to be no older than eighteen years of age. He was a typical spit and polish office pinky with a baby face and a runny nose. He was polite but at the same time a little on the arrogant side leaving no doubt that he considered himself the boss. He readily agreed with me that my first priorities were to take a hot shower, shave with warm water, and get some clean clothing. Before the day had ended, I, too, had discarded my helmet for a dungaree cap.

The tent that was to be my home for the next three or four weeks contained three cots, a small stove, table, folding chairs, and was illuminated by one bare electric light bulb. After sleeping in a hole in the ground, it looked as plush, comfortable and inviting as the Benson Hotel in downtown Portland. But, to my chagrin, this was also Corporal Fox's quarters.

Another short-timer Marine fresh from combat joined me. He, too, was assigned temporarily to division awaiting orders to go home. Gibson, whose nickname was *Hoot*, was a likeable, agreeable Southern boy. We found that we had a lot in common, our companies, our platoons, the guilt we felt leaving friends behind. And we both noticed the quietness of this place. No noise. No booming artillery or the distant clatter of machine guns. Not hearing the sounds of war was strange, eerily strange and almost spooky.

Fox didn't bother us nor did he speak but a few words to us during the first few days, probably because he had orders to leave us alone. But when he finally gave us some assignments, they were menial tasks such as running errands, policing the area around the PIO tents and delivering messages. The most interesting chore given us was disposing of thousands and thousands of old military photographs. It was easy duty—very easy duty—and the hot chow was pretty good too. Thank God, no more c-rations.

Fox was not very demanding of me but for some reason he kept harping at Gibson. Once, he made Gibby remake his bunk and another time, he got on Gibson for slouching. I soon found out why he left me alone. He'd spotted the faded, barely visible stenciled sergeant's chevrons on the sleeves of my dungaree jacket when I first reported in and he believed that I was a sergeant. It was the same jacket that I'd gotten when we moved to the West Coast a couple of months ago. Gibson knew that I was a PFC but he never let on to Corporal Fox and neither did I.

Several days passed when I was summoned to the lieutenant's office and informed that I'd been promoted to corporal. By the end of day, I had stenciled the new rank of corporal on my sleeves. Fox was startled when he saw the bold, black corporal stripes and asked if I'd been busted.

"Naw, I just got promoted."

Momentarily stumped, he suddenly became livid.

"You mean to tell me that you weren't a sergeant but a PFC all along?"

"That's right!"

He stammered and sputtered like an idiot.

"Well, I'm still your senior. You just remember that."

I'd really had my fill of the little bastard and told him so.

"Why don't you grow up, Foxy? Having two stripes doesn't make you a man or better than anyone else. And you'd better lay off Gibson. We'll do our jobs but if you keep screwin' with him and giving him your smart mouth crap, he's gonna shove an M1 up yer ass and, he won't just squeeze the trigger, he'll jerk it."

We had no more trouble with Fox. He gave us our daily assignments, we completed them, and he left us alone.

Hurry Up and Wait

After three-plus weeks, Gibson and I left Division Headquarters and joined a couple thousand other Marines bivouacked near Inchon Harbor, all short-timers and all waiting to board a ship destined to take us home. The men were giddy and euphoric and especially elated when they ran into old buddies they hadn't seen for a year. The story telling was non-stop. The scene was mostly joyful but sometimes it turned sad when one of us found out a friend had been killed. While wandering around through a horde of guys, I heard a familiar voice behind me say,

"*Hey, Pledge, youse big ox.*"

"*Holy Catfish! Louie Caruso!*"

I wheeled around and there he stood with his hands on his hips and his head cocked to one side, smoking a cigarette. What a sight he was. The dumb little jerk was safe and sound and all the worrying I did about him had been for naught. I damned near bawled but I couldn't have been happier. And then we found Leo Plick, Johnny Pompeo, John O'Malley, Prevost and Proietti and a host of others from Easy Company, all bound for home. It felt good to be together again and to know that we would soon be out of harm's way.

Some of the others had been transferred out to various units in the rear also but those who remained with the Company soon brought us up to date about what had happened after we'd gone. The rumored tank patrol became a reality and we took some casualties. Then the platoon pulled dreaded outpost duty and were hit hard one night, suffering several wounded and a few killed. The names of the dead were not familiar to me but several of the wounded were. Dickie Haymon was one but, thankfully, his wound wasn't serious enough to keep him out of action. But a few had suffered injuries so grievous that they never returned.

And when the company went back into reserve, early one morning, some jerk blew up the big "E" shaking the men out of their sleep. They found it shattered, blown to pieces. The consensus was that the culprit was from another company and he'd used an explosive called *primer cord* wrapping it around the poles that held the Company symbol in place. The top sergeant was so damned angry that an egg could have been fried on his forehead. It was soon restored to its place in front of the company command tent and a 24-hour armed sentry was assigned to patrol around it with orders to shoot anyone loitering too close, and that included officers.

We all were antsy and wanted to get underway but it just wasn't going to happen that quickly. We hung around and waited and waited and waited for orders to assemble for boarding our ship. Reclaiming the sea-bag I hadn't seen for a year, I pawed through my belongings and found that nothing fit except my dress shoes. Because I'd lost so much weight, everything hung on me like a sack. The clothing smelled stale and was horribly wrinkled but at least it was clean, cleaner than anything we'd been wearing for the past year.

After a couple of boring days, we finally got the word to *saddle up* and prepare to board ship. But it was the same old thing, hurry up and wait. And that's exactly what we did, waiting in line for another three or four hours before being allowed to go aboard. The first thing I did was claim a top rack remembering what could happen to those sleeping below if someone above them got sick.

Finally underway, we left Korea, some of our friends, and the war behind. The ship was a magnificent, new, modern U. S. Navy troop ship. It didn't take long, though, maybe three or four hours at sea, before this beautiful, new, modern U. S. Navy troop ship had turned into one huge puke-bucket. As I claimed a place at the rail, I recalled how sick I'd been on the old Cavalier. At least this thing was headed in the right direction and I figured I could at least put up with being seasick for a couple of weeks.

Just before departure, twin brothers, who had been assigned to different units, had heard the other brother had been killed in combat. But it wasn't true and they found each other on the ship. I could never, never describe the tearful, emotional reunion those two had and the raucous celebration that followed. Watching them hug each other and cry and laugh made us all feel good, anticipating that our own happy homecoming would soon take place.

The ship stopped in Sasebo, Japan remaining one full day to pick up several hundred Air Force personnel. These were the same guys who were on the ship when we left the States to go to Korea. But now, instead of being lowly airmen, nearly every one of them had been promoted to staff or technical sergeant. With the exception of a few corporals, most of us Marines were still privates first class. Immediately, there was grumbling among us. We'd been sleeping in mud and getting our asses shot off while the crumbs in the Air Force ate hot chow, slept in cozy beds in a heated building, went out on the town at night, and then got promoted with big increases in pay. What kind of crap was that? Adding insult to injury, we had to pull mess duty on the ship and wait on the cruds.

Four or five days before reaching San Diego, we encountered rough weather. The tossing of the ship was exaggerated three-fold caused by the large ocean swells. One of us walking across the mess-deck carting a vat of hard-boiled eggs tripped and suddenly there were several hundred boiled eggs rolling loose, back and forth on the ship's deck. It was ugly. We seasick bastards tried to corral the runaway eggs but, even on our hands and knees, it was like trying to pick overripe grapes while wearing boxing gloves. Every single one was smashed, the deck covered with a gooey stinking yellow paste. It was awful ugly. The foul stench of vomit mixed with the offensive odor of crushed hard-boiled eggs would have turned the stomach of a turkey buzzard.

The Good Old U. S. A.

Not many slept during our last night on the ship. Every man picked the cleanest, neatest uniform he could find, even if it was a mix of summer and winter clothing. The best I had was a set of khakis that sagged on me like a hop-picker's sack. Everyone who was able had gone topside and had crowded against the rails of the ship, straining and craning their necks, looking for land. Even seasickness couldn't dampen my jubilation when I first saw the faint outline of the good old United States on the horizon. As our ship sailed ever closer to land, buildings began to appear. Strangely, we were quiet and tense, almost taut like bowstrings. You could have heard a pin drop on the deck. We were waiting, just waiting to see people, our families, anyone, just as long as they were Americans.

As we entered San Diego bay, a flotilla of fireboats, yachts, and skiffs greeted us with blasts of horns, sirens and streams of water shooting skyward. A deafening, escalating chorus of whistles and cheers suddenly broke the dead silence as a bevy of beautiful young girls appeared atop one of the yachts, dancing and waving and throwing kisses. The men went nuts and it's somewhat of a miracle that no one fell overboard. The yacht with the girls swung around from one side of the ship to the other and as they did, Marines and Air Force personnel followed them running from one side of the ship to the other. Over the roar and cheers of the men, one girl shouted out a telephone number and, if it was hers, I'll bet money she got no less than eight hundred telephone calls that night.

Feeling caged, we wanted off that ship in the worst way but it seemed to take forever to dock and secure it. A crowd of people, families, dads, moms, girlfriends, waited anxiously on the dock waving, screaming, laughing joyously, and dancing. I knew that my mom and dad weren't there to greet me but, even so, my time would soon come. For now, I wanted off that bucket just to put my feet back on American soil.

As we stepped off the gangplank, boot Marines took our seabags and escorted us to waiting buses ready to transport us to the Marine Corps Recruit Depot. A cordon of Marines held the crowd back but one of

Somebody's mom

the guys spotted his mother in the crowd and made a mad dash for her. No force on this earth could have kept them apart and he easily broke through, sweeping her up in his arms. Many of us, including me, stopped to watch this tearful but joyful reunion of a grateful mother and her loving son.

Transported to MCRD, we were housed in Quonset huts. But we weren't allowed to go anywhere, restricted to the base until we had been given a thorough physical examination and instructions about reentering the civilian world. We'd been living like animals for a year and had developed several bad habits. For instance, our language was so foul it would have embarrassed a longshoreman and we had to be reminded to use toilets now instead of peeing in roadside ditches.

The cots in the huts were comfortable but, nonetheless, I couldn't sleep feeling too much excitement and wanting desperately to get on the road for home. When morning came, we took soothing, luxurious, warm showers and ate a true American breakfast. The day began serenely enough but then around 9:00 A.M. a rumor of a clothing inspection went through our ranks like bean soup through a duck. A clothing inspection! Why in the hell, I wondered, do we have to have a clothing inspection?

We soon found out when we fell into formation for roll call and to receive instructions for the day. An officer informed us that our sea-bags were to be emptied on our racks and the contents arranged in some kind of order for inspection. They weren't just checking our clothing, though.

> *"In two hours, two officers will enter each of the huts looking for weaponry, any military ordnance, ammunition or explosives. It is a court martial offense to possess these things. You cannot take any of it home with you. And we know some of you have this stuff. We've placed ponchos at the entry of every hut. After dismissal from this formation, you will have two hours to get rid of it. Place it on the ponchos outside your huts and no questions will be asked. That's all. Fall out!"*

Ponchos had indeed been placed at the entry to every Quonset hut. Nearly two hours later, I stepped out of my hut and saw piles and piles of military hardware including BARs, burp guns, hand grenades, rockets, sixty-millimeter mortar tubes, flares and thousands of rounds of ammunition. There was enough crap on those ponchos to launch a revolution in just about any South American country. When the two Marine officers entered our Quonset hut, they merely looked around, walking from one end to the other, and then left not bothering to ruffle through one single bunk or sea-bag. It was a good thing too, because I gambled and kept a fragmentation grenade, a bayonet and a dozen rounds of the Red Army's rifle ammunition as souvenirs.

Passing my physical examination, three days after leaving the ship, I was handed my orders and given a thirty-day leave. I was finally going home.

Home

Leaving San Diego Recruit Depot early in the morning, I boarded a passenger train with another Marine who was destined for his home in Vancouver, Washington. It had been a year and a half since I'd last seen my family. The last letter I'd written to Mom and Dad was three weeks earlier when I was still in Korea, telling them that I would soon be aboard a ship returning to the States. They knew that I was coming but they had no idea when I would arrive. Neither had I. To pass the time trying to escape the memories of that horrible, dreadful war, I daydreamed just like I had during those lonely, dismal nights on the lines.

With every bump and groan the train made, I knew I was getting closer and closer to home and my family. Listening to the *clickity-clack* sound of the Pullman coach wheels on the uneven rails as the train lumbered along reminded me of a movie that Dad had taken us to when I was in the eighth grade. In one of the scenes, a train going down railroad tracks, quite like the train I was riding, made similar sounds prompting one of the movie characters to imitate them, *clickity-clack, clickity-clack, clickity-clack.* On the way home from the movie, Dad did the same as the actor, mimicking the sounds our car's tires made on the highway. "*Heinemehnooshka, Heinemehnooshka, Heinemehnooshka!*" My little brother Dee loved what Dad was doing so much that he giggled and giggled like little boys do when they are happily entertained. For several years thereafter, Dad called him, *Heinemehnooshka.*

The train finally arrived in Portland in the early evening of the second day. Hoisting my sea-bag onto my shoulder, I exited the Pullman, found a taxicab, and asked the driver how much he'd charge to take me to Sherwood. He looked at my dress uniform and said,

"Normally, it would be fifteen dollars but for a Leatherneck I'll do it for ten."

He put the sea bag in the trunk and opened the cab's back door for me. But, I didn't want to ride in the back,

"This is really great, but would you mind if I ride in the front with you?"

With a big grin, he nodded and said,

"Not at all, Marine. Hop in."

The cab driver was a swell guy, easy to talk to, and I'm sure he sensed my elation and also my nervousness. By the time we arrived home, it was completely dark. I asked him not to drive down the driveway to the house, but to stop on the railroad tracks so I could walk the final one-hundred-fifty-feet. But I didn't get out right away. I sat there for just a moment, drinking in the scene before me. When I offered him an extra two dollars as a tip, he refused and, with a smile, shook my hand.

"No! You keep it son and good luck to you."

I threw my sea-bag on my shoulder, and as I began to walk slowly down the familiar, rutted drive to the house, tears began welling up in my eyes. Everything looked so good to me, so inviting, so memorable: the railroad tracks, the pump house, outline of the trees in the dark. And the house windows—they were lit up as if it were Christmas...just like they'd done it for me.

By then, the family had seen the headlights of the cab. At first they had no inkling of who had come. But the kids, sticking their heads out the door, suddenly realized it was their big brother. Pouring out of the house, they yelled, screamed, laughed and cried—nonstop for minutes. I was so overwhelmed by their joy and loving welcome that I could do nothing but sob uncontrollably and hold onto them, hugging each and every one of them over and over. Dee took my sea bag and, surprisingly, slung it up on his shoulder with ease. As we entered the house, I noticed the cab was just leaving. The driver had been sitting there, taking in the entire joyous reunion of one grateful Marine.

Grandmother had retired early and, still in bed, was calling for someone to tell her what all the commotion was about. Sliding the curtain open to her bedroom, I said,

"It's me, Grandma."

Kneeling beside her bed, we embraced in a teary reunion, as the rest of the family crowded in with us, everyone talking at the same time. Over and over, she cried,

"Thank God, Oh, thank God."

Charla, still too young to understand why all the tears, asked her grandmother,

"Why are you crying, Grandma? Are you sad?"

"Gosh no, child. I'm cryin' because I'm so durned happy."

Confessing, I told her there were times that, while under fire, I had serious doubts that I'd survive the war and worried that I'd never again see her, wishing I'd been a better kid and not so blasted ornery.

"Yes, you were a little stinker at times, but, you were a good boy, Teddy."

My brothers and sisters had grown so much during the time I had been gone and I missed being involved in the family's activities. My youngest sister, Charla, was no longer a small child but an impish little rascal who could run like a jackrabbit. It was impossible to catch her whenever she did something mischievous. My sister Theresa was turning into a sweet young lady and Tom was soon to leave home to be married. Dick had become the mechanic in the family, repairing our old outdated farm machinery, and Dee, as tall and nearly as strong as Dad, had assumed the role as protector of our little sisters. And Mom, Dad and Grandma…gosh, they looked so good to me.

Sitting around the kitchen table for several hours, we talked nonstop about everything under the sun. So accustomed to talking to Marines, an occasional expletive slipped out of my mouth, causing me a good deal of embarrassment. Asking question after question, I couldn't get answers quickly enough and Maggie, my sweetheart, was also on my mind. And, of course, I hungered for Mom's cooking and was determined to regain some of the forty pounds I'd lost. We went to bed late but, too excited, I couldn't sleep. I don't believe anyone did.

Nearly two months had passed since I'd left Easy Company and my friends. And yet, the confusion and unsettled feelings still persisted; like none of this was permanent and I'd have to go back. Feelings of guilt constantly tormented me too. It seemed unfair that I was home enjoying life with my family while my Marine friends were still in harm's way with the likelihood that some would never again see their loved ones. And I was still jumpy and nervous; odd noises sent me diving to the ground or darting behind things. I wanted to be a normal person again but I wasn't…I just wasn't.

The following afternoon, as we were sitting around the kitchen table having a snack and catching up on recent events that had occurred in the family, a neighbor clearing land set off a charge of dynamite to blow a stump. When I heard the blast, to everyone's utter amazement, I instinctively ducked under the table, covering my head. That was not the last time I reacted that way, either. A few days later, while walking down the driveway with Dee and Charla, I heard a twig snap in the nearby underbrush. To me, it sounded much like the pop a hand grenade makes when the spoon has been released. Again, instinctively, I grabbed my surprised brother, who was walking beside me, and took him with me, diving into the ditch.

A few days later, Dad and I went for a stroll down the familiar rutted dirt road through the woods to the barn. Alone for a change, neither of us said much but I didn't care whether we talked or not; I just wanted to soak up the surroundings and be with my Pop.

Walking beside this pudgy little man that I loved so much, I realized just how much I'd missed his fatherly protection, his strength, his guidance. At that very moment, I knew that I needed him then more than ever.

"Dad!"

My voice barely audible, I thought surely he hadn't heard me. But he had. As if he knew that I was struggling with my emotions, as if he knew that I needed his help, his solace, his support, he said nothing, just put his arms around me and embraced me with the strength, warmth and comfort that I'd missed for so long. In an instant, the hopelessness, the despair, the uncertainty of that horrible war gushed from me like a flood. With my head buried in his shoulder, I broke down, utterly and completely, sobbing like a helpless little child suffering from a terrible hurt.

In my dad's arms, I found relief; I found hope and security. I was home.

END

BATTLE HONORS

Recommendation

Citation of Unit

The 2nd Battalion, 7th Marines, 1st Marine Division (reinforced) is cited for extraordinary heroism, superb professional performance in battle, and outstanding devotion to duty in action against the armed enemy in the Chunchon-Hwachon-Yanggu area during the period April 1, 1951 to June 21, 1951.

The 2nd Battalion, 7th Marines, fighting for an extended period, over extremely rugged and mountainous terrain, successfully executed every combat mission assigned and inflicted staggering losses of personnel and materiel on the enemy forces encountered. Without exception, the Battalion decisively and efficiently accomplished each of its missions within the time specified by higher headquarters.

The advances of the Battalion from Hongchon to the Kunn-ni Korea (Quantico Line) from April 1 to April 23 and again the advance from Hongchon to Muhak (Brown Line) from May 24 to June 21 were executed with aggressiveness, skill and decisive action. The oppressing enemy was well disciplined, well armed, and stubborn. He defended fanatically from heavily reinforced bunker and earthworks, located on commanding precipitous terrain, and employed to his utmost advantage artillery, mortar, small arms, mines and grenades in his attempts to halt the advance of the Battalion. On one occasion during the period June 8 to June 21 Northeast of Yanggu, this Battalion virtually annihilated two Battalions of the 152nd Infantry Division, 5th North Korean Corps by a series of determined bloody attacks.

During the period April 23 to April 27, the Battalion executed with particular precision and skill an extremely difficult retrograde movement from Kunn-ni to Hongchon under heavy enemy pressure. Assigned the missions of disengaging from action with the enemy, providing support for adjacent friendly units and protecting the withdrawal of the other disengaging units this Battalion displayed outstanding heroism and tactical coordination in the execution of the regimental plan. Despite the enemy's overwhelming numbers and the skillful employment of his forces, his attacks against friendly units were effectively prevented. During this time on April 24 southwest of Hwachon, the 2nd Battalion completely destroyed one Battalion of the 358th Regiment, 120th Infantry Division, the 40th CCF corps and decimated other elements of that Regiment during a savagely fought battle.

For 75 of the 82 days of the period covered by this citation, this Battalion was in constant contact with the enemy and continually carried the fight to him. The heavy physical demands made on the troops by the long hours of attacking over mountainous torturous terrain, the strain induced by maintaining fifty percent of all personnel on watch each night, and the exhaustion arising from the protracted period of combat without rest or relief accentuates the accomplishments of the Battalion in battle.

Although sustaining fifty percent casualties and experiencing an additional marked replacement of key personnel during this period, the Battalion continued to perform its duties with the undiminished spirit, courage and skill which have characterized all its operations.

Battle Honors

The 2nd Battalion during this period inflicted over 2600 casualties, including prisoners of war, on the enemy. Tremendous amounts of equipment and supplies which the enemy could ill-afford to lose, were captured or destroyed including large quantities of medical supplies, demolitions, food, transportation, rifles, and pistols. This material included: 150,000 rounds small arms ammunition, 21,000 mortar shells, 11,000 hand grenades, 1600 artillery shells, 30 mortars and machine guns.

By their gallantry in action, aggressiveness in battle and devotion to duty, the members of the 2nd Battalion, 7th Marines reflect great credit on themselves and their organization and have upheld the highest tradition of the United States Armed Forces.

/s/ *Major James F. Lawrence, S3*

A Tribute To A Valiant Marine – One Hero of Many

Vonnie Pitts was just an average guy who hailed from the state of Texas. He was my friend and, although he wasn't an Easy Company Marine, I need to tell you this story about him, to tell you what torture he'd endured during a brief but traumatic period in his life. For all I know, he might still be suffering.

During the fall of 1951, the entire First Marine Division was involved in a general offensive in the eastern sector of Korea. Vonnie's company, having successfully taken some nameless ridge, had come under a ferocious counterattack by North Korean suicide squads. One of his company's machine gun sections, trapped on the forward slope of the ridge, was running perilously low on ammunition and desperately needed help. Enemy dead were piling up barely fifty yards in front of the gun; so many that other enemy soldiers were able to crawl close to the beleaguered squad, using their comrades' bodies for cover.

Vonnie's squad was on the reverse slope of the ridge trying to re-supply the gunners with ammunition. But each time a man darted toward them, he was downed by enemy fire. It was Vonnie's turn to go. He was no hero; he wasn't looking for medals but the Marines are trained to do things without thinking of themselves. And Vonnie was well trained. Even though frightened beyond belief, he was ready and determined. He grabbed two cans of machine gun ammunition but before his squad leader could get the word *GO* out of his mouth, the young Marine's shoes had already kicked up dirt, propelling him forward. The distance to the gun was only some fifty yards but it might as well have been five hundred. Fearing he'd step on a mine if he ran too far off the narrow trail, he crouched, bobbed and weaved as he sprinted forward, trying to make a poor target. Leaping over the body of one of his buddies who'd gone down on a previous attempt, he was about to hurdle another when he was hit. His body slammed to the earth but, somehow, he managed to hang onto both cans of ammunition. Still conscious, he rolled onto his right side and found a gaping hole in his left shoulder. He'd been shot from behind.

He screamed a warning to his squad,

"They're behind us! They're behind us!"

The roar of gunfire, grenades and mortars was deafening but Vonnie's squad leader heard his desperate cries. They knew it had to be a sniper. Turning their attention to the terrain behind them, they determined the only place one could be hidden and able to see the trail was from a tree seventy-five yards to their rear. Every man in the Texan's squad, who was still alive and still able in body, turned his weapon on it and riddled every inch of its foliage. They were right; a North Korean sniper fell dead from its branches.

With the threat eliminated, Marines poured over the ridge, re-supplying the machine gunners and, with the added men, repelled the attackers. Vonnie was still conscious but barely when they got to him. And he was still clutching the cans of ammunition and trying to crawl forward.

His wound treated, he was placed on a stretcher and prepared for evacuation. But, the enemy got one more crack at him before he could be carried to safety. The entire ridge was plastered by a devastating barrage of mortars, one of them striking so close that it literally blew him out of the stretcher. He was wounded a second time, peppered by bits of shrapnel. Again treated, the second attempt to get him off the hill was successful and he was eventually transported to a hospital in Japan. He recovered from his wounds but his life was changed forever.

A Tribute to a Valiant Marine

Back in the States, Vonnie and I were assigned to the same infantry platoon in Camp Pendleton, California, training young Marines, preparing them for combat in Korea. We often used blank ammunition to create a little realism during training exercises, trying to simulate actual combat. It proved too real.

One day, Vonnie acted as a defender in a foxhole as several young Marines charged his position, firing blanks at him. Without warning, he exploded from his hole, screaming, and attacked them, using his rifle as a club. In self-defense, they overwhelmed him and pinned him to the ground. Sobbing, he whimpered over and over,

"They're behind us! They're behind us!"

His mind had snapped and he'd reverted back to the battles he'd fought in Korea.

The last time I saw this valiant Marine; he was again strapped to a stretcher, his body quivering and convulsing uncontrollably. He was never again to be a completely whole and sane person, living the war over and over again in his mind.

It was a nightmarish fate for a true hero. Vonnie Pitts, my friend, was just one of many.

Acknowledgments

With my gratitude, I thank these people who helped me immensely in compiling this story.

Carol Dunlap, editing
Patricia Love, editing
Susie Pileggi, editing
Ardis Schroeder, editing
Stuart Sparkman, editing
Rebekah Wozniak-Gelzer, editing
Hinrich Muller, design, graphics, and page layout

James F. Lawrence, Brigadier-General USMC retired
John (Jack) Lilley, Colonel USMC retired
Embree Maxson, Lt. Colonel USMC retired
Timothy O'Reilly, Colonel USMC retired
James VanAirsdale, Lt. Colonel USMC retired
Jerry (J. J.) Miller, Major USMC retired
Donald Greenlaw, Captain USMC retired
George E. Foster, CWO4 USMC
Clyde H. Bridge, Jr.
Lehman (Chief) Brightman
Thomas Edward Bullock
Louis J. Caruso

Lewis (John) Channey
Earl Boyce Clark, USMC retired
Hoyt Hutchinson
Donald Francis Kirk, USN
Harry Levitt
William Jon (W. J.) Miller
Alan Murphy
Jack Wilkins Mills
John J. O'Malley
Bobby Ogden
Robert Oliver
Johnny Pompeo
Larry L. Pressley
Edward Prevost
Danny Proietti
Robert C. Rice, USN
Loren Tracy
Troy Watson
Donald Young

Marines E-2-7 Roster, August 1951, Korea

Lilley, John R. II	2Lt	Burdick, Charles J.	PFC
Martin, Reginald G.	2Lt	Burke, Richard J.	Cpl
Mc Kelvey, James E.	2Lt	Burkett, William B.	Sgt
Monti, Anthony A.	2Lt	Burkhardt, Frank G.	Cpl
Pelham, George F. II	2Lt	Burzumato, Carmine	PFC
		Busby, Milburn E.	Cpl
Bingaman, William L.	Cpl	Byerley, Philip T.	PFC
Birney, Gerald D.	Cpl	Caffiero, Joseph W.	PFC
Bitting, Jack H.	PFC	Cairns, Forrest B.	PFC
Blackburn, James A.	PFC	Caltry, Paul C.	PFC
Blackwater, Louis T.	PFC	Campbell, Clair D.	PFC
Blake, John L.	Cpl	Campbell, Donald L.	Sgt
Blankenship, John M.	Cpl	Campbell, Virgil R.	Sgt
Blanton, Charles B.	PFC	Capper, James S.	PFC
Blayney, William V.	Sgt	Carlson, William H.	PFC
Bode, William N.	PFC	Caruso, Louis J.	PFC
Bogue, Thomas, Jr.	Cpl	Chalcraft, Walter J.	Sgt
Bolduc, Donald N.	Cpl	Channey, Lewis E.	Cpl
Bolton, William E.	Cpl	Chavez, Alfonso V.	Cpl
Bouchard, Robert J.	PFC	Chino, Lawrence A.	Cpl
Bowman, Donald L.	Cpl	Clabby, Vernon E.	Sgt
Brabham, Keith H.	PFC	Collins, John J.	Cpl
Brannon, William E.	PFC	Corcoran, Matthew G.	PFC
Brazell, Burnett C.	Cpl	Cornelius, Earl F.	PFC
Brelet, Clayton P.	PFC	Coulter, James R.	PFC
Bridge, Clyde H. Jr.	PFC	Couser, Robert H.	PFC
Brinlee, Henry L.	PFC	Cowan, Wallace R.	PFC
Brown, Lonnie R.	PFC	Cox, Bernard W.	Cpl
Broz, Eugene E.	PFC	Cranmer, Paul I.	PFC
Brubaker, Dale F.	Cpl	Crawford, Ian C.	PFC
Buie, Chauncey G.	PFC	Creaghe, Charles S.	PFC
Bullock, Thomas E.	PFC	Creel, Charles E.	PFC
Bunce, Donald E.	PFC	Cremin, Edward J.	PFC

Crockett, David	PFC	Hallett, Richard R.	PFC
Cunningham, Gerald	PFC	Hamlet, Ben F.	PFC
Curtin, Richard E.	PFC	Hanks, Francis H.	Cpl
Danna, Charles A.	PFC	Hanson, Dougles M.	PFC
Daray, Louis F.	PFC	Hanson, Robert E.	Cpl
Daughtery, Ebb	PFC	Harding, Robert F.	PFC
Deluise, Alphonse J.	Cpl	Hargis, Robert L.	Cpl
Donald, Charles W.	PFC	Harvey, John F.	Cpl
Douglas, William H.	PFC	Haumacher, Joseph C.	PFC
Ellison, Carl A. Jr.	PFC	Hawkins, Buddy D.	PFC
Evans, Edward S.	PFC	Heidrick, George A.	SSgt
Fank, Earl T. Jr.	PFC	Helms, Billy G.	Cpl
Faulstich, Charles	PFC	Hirata, Manuel H.	Sgt
Fenton, Robert A.	Sgt	Hoga, James F.	Pvt
Feola, Phillip	PFC	Holmes, John B.	Cpl
Ferrell, Charles F.	PFC	Houlihan, Thomas J.	Sgt
Fields, Ralph E.	PFC	Hurt, Toulman W. Jr.	PFC
Finley, Glenn G.	PFC	Huth, Charles J.	PFC
Fisher, William E.	Sgt	Jackson, John L.	PFC
Fitzgerald, Patrick	PFC	Jaramillo, Victor	PFC
Flores, Delfino C.	Cpl	Johnson, Luther L.	PFC
Fox, Harry W.	PFC	Jones, Don D.	Cpl
Galan, Henry G. Jr.	PFC	Jones, Donald R.	PFC
Garcia, Charles	Sgt	Just, John	SSgt
Gaugenmaier, Robert	Sgt	Kenifick, Walter M.	PFC
Gauvin, Henry P.	PFC	Killheffer, Edmund	PFC
Geier, William E.	PFC	Kindt, Glenn J.	PFC
Graham, James E.	Sgt	Kollar, Andrew M.	Sgt
Gray, Charles R.	PFC	Kolling, Donald E.	PFC
Gutierrez, Jesus B.	Sgt	Kozikowski, Edmund	Sgt
Haimje, John A.	Cpl	Lachman, Anton E.	PFC
Halevan, Alfred W.	PFC	Lander, Richard R.	Cpl
Hallberg, James D.	PFC	Lapchynski, Stanley	Cpl

Marines E-2-7 Roster, August 1951, Korea, cont.

Larsen, Robert R.	Cpl	O'Malley, John J.	PFC
Leach, Ronald F.	PFC	Page, Paul	Cpl
Lyons, Dennis J.	PFC	Parra, Henry V.	PFC
Martin, W. L.	SSgt	Partridge, Everett	PFC
McCardell, Theodore	Cpl	Pavelcik, Otto	PFC
McSweeney, Frederic	PFC	Payer, Forrest L.	PFC
Medlin, Alfred J.	Cpl	Peak, Paul H.	PFC
Mee, Robert E.	Cpl	Peregoy, Frederick	Cpl
Meek, Phillip E.	PFC	Perigo, Carl W.	Sgt
Michels, Harland R.	Cpl	Perkins, John C.	PFC
Mill, Richard S.	PFC	Phillips, Roy D.	PFC
Miller, Emmett	PFC	Phillips, William L.	PFC
Miller, Jerry J.	Cpl	Pianecki, John V.	PFC
Miller, William J.	Cpl	Pier, Robert P.	Cpl
Mills, Jack W.	PFC	Pileggi, Vito P.	PFC
Milner, John W.	Cpl	Polon, Jack D.	Cpl
Miner, Clarence R.	PFC	Pompeo, John	PFC
Moody, Kenneth A.	Cpl	Poole, Rupert C.	PFC
Moreno, Joseph J.	Cpl	Poutz, William E.	PFC
Mote, James F.	Cpl	Powell, Lloyd H.	Cpl
Motley, James V.	Cpl	Powers, Darrell E.	PFC
Mueller, Lennis W.	Cpl	Pradragovich, John	PFC
Muncy, James E.	PFC	Pressley, Larry L.	Sgt
Murphy, Alan F.	Cpl	Prevost, Edward F.	PFC
Myers, Louis H.	PFC	Proietti, Daniel	PFC
Narvaez, Antonio	PFC	Pruett, Ben J.	Cpl
Nelson, Richard H.	PFC	Quinn, John P.	Cpl
Nelson, Walter L.	Cpl	Quinones, Sigifredo	SSgt
Nesbitt, Stanley R.	PFC	Ramos, John Jr.	PFC
Nichols, James C.	PFC	Rauschmier, William	Cpl
Ogden, Bobby J.	Cpl	Richardson, Everett	PFC
Olesen, Donald L.	PFC	Richardson, Paul E.	PFC
Olson, Leslie G.	Cpl	Ridenour, Raymond A.	Cpl

Rock, John J. Jr.	PFC	Spradlin, Jack	Sgt
Rodriguez, Joel S.	Cpl	Spring, Vernon M.	PFC
Rogers, Edgar E. Jr.	PFC	Spurrier, James H.	PFC
Rosalles, Abb J.	Cpl	Srebroski, Joseph L.	PFC
Rose, James C.	Cpl	Stanley, James F.	Sgt
Roseland, John R.	Cpl	Stewart, Robert C.	Cpl
Rost, Edwin F.	PFC	Stieg, Wallace G.	PFC
Sambol, John A.	PFC	Sullivan, George R.	SSgt
Schaus, Raymond A.	Cpl	Tastet, Lester J.	SSgt
Segel, Thomas D.	PFC	Torres, David R.	PFC
Shackle, Richard L.	PFC	Torres, Raymond J.	PFC
Sharp, Charles F.	PFC	Tracy, Loren E.	PFC
Simmons, Buck S.	Cpl	Vandenhende, Gerald	Cpl
Simmons, Charles J.	Cpl	Varela, Joe R.	Sgt
Simmons, John F.	Cpl	Virili, Morris	Tsgt
Sindrick, Joseph M.	PFC	Vogelsang, Carl E.	PFC
Sitton, Charles R.	Cpl	Whitehead, Ernest E.	PFC
Smith, Phillip M.	PFC	Wingsted, Robert L.	Sgt
Snyder, Charles M.	PFC	Young, Donald	Cpl
Sommerhoff, Roy F.	Cpl	Young, Herschell B.	Cpl
Soria, Joseph A.	PFC	Young, Willard H.	Sgt

Source: E-2-7 Marines Company Log

List of photos and maps

- 14 Alan Hannigan, Vito Pileggi, and Eddie Wager
- 27 Louie Caruso
- 31 Larry Pressley, Lt. John Lilley, and SSgt Quinones
- 33 Jerry Miller
- 34 Loren Tracy
- 35 Jack Mills
- 36 J. J. Miller and Daughtery
- 37 Don Young manning a heavy .30 caliber machine gun
- 38 Doc Kees
- 39 Caruso, O'Malley, and Pileggi
- 41 Richardson, Phillips, Miller, and Daughtery in back; Pileggi with the BAR, Creel, and Bridge holding an M1
- 42 L to R: Name forgotten, Bullock, Meek, Pileggi, Name forgotten, Plick, Mills, and in front Creel and Nelson
- 44 Pileggi and Meek in back; Plick, Bitting, and Tracy in front
- 46 Moving forward and moving upward
- 63 Hand grenade
- 68 Jerry Miller
- 70 Assault route to Hill 749
- 71 Moving to attack Hill 749, September 1951
- 83 Ebb Daughtery
- 91 Bobby Ogden
- 96 Script money
- 97 Earl Boyce Clark
- 99 William Jon (W. J.) Miller, the Oregon con-artist
- 100 Sgt. Manuel Hirata
- 101 O'Malley, Schaus, and Miller
- 102 Jon Miller
- 104 Seamen Robert Rice with his childhood friend, Marine Corporal Donald Young, September 1951
- 108 Alan Murphy & Ken Moody
- 109 Red & Daughtery
- 112 North Korean surrendering
- 113 Safe Conduct Pass
- 119 Chiggy bearers
- 121 Dog tags
- 128 AWOL Seamen Robert Rice and Donald Kirk, serving with Easy Company in September 1951, prior to returning to the Navy
- 130 Souvenirs: "Itiwa" spoons, opium pipe, Communist red star hat emblems
- 131 Korean bank note
- 134 Jimmy Richardson, October 1951
- 135 Lehman Brightman, our own Indian Chief
- 137 Korean hut
- 138 Bridge and Miller
- 139 Ray "Butch" Schaus and Don Young on the old two-holer
- 146 The author holding a Thompson .45 caliber submachine gun
- 159 The Veep
- 160 Thanksgiving dinner, Lieutenant Jack Lilley eating turkey
- 162 Lieutenant John "Jack" Lilley, getting warm
- 164 Eddie Newman next to his bunker
- 173 O'Malley and Schaus
- 174 2nd squad, O'Malley (partially hidden), Chief Brightman, Name forgotten, Evans, Louie Racca, Squad Leader Butch Schaus,

Pavelcik in front of Schaus, Name forgotten, and Roy Phillips
176 Near the spring
178 Winter patrol
183 Bill Poutz, machine guns
184 Checking an abandoned Korean house
187 Willie Schlei and his squad leader Butch Schaus at Camp Tripoli
188 Camp Tripoli. Left to right: Norm Wagner, Bob Urban, Jack Mills, Lieutenant Lilley, Jimmy Richardson, "Hoyt" Vandenburg, and Charles Creel (squatting)
189 Back, L to R: L. Blackwater, C. Snyder. Dan Proietti and Ed Prevost. Front, L to R: J. Nichols and Carl Radwanski (note MG muzzle)
191 Jimmie
193 Piss tube
194 Camp Tripoli. Jerry Rogalla, Hoyt Hutchinson, Charles Long, Jimmie, our washy-washy boy, and Louie Caruso
197 Sikorsky helicopter
198 Line of bunkers on the Main Line of Resistance
199 Winter scene
201 1st Squad machine guns. Standing L to R: Brinlee, Hurt, Phillips, Pompeo, and Sommerhoff. Kneeling L to R: Poutz, Blackburn, Jones, and Bingaman
202 The ridge in front of Blood and Guts
203 Dan Proietti, machine guns
204 Front line bunkers on Hill 884
205 Building bunkers
206 Johnny Pompeo holding a thirty caliber M.G.
207 On the front lines, January 1952
209 Pet crow
210 Standing: Joe Caffiero and Leo Plick. Squatting: Louie Caruso (with sunglasses) and Hoyt Hutchinson
212 Winter combat patrol
213 Otto Pavelcik
216 Korean prisoners
222 Second Lieutenant James VanAirsdale, Winter 1952
223 The arm
227 Left to right: Gunnery Sargeant Morris Virili, Captain Embree Maxson, Lt. General Franklin A. Hart, Lt. Colonel Kirgil, and the assistant Battalion Commander. Winter 1952
228 Charles Creel and Lt. Tim O'Reilly
232 Vito Pileggi. Weight: Under 150 pounds. February 1952
233 Dead North Korean
235 The author and our Korean interpreter, Charlie
238 Thomas "Ed" Bullock. Fixin' to go home.
239 Easy Company Command Post
240 Captured Russian truck
243 Korean family
245 John O'Malley; a haircut, a shave, and a shower. Now for a can of pork and beans.
248 Korean kids
256 Korean girl
262 Panmunjom map
265 Morrisey and Oliver
266 Haymon and Brock
273 West coast of the Korean Peninsula, May–June 1952
276 Harry Levitt, May–June 1952
277 Troy Watson, May–June 1952
297 Somebody's mom

Made in the USA
San Bernardino, CA
13 February 2016